enVisionmath 2.0
SCOTT FORESMAN · ADDISON WESLEY

Volume 1 Topics 1–4

Authors

Robert Q. Berry, III
Associate Professor of Mathematics Education, Department of Curriculum, Instruction and Special Education, University of Virginia, Charlottesville, Virginia

Zachary Champagne
Assistant in Research Florida Center for Research in Science, Technology, Engineering, and Mathematics (FCR-STEM) Jacksonville, Florida

Eric Milou
Professor of Mathematics Rowan University, Glassboro, New Jersey

Jane F. Schielack
Professor Emerita Department of Mathematics Texas A&M University College Station, Texas

Jonathan A. Wray
Mathematics Instructional Facilitator, Howard County Public Schools, Ellicott City, Maryland

Randall I. Charles
Professor Emeritus Department of Mathematics San Jose State University San Jose, California

Francis (Skip) Fennell
L. Stanley Bowlsbey Professor of Education and Graduate and Professional Studies, McDaniel College Westminster, Maryland

PEARSON

Glenview, Illinois   Boston, Massachusetts   Chandler, Arizona   Hoboken, New Jersey

Mathematician Reviewers

Gary Lippman, Ph.D.
Professor Emeritus
Mathematics and Computer Science
California State University, East Bay
Hayward, California

Karen Edwards, Ph.D.
Mathematics Lecturer
Arlington, MA

Copyright © 2017 by Pearson Education, Inc., or its affiliates. All Rights Reserved.
Printed in the United States of America. This publication is protected by copyright, and permission should be obtained from the publisher prior to any prohibited reproduction, storage in a retrieval system, or transmission in any form or by any means, electronic, mechanical, photocopying, recording, or otherwise. For information regarding permissions, request forms from the appropriate contacts within the Pearson Education Global Rights & Permissions Department. Please visit www.pearsoned.com/permissions/.

PEARSON, ALWAYS LEARNING, SCOTT FORESMAN, PEARSON SCOTT FORESMAN, and enVisionmath are exclusive trademarks owned by Pearson Education, Inc. or its affiliates in the U.S. and/or other countries. Unless otherwise indicated herein, any third-party trademarks that may appear in this work are the property of their respective owners and any references to third-party trademarks, logos or other trade dress are for demonstrative or descriptive purposes only. Such references are not intended to imply any sponsorship, endorsement, authorization, or promotion of Pearson's products by the owners of such marks, or any relationship between the owner and Pearson Education, Inc. or its affiliates, authors, licensees or distributors.

PEARSON

ISBN-13: 978-0-134-93016-9
ISBN-10: 0-134-93016-9

CONTENTS

TOPICS

1. Integers and Rational Numbers
2. Analyze and Use Proportional Relationships
3. Analyze and Solve Percent Problems
4. Generate Equivalent Expressions
5. Solve Problems Using Equations and Inequalities
6. Use Sampling to Draw Inferences About Populations
7. Probability
8. Solve Problems Involving Geometry

KEY

- Numbers and Computation
- Algebra and Functions
- Proportionality
- Geometry
- Data Analysis and Probability

DIGITAL RESOURCES

Go Online | PearsonRealize.com

INTERACTIVE ANIMATION
Interact with visual learning animations

ACTIVITY
Use with *Solve & Discuss It, Explore It,* and *Explain It* activities and Examples

VIDEOS
Watch clips to support *3-Act Mathematical Modeling* Lessons and *STEM Projects*

PRACTICE
Practice what you've learned and get immediate feedback

TUTORIALS
Get help from *Virtual Nerd* any time you need it

KEY CONCEPT
Review important lesson content

GLOSSARY
Read and listen to English and Spanish definitions

ASSESSMENT
Show what you've learned

MATH TOOLS
Explore math with digital tools

GAMES
Play math games to help you learn

ETEXT
Access your book online

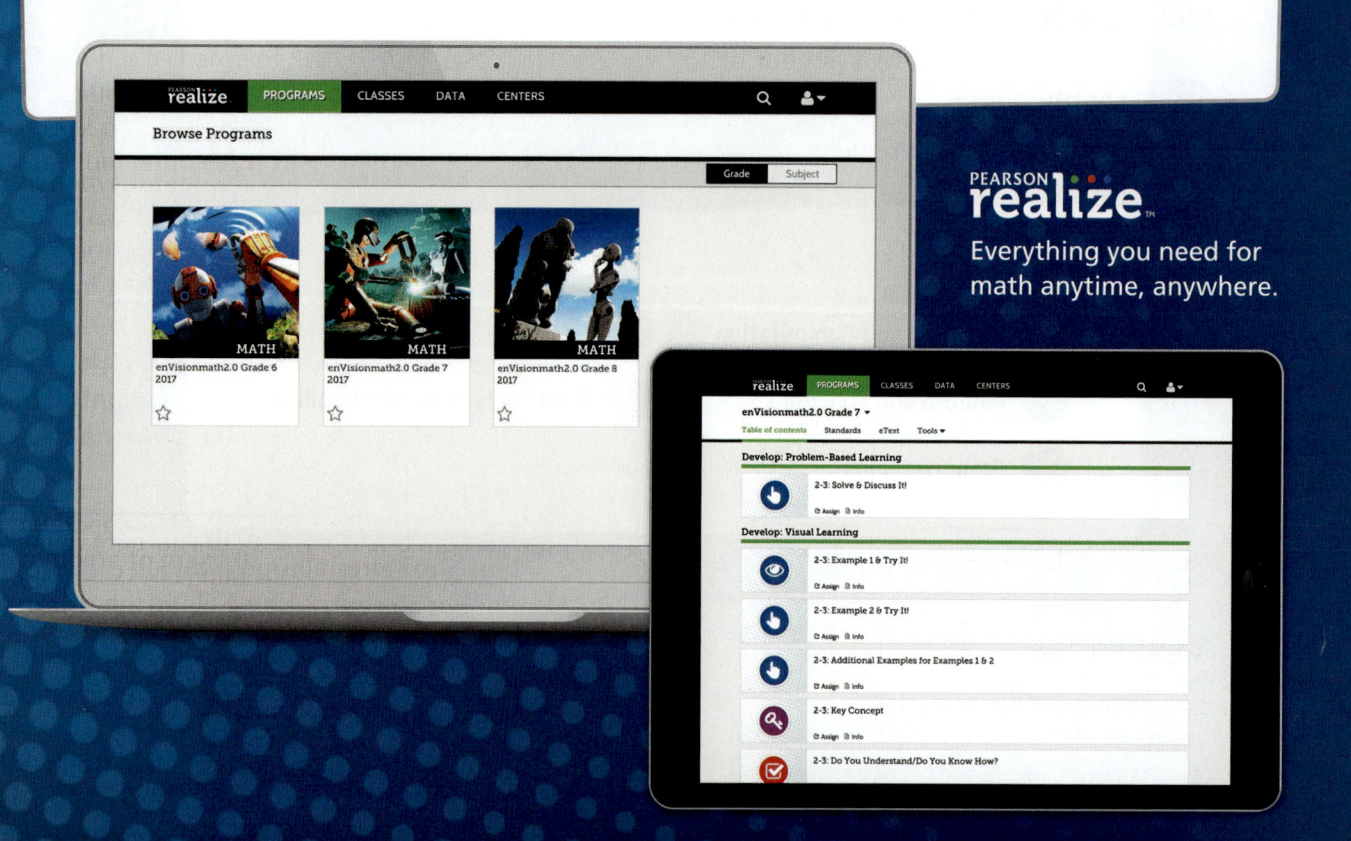

PEARSON realize.
Everything you need for math anytime, anywhere.

TOPIC 1: Integers and Rational Numbers

STEM Project	4
Review What You Know	5
Math Literacy Activity	6
1-1 Relate Integers and Their Opposites	7
1-2 Understand Rational Numbers	13
1-3 Add Integers	19
1-4 Subtract Integers	25
1-5 Add and Subtract Rational Numbers	31
Mid-Topic Checkpoint	37
Mid-Topic Performance Task	38
1-6 Multiply Integers	39
1-7 Multiply Rational Numbers	45
1-8 Divide Integers	51
1-9 Divide Rational Numbers	57
1-10 Solve Problems with Rational Numbers	63
3-Act Mathematical Modeling: Win Some, Lose Some	69
Topic Review	73
Fluency Practice Activity	79

TOPIC 2: Analyze and Use Proportional Relationships

STEM Project	82
Review What You Know	83
Math Literacy Activity	84
2-1 Connect Ratios, Rates, and Unit Rates	85
2-2 Determine Unit Rates with Ratios of Fractions	91
2-3 Understand Proportional Relationships: Equivalent Ratios	97
2-4 Describe Proportional Relationships: Constant of Proportionality	103
Mid-Topic Checkpoint	109
Mid-Topic Performance Task	110
3-Act Mathematical Modeling: Mixin' It Up	111
2-5 Graph Proportional Relationships	115
2-6 Apply Proportional Reasoning to Solve Problems	121
Topic Review	127
Fluency Practice Activity	131

TOPIC 3: Analyze and Solve Percent Problems

STEM Project	134
Review What You Know	135
Math Literacy Activity	136
3-1 Analyze Percents of Numbers	137
3-2 Connect Percent and Proportion	143
3-3 Represent and Use the Percent Equation	149
Mid-Topic Checkpoint	155
Mid-Topic Performance Task	156
3-4 Solve Percent Change and Percent Error Problems	157
3-Act Mathematical Modeling: The Smart Shopper	163
3-5 Solve Markup and Markdown Problems	167
3-6 Solve Simple Interest Problems	173
Topic Review	179
Fluency Practice Activity	183

TOPIC 4: Generate Equivalent Expressions

STEM Project	186
Review What You Know	187
Math Literacy Activity	188
4-1 Write and Evaluate Algebraic Expressions	189
4-2 Generate Equivalent Expressions	195
4-3 Simplify Expressions	201
4-4 Expand Expressions	207
4-5 Factor Expressions	213
Mid-Topic Checkpoint	219
Mid-Topic Performance Task	220
3-Act Mathematical Modeling: I've Got You Covered	221
4-6 Add Expressions	225
4-7 Subtract Expressions	231
4-8 Analyze Equivalent Expressions	237
Topic Review	243
Fluency Practice Activity	247

TOPIC 5
Solve Problems Using Equations and Inequalities

In Volume 2

STEM Project	250
Review What You Know	251
Math Literacy Activity	252
5-1 Write Two-Step Equations	253
5-2 Solve Two-Step Equations	259
5-3 Solve Equations Using the Distributive Property	265
Mid-Topic Checkpoint	271
Mid-Topic Performance Task	272
5-4 Solve Inequalities Using Addition or Subtraction	273
5-5 Solve Inequalities Using Multiplication or Division	279
3-Act Mathematical Modeling: Digital Downloads	285
5-6 Solve Two-Step Inequalities	289
5-7 Solve Multi-Step Inequalities	295
Topic Review	301
Fluency Practice Activity	305

F9

TOPIC 6
Use Sampling to Draw Inferences About Populations

In Volume 2

STEM Project	308
Review What You Know	309
Math Literacy Activity	310
6-1 Populations and Samples	311
6-2 Draw Inferences from Data	319
Mid-Topic Checkpoint	327
Mid-Topic Performance Task	328
6-3 Make Comparative Inferences About Populations	329
6-4 Make More Comparative Inferences About Populations	335
3-Act Mathematical Modeling: Raising Money	341
Topic Review	345
Fluency Practice Activity	349

TOPIC 7
Probability
In Volume 2

STEM Project	352
Review What You Know	353
Math Literacy Activity	354
7-1 Understand Likelihood and Probability	355
7-2 Understand Theoretical Probability	361
7-3 Understand Experimental Probability	367
7-4 Use Probability Models	373
Mid-Topic Checkpoint	379
Mid-Topic Performance Task	380
3-Act Mathematical Modeling: Photo Finish	381
7-5 Determine Outcomes of Compound Events	385
7-6 Find Probabilities of Compound Events	391
7-7 Simulate Compound Events	397
Topic Review	403
Fluency Practice Activity	409

TOPIC 8: Solve Problems Involving Geometry

In Volume 2

STEM Project	412
Review What You Know	413
Math Literacy Activity	414
8-1 Solve Problems Involving Scale Drawings	415
8-2 Draw Geometric Figures	421
8-3 Draw Triangles with Given Conditions	427
8-4 Solve Problems Using Angle Relationships	435
8-5 Solve Problems Involving Circumference of a Circle	441
Mid-Topic Checkpoint	447
Mid-Topic Performance Task	448
8-6 Solve Problems Involving Area of a Circle	449
3-Act Mathematical Modeling: Whole Lotta Dough	455
8-7 Describe Cross Sections	459
8-8 Solve Problems Involving Surface Area	465
8-9 Solve Problems Involving Volume	471
Topic Review	477
Fluency Practice Activity	483

Math Practices and Problem Solving Handbook

CONTENTS

Math Practices	F14–F15
1	F16
2	F17
3	F18
4	F19
5	F20
6	F21
7	F22
8	F23
Bar Diagrams with Operations	F24
Bar Diagrams in Proportional Reasoning	F25–F26
Bar Diagrams in Quantitative Reasoning	F27

Math Practices

1 Make sense of problems and persevere in solving them.

Mathematically proficient students:
- can explain the meaning of a problem
- look for entry points to begin solving a problem
- analyze givens, constraints, relationships, and goals
- make conjectures about the solution
- plan a solution pathway
- think of similar problems, and try simpler forms of the problem
- evaluate their progress toward a solution and change pathways if necessary
- can explain similarities and differences between different representations
- check their solutions to problems.

2 Reason abstractly and quantitatively.

Mathematically proficient students:
- make sense of quantities and their relationships in problem situations:
  - They *decontextualize*—create a coherent representation of a problem situation using numbers, variables, and symbols; and
  - They *contextualize* – attend to the meaning of numbers, variables, and symbols in the problem situation
- know and use different properties of operations to solve problems.

3 Construct viable arguments and critique the reasoning of others.

Mathematically proficient students:
- use definitions and problem solutions when constructing arguments
- make conjectures about the solutions to problems
- build a logical progression of statements to support their conjectures and justify their conclusions
- analyze situations and recognize and use counterexamples
- reason inductively about data, making plausible arguments that take into account the context from which the data arose
- listen or read the arguments of others, and decide whether they make sense
- respond to the arguments of others
- compare the effectiveness of two plausible arguments
- distinguish correct logic or reasoning from flawed, and—if there is a flaw in an argument—explain what it is
- ask useful questions to clarify or improve arguments of others.

4 Model with mathematics.

Mathematically proficient students:
- can develop a representation—drawing, diagram, table, graph, expression, equation–to model a problem situation
- make assumptions and approximations to simplify a complicated situation
- identify important quantities in a practical situation and map their relationships using a range of tools
- analyze relationships mathematically to draw conclusions
- interpret mathematical results in the context of the situation and propose improvements to the model as needed.

5 Use appropriate tools strategically.

Mathematically proficient students:
- consider appropriate tools when solving a mathematical problem
- make sound decisions about when each of these tools might be helpful
- identify relevant mathematical resources, and use them to pose or solve problems
- use tools and technology to explore and deepen their understanding of concepts.

6 Attend to precision.

Mathematically proficient students:
- communicate precisely to others
- use clear definitions in discussions with others and in their own reasoning
- state the meaning of the symbols they use
- specify units of measure, and label axes to clarify their correspondence with quantities in a problem
- calculate accurately and efficiently
- express numerical answers with a degree of precision appropriate for the problem context.

7 Look for and make use of structure.

Mathematically proficient students:
- look closely at a problem situation to identify a pattern or structure
- can step back from a solution pathway and shift perspective
- can see complex representations, such as some algebraic expressions, as single objects or as being composed of several objects.

8 Look for and express regularity in repeated reasoning.

Mathematically proficient students:
- notice if calculations are repeated, and look both for general methods and for shortcuts
- maintain oversight of the process as they work to solve a problem, while also attending to the details
- continually evaluate the reasonableness of their intermediate results.

1 > Make sense of problems and persevere in solving them.

The student council plans to build a brick "walk of fame" in the town center as a fund-raising activity to raise $15,000. Town residents can buy a brick and have a name engraved on the top.

The cost to build the walk is $6,713.75. If the student council sells bricks for $125 each, how many will they need to sell to reach their fund-raising goal?

What am I asked to find? The number of bricks that the council needs to sell to reach its fund raising goal.

250 total bricks

What are the known quantities and variables? How do they relate? Target fund-raising amount and cost to build the walk are expenses.

Amount earned by selling the bricks is income.

What can I do if I get stuck? Start by finding how much money the council will raise if they sell 100 bricks, then 200 bricks.

What is a good plan for solving the problem? Find the total expenses, including target fund-raising amount. Then divide by planned selling price.

Other questions to consider:
- Have I solved a similar problem before?
- What information is necessary and unnecessary?
- How can I check that my answer makes sense?
- How is my solution pathway the same as or different from my classmate's?

2 Reason abstractly and quantitatively.

The student council treasurer determines the percent of the total bricks that the council will need to sell to reach their fund-raising goal.

How can I represent this problem situation using numbers, variables, and symbols? I can write a proportion with a variable for the percent.

What do the numbers, variables, and symbols in the expression or equation mean/represent to the problem situation? 15,000 + 6,713.75 represent the total expenses.

$(15,000 + 6,713.75) \div 125 =$ — the expenses to build the walk of fame divided by the selling price of each walk of fame brick

173.71 or 174 — the number of bricks the council needs to sell to reach its fund-raising goal (Can't sell part of a brick!)

Percent equation: part = whole × percent

$174 = 250 \times n$
$0.696 = n$
$69.6 = n$ — the percent of the total number of bricks the council needs to sell to reach its fund-raising goal

3 Construct viable arguments and critique the reasoning of others.

Avery and Amelie are shopping for jeans. At the store, they find that all jeans are on sale for 25% off. They also each have a 25% off coupon. Whose cost for one pair of jeans is correct?

Avery: With the sale and my coupon, I'll pay only $40.

Amelie: When I figure it out, I get $45.

What assumptions can I make when constructing an argument? One of the two costs presented—or neither—may be correct.

What questions can I ask to understand other people's thinking? Why does Amelie think the cost will be higher than what Avery says?

What conjectures can I make about the solution to the problem? The correct solution may be either $40 or $45.

What arguments can I present to defend my conjectures? Two discounts of 25% result in a discount of about half.

Other questions to consider:
- How can I determine the accuracy of my conjectures?
- How can I justify my conclusions?
- What flaws, if any, do I note in my classmate's thinking?
- Which argument do I find more plausible?

4 Model with mathematics.

Sale!
Jeans
ORIGINAL PRICE **$80**
NOW **25%** OFF!
additional discounts taken off of sale price

What representation can I use to show the relationship among quantities or variables? A bar diagram can help me see the relationship among the quantities.

- 100% -
Original Price
Sale Price — 25% off
Sale Price with Coupon — 25% off
— 50% off —

Other questions to consider:
- Can I use a drawing, diagram, table, graph, expression, or equation to model the problem?
- How can I make my model better if it doesn't work?
- What assumptions can I make about the problem situation to simplify the problem?
- Does my solution or prediction make sense?
- Is there something I have not considered or forgotten?

5 Use appropriate tools strategically.

The monorail at an amusement park operates over $3\frac{1}{2}$ miles and has 4 stops equally spaced along the track. What is the distance between each stop?

What tool—objects, technology, or paper and pencil—can I use to help solve the problem? The scaled map will serve as a tool to help me visualize the monorail's path. I will need to solve a numeric equation, so I can use a calculator.

Could I use a different tool? Which one? I could use paper and pencil and solve the equation without a calculator.

Other questions to consider:
- How can technology help me with a solution strategy?
- What other resources can I use to help me reach and understand my solution?

6 Attend to precision.

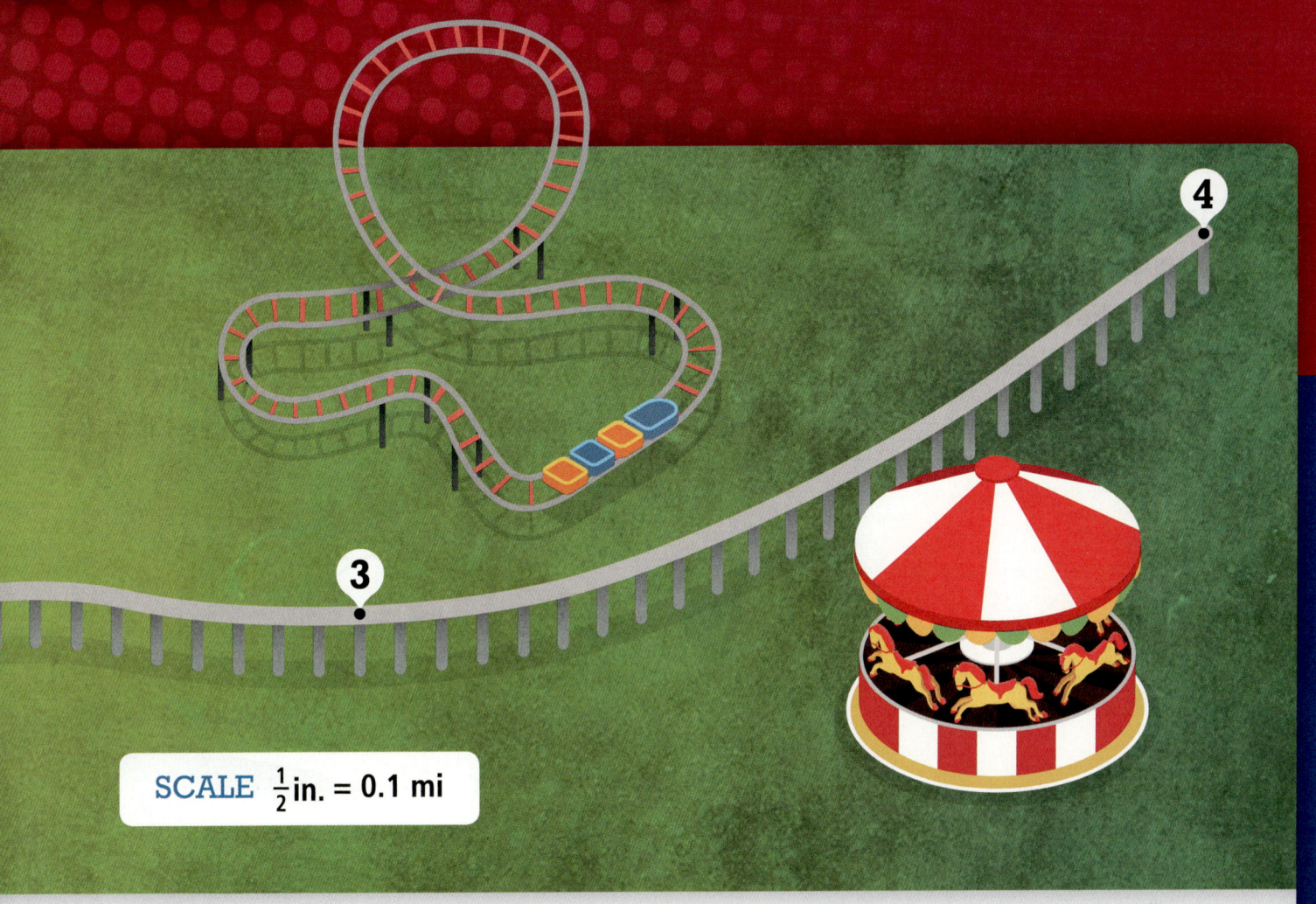

SCALE $\frac{1}{2}$ in. = 0.1 mi

Have I stated the meaning of the variables and symbols I am using? I'm looking for the distance between stops, so the variable in my equation represents the distance between stops.

Have I specified the units of measure I am using? The units in the problem are miles, so I need to specify miles in my solution.

Have I calculated accurately and efficiently? I can check my worked out solution on a calculator.

Other questions to consider:
- Is my work precise/exact enough?
- Am I using the precise definitions?
- Did I provide carefully formulated explanations?
- Am I using accurate vocabulary to communicate my reasoning?

Go Online | PearsonRealize.com

7 Look for and make use of structure.

Jordan helps his uncle set up for an event. Jordan's uncle drew a diagram to show Jordan how he wants the tables set up. Jordan needs to set up enough tables for 42 guests. How can Jordan figure out how many tables to set up?

Can I see a pattern or structure in the problem or solution strategy?
I can see that each end table has 5 seats and each middle table has 4 seats. Each additional table increases the number of seats by 4.

How can I use the pattern or structure I see to help me solve the problem?
I can write an equation that includes a term for the two end tables and a term for the middle tables.

Other questions to consider:
- Are there attributes in common that help me?
- Can I see the expression or equation as a single object? Or as a composition of several objects?

8 Look for and express regularity in repeated reasoning.

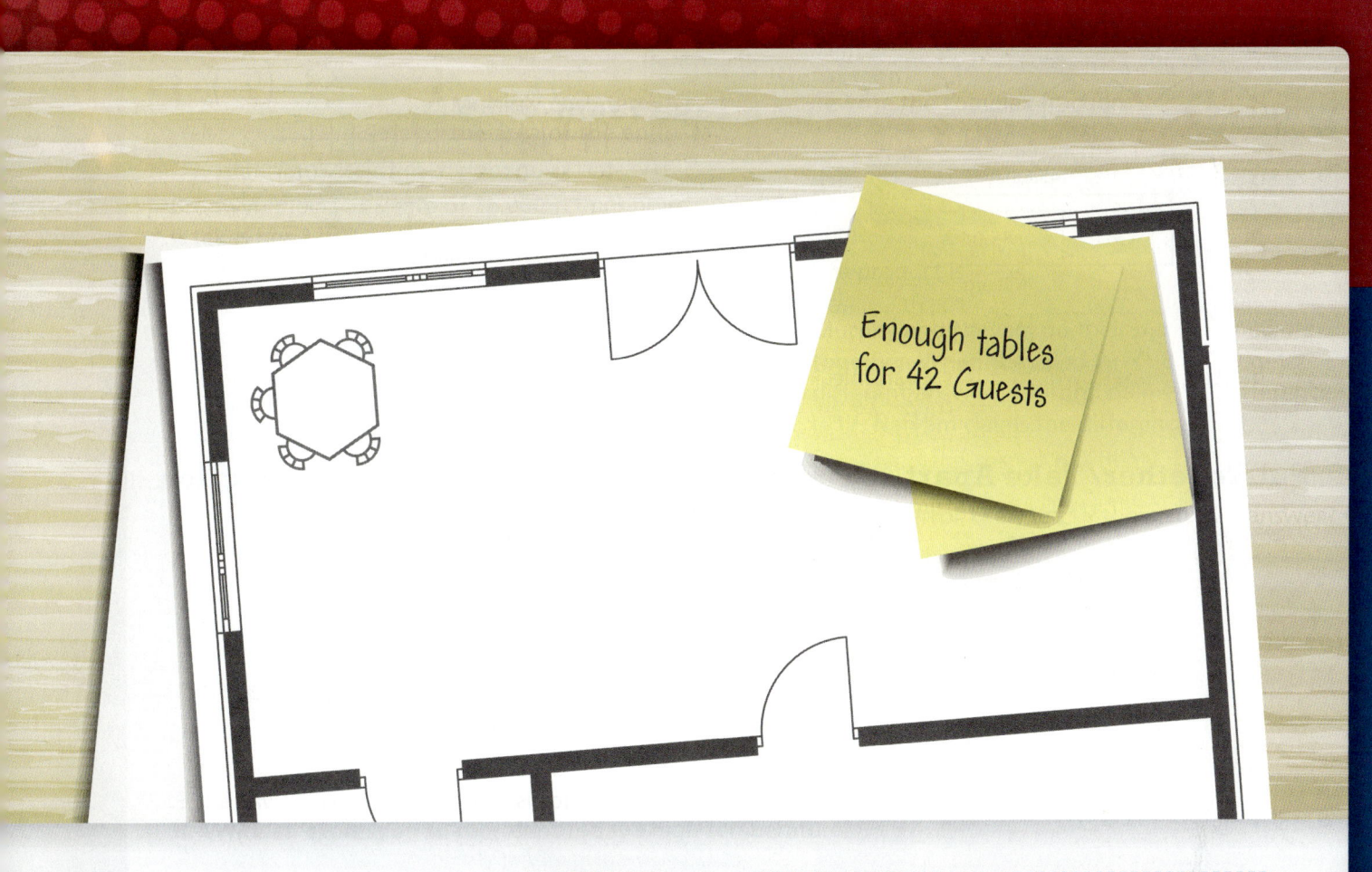

Enough tables for 42 Guests

Do I notice any repeated calculations or steps? Each additional table adds 4 seats.

Are there general methods that I can use to solve the problem? I can multiply the number of middle tables by 4 and then add the seats on the two end tables.

Other questions to consider:
- What can I generalize from one problem to another?
- Can I derive an equation from a series of data points?
- How reasonable are the results that I am getting?

Bar Diagrams with Operations

You can draw bar diagrams to show how quantities are related and to write an equation to solve the problem.

Add To

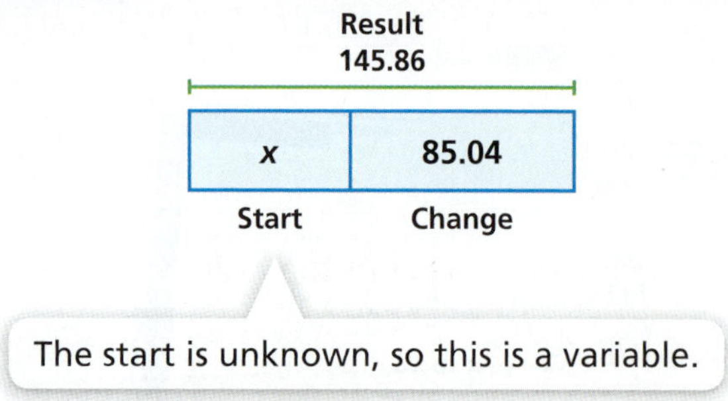

Result
145.86

x	85.04
Start	Change

The start is unknown, so this is a variable.

Take From

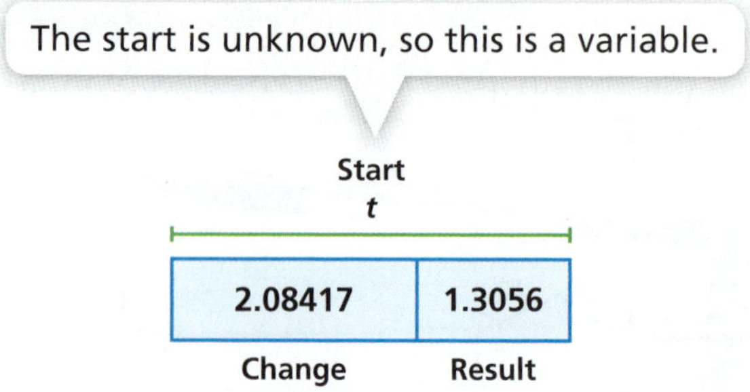

The start is unknown, so this is a variable.

Start
t

2.08417	1.3056
Change	Result

Put Together/Take Apart

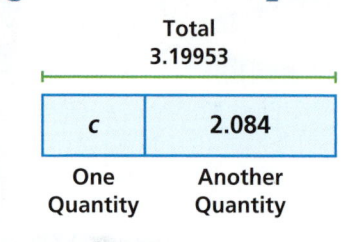

Total
3.19953

c	2.084
One Quantity	Another Quantity

One of the quantities is unknown, so this is a variable.

Compare: Addition and Subtraction

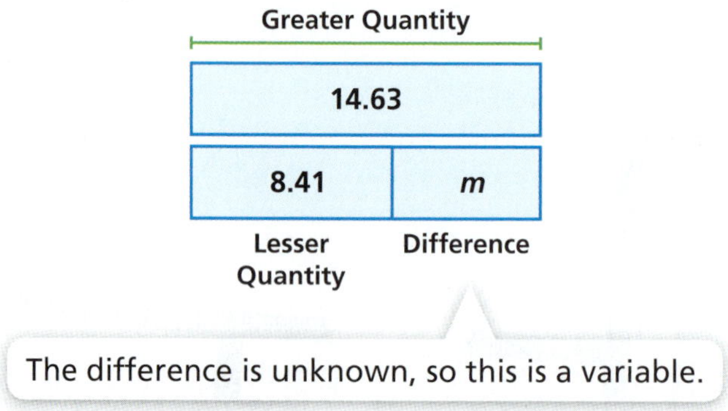

Greater Quantity

14.63

8.41	m
Lesser Quantity	Difference

The difference is unknown, so this is a variable.

Equal Groups: Multiplication and Division

The number of equal groups is unknown, so this is a variable.

Total
s

$3\frac{2}{5}$	$3\frac{2}{5}$	$3\frac{2}{5}$	$3\frac{2}{5}$

↑ Group Size

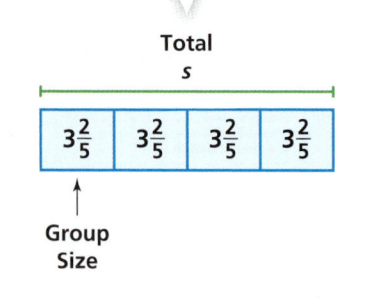

Compare: Multiplication and Division

The bigger quantity is unknown, so this is a variable.

m

Greater Quantity: $\frac{7}{8}$ | $\frac{7}{8}$ | $\frac{7}{8}$ | $\frac{7}{8}$ Multiplier: 4 times as many

Lesser Quantity: $\frac{7}{8}$

3.5

Greater Quantity: 0.7 → n Multiplier: n times as many

Lesser Quantity: 0.7

The multiplier is unknown, so this is a variable.

Math Practices and Problem Solving Handbook — BAR DIAGRAMS

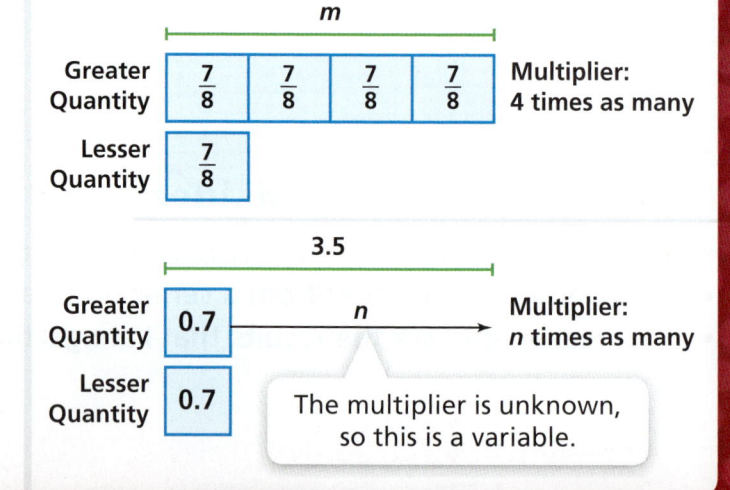

Bar Diagrams in Proportional Reasoning

You can draw bar diagrams to show how quantities are related in proportional relationships.

Ratios and Rates

Draw this bar diagram to show ratios and rates.

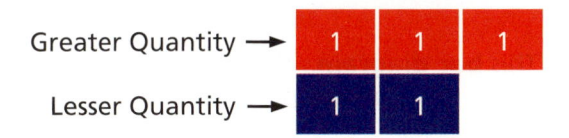

Greater Quantity → | 1 | 1 | 1 |
Lesser Quantity → | 1 | 1 |

This **bar diagram** represents the ratio **3 : 2**.

Greater Quantity Unknown

For every 3 cashews in a snack mix, there are 5 almonds. A package contains 42 cashews. How many almonds are in the same package?

Draw a bar diagram to represent the ratio of cashews to almonds.

Cashews
3 | | | |
5 | | | | | |
Almonds

Use the same diagram to represent 42 cashews and to determine the number of almonds.

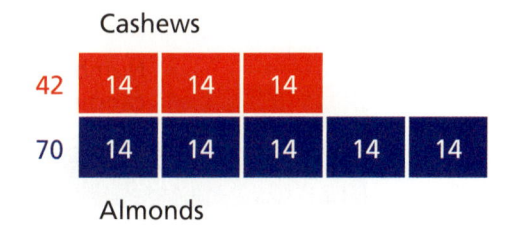

Cashews
42 | 14 | 14 | 14 |
70 | 14 | 14 | 14 | 14 | 14 |
Almonds

There are 70 almonds in the package.

Bar Diagrams in Proportional Reasoning

You can draw bar diagrams to show how quantities are related in proportional relationships.

Percents

Draw this bar diagram to show percents.

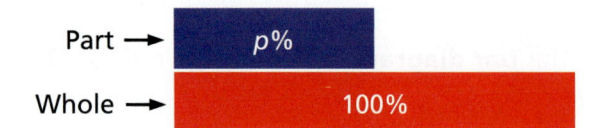

Part → $p\%$
Whole → 100%

This **bar diagram** relates a part to a whole to represent percent.

Part Unknown

A candy company creates batches of colored candies so that, on average, 30% of the candies are orange. About how many orange candies should be included in a batch of 1,500 candies?

Use the bar diagram to write an equation.

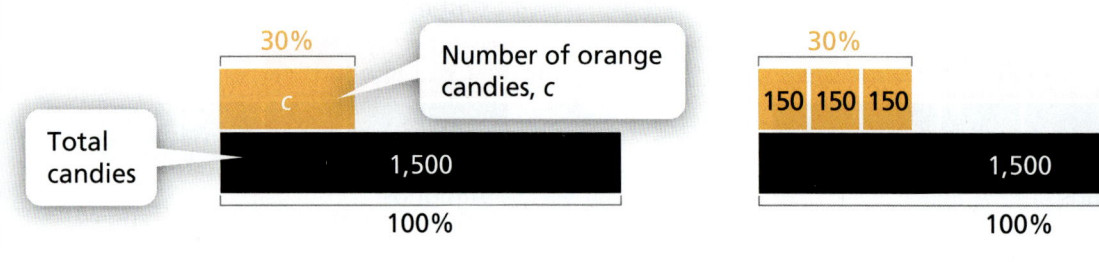

30%
Number of orange candies, c
Total candies
1,500
100%

30%
150 150 150
1,500
100%

$$\frac{30}{100} = \frac{c}{1,500}$$

There should be about 450 orange candies in the batch.

Math Practices and Problem Solving Handbook — BAR DIAGRAMS

F26

Bar Diagrams in Quantitative Reasoning

You can use bar diagrams to solve one-variable equations.

Solve for x: $2x + 5 = 19$

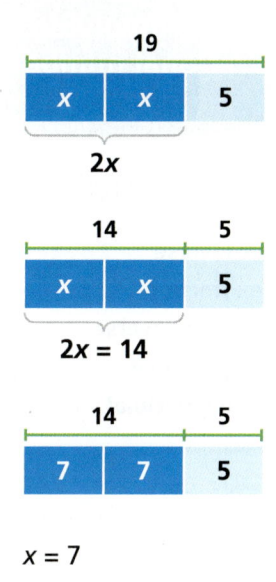

$2x = 14$

$x = 7$

Solve for y: $4(y - 2) = 24$

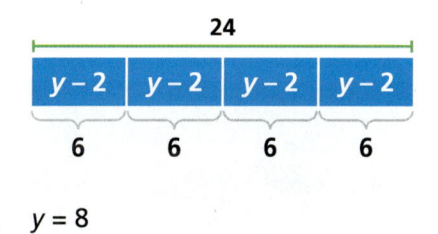

$y = 8$

Solve for m: $4m + 2 = 3m + 4$

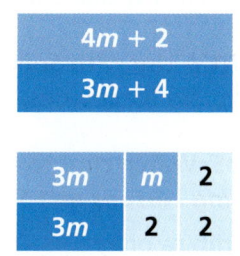

$m = 2$

Andy's brother can spend $80 each month on his cable bill. The local cable company charges a $45 monthly fee for basic cable and $8 per month for each premium channel a customer orders.

How many premium channels can Andy's brother order?

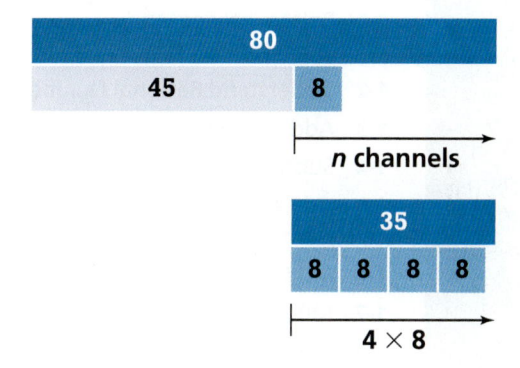

He can order 4 premium channels.

Ella opens a savings account with the $150 she got for her birthday. She plans to deposit $25 each month.

Assuming she does not withdraw any money, how much will she have saved after 2 years?

24 months × $25 = $600

$600 + $150 = $750

She will have saved $750 after 2 years.

TOPIC 1
INTEGERS AND RATIONAL NUMBERS

? Topic Essential Question

How can the properties of operations be used to solve problems involving integers and rational numbers?

Topic Overview

1-1 Relate Integers and Their Opposites
1-2 Understand Rational Numbers
1-3 Add Integers
1-4 Subtract Integers
1-5 Add and Subtract Rational Numbers
1-6 Multiply Integers
1-7 Multiply Rational Numbers
1-8 Divide Integers
1-9 Divide Rational Numbers
1-10 Solve Problems with Rational Numbers
3-Act Mathematical Modeling: Win Some, Lose Some

Topic Vocabulary

- additive inverse
- complex fraction
- multiplicative inverse
- repeating decimal
- terminating decimal

Lesson Digital Resources

INTERACTIVE ANIMATION Interact with visual learning animations.

ACTIVITY Use with *Solve & Discuss It, Explore It*, and *Explain It* activities, and to explore Examples.

VIDEOS Watch clips to support *3-Act Mathematical Modeling Lessons* and *STEM Projects*.

PRACTICE Practice what you've learned.

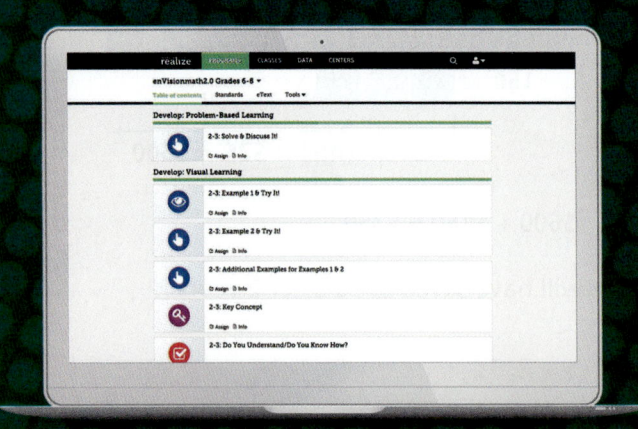

Go online | PearsonRealize.com

3-ACT MATH

Win Some, Lose Some

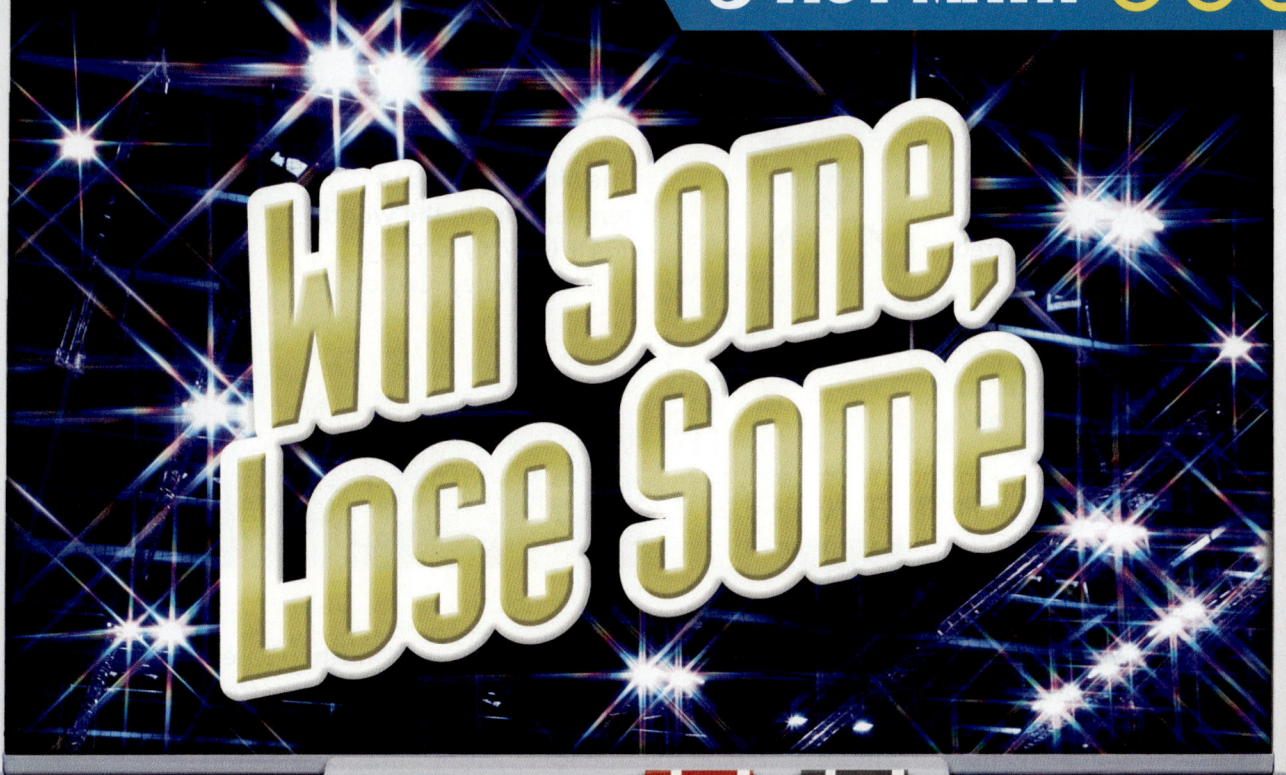

Are you the kind of person who has a lot of knowledge about history, literature, or science? What about pop culture, music, sports, and current events? Some schools have an academic bowl team that competes in tournaments against other schools. The teams are made up of members with strengths in different subject areas.

In any quiz competition, it's important to understand the rules and scoring. Think about this during the 3-Act Mathematical Modeling lesson.

TUTORIALS Get help from *Virtual Nerd*, right when you need it.

KEY CONCEPT Review important lesson content.

GLOSSARY Read and listen to English/Spanish definitions.

ASSESSMENT Show what you've learned.

Additional Digital Resources

MATH TOOLS Explore math with digital tools.

GAMES Play Math Games to help you learn.

ETEXT Interact with your Student's Edition online.

Topic 1 Integers and Rational Numbers 3

TOPIC 1 STEM Project

Did You Know?

The **lowest recorded temperature in the world, −136°F (−93.2°C)**, occurred in Antarctica.

The **highest recorded temperature in the world, 134°F (56.7°C)**, occurred in Death Valley, California.

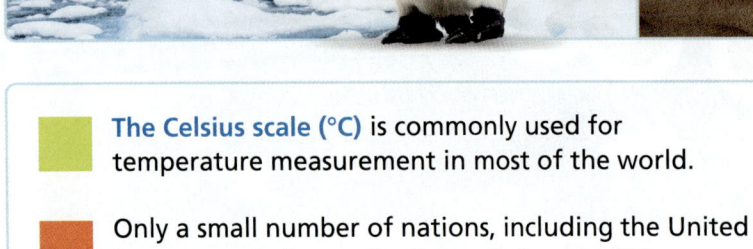

The Celsius scale (°C) is commonly used for temperature measurement in most of the world.

Only a small number of nations, including the United States, **regularly use the Fahrenheit scale (°F)**.

Windchill, based on the rate of heat loss from exposed skin, can make it feel colder outside than the actual air temperature indicates. Wind chills in some places of the world can **dip into the −100°F range**.

Your Task: How Cold is Too Cold?

There are many regions of the world with cold temperatures and extreme conditions. How do the inhabitants of these regions adapt and thrive? Do conditions exist that make regions too cold for human living? You and your classmates will explore and describe the habitability of regions with low temperatures.

Review What You Know!

GET READY!
TOPIC 1

Vocabulary
Choose the best term from the box. Write it on the blank.

> absolute value
> Associative Property
> Commutative Property
> Distributive Property
> integers
> rational number

1. The _____ explains why $a \times b = b \times a$ and $a + b = b + a$.

2. The _____ of -6 is 6, because it is 6 units from zero on the number line.

3. The number $\frac{5}{3}$ is a _____ because 5 and 3 are integers and $3 \neq 0$.

4. The set of _____ consists of the counting numbers, their opposites, and zero.

5. The sum of $(a + b) + c$ is equal to the sum of $a + (b + c)$ as explained by the _____.

6. If you evaluate $n \times (y + z)$ by writing it as $(n \times y) + (n \times z)$, you have used the _____.

Add and Subtract Fractions and Decimals
Add or subtract.

7. $2\frac{1}{3} + 6\frac{3}{5}$

8. $9\frac{1}{10} - 4\frac{3}{4}$

9. $19.86 + 7.091$

10. $57 - 10.62$

Multiply and Divide Fractions and Decimals
Multiply or divide.

11. 4.08×29.7

12. $15{,}183.3 \div 473$

13. $\frac{15}{16} \times 9\frac{1}{5}$

14. $4\frac{7}{9} \div 1\frac{7}{12}$

15. Byron has $1\frac{7}{10}$ kilograms of black pepper. He uses $\frac{7}{8}$ of the pepper and splits it between 7 pepper shakers. How much pepper will be in each shaker?

   Ⓐ $\frac{119}{80}$ kg

   Ⓑ $\frac{1}{8}$ kg

   Ⓒ 1.4125 kg

   Ⓓ $\frac{17}{80}$ kg

Go Online | PearsonRealize.com   Topic 1 Integers and Rational Numbers

Prepare for Reading Success

Use the following questions to help you understand the new ideas in Topic 1.

Questions Before Reading

What do I know about integers and rational numbers?

What do I know about fractions and decimals?

What does it mean when two things are opposites?
How can numbers be opposites?

Questions During Reading

Why might a number be positive or negative?

Who uses positive and negative numbers?
How are integers and rational numbers used in real life?

Where are opposite numbers located on a number line?

Questions After Reading

When might I use integers and rational numbers in real life?

Why is it important to know whether a number is positive or negative?

How is adding a positive number to a negative number different from adding two positive numbers or two negative numbers?

Lesson 1-1
Relate Integers and Their Opposites

Go Online | PearsonRealize.com

I can... relate integers, their opposites, and their absolute values.

Solve & Discuss It!

When preparing for a rocket launch, the mission control center uses the phrase "T minus" before liftoff.

...T minus 3, T minus 2, T minus 1, ...

After the rocket has launched, "T plus" is used while the rocket is in flight.

...T plus 1, T plus 2, T plus 3, ...

When does the rocket launch? What could "T" represent?

Reasoning What integers can you use to represent this situation?

Focus on math practices

Reasoning How are "T minus 4" and "T plus 4" related?

? Essential Question How are integers and their opposites related?

EXAMPLE 1 Combine Opposite Quantities to Make 0

Alexis was shopping on the ground floor of the mall when she realized she had left her phone in her car. She walks down 6 floors to her car in the underground parking garage.

How far will Alexis walk to get back to the ground floor? Use integers to explain.

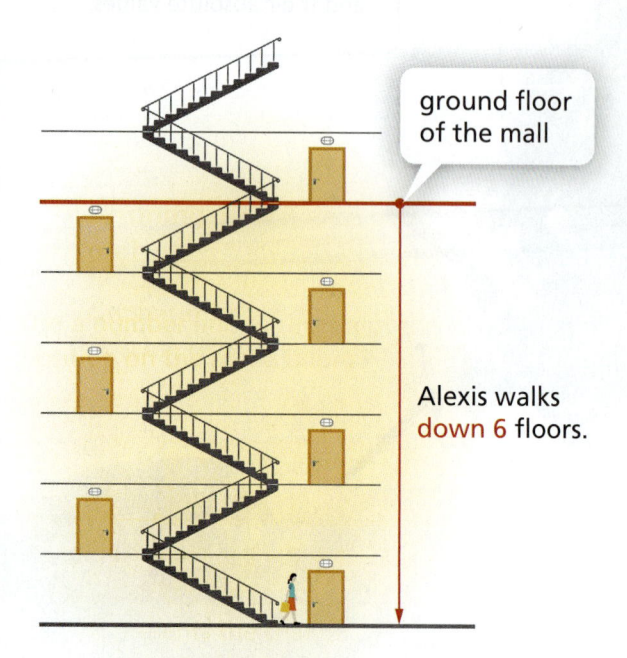

Alexis walks down 6 floors.

ground floor of the mall

Use integers on a number line to represent the situation.

The integer 0 represents the location of the ground floor.

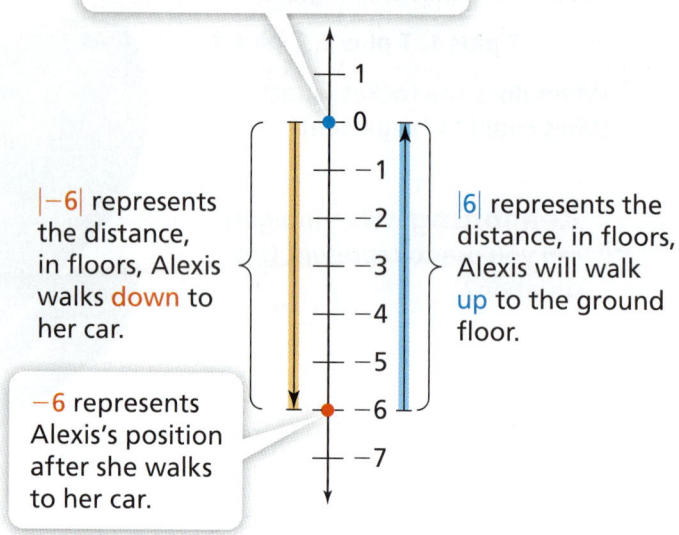

$|-6|$ represents the distance, in floors, Alexis walks down to her car.

$|6|$ represents the distance, in floors, Alexis will walk up to the ground floor.

−6 represents Alexis's position after she walks to her car.

$|-6| = |6| = 6$

−6 and 6 are opposites. Opposite quantities combine to make 0.

Alexis will walk the same distance, 6 floors, in the opposite direction to get back to the ground floor.

✓ Try It!

Xavier climbs 9 feet up into an apple tree. What integer represents the direction and how far he will climb to get back down to the ground? What does the integer 0 represent in this situation?

The integer ☐ represents Xavier's climb down.

The integer 0 represents ☐.

Convince Me! How are the absolute values of opposite integers related?

8   1-1 Relate Integers and Their Opposites

EXAMPLE 2 — Combine Opposite Quantities

Samuel has $20 in his savings account before he makes a deposit of $160. After 2 weeks, he withdraws $160. How did Samuel's savings account balance change?

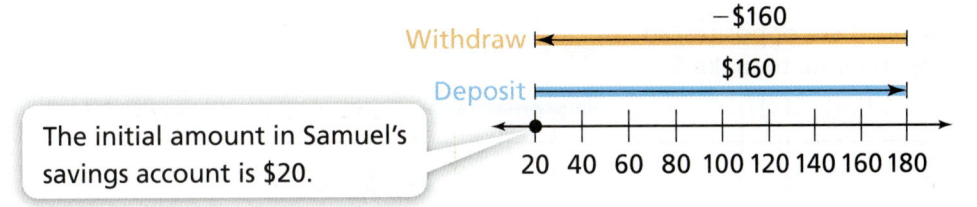

The initial amount in Samuel's savings account is $20.

The amounts deposited and withdrawn are opposite quantities and combine to make 0. Samuel's account balance did not change because the amounts deposited and withdrawn combine to make 0.

Try It!

The temperature was 75°. At noon, the temperature increased 7°. By evening, the temperature decreased by 7°. How did the temperature change?

EXAMPLE 3 — Represent Change Using Integers

One winter morning, the temperature was −2°C. By 11:00 A.M., the temperature had decreased by 3°. At 4:00 P.M., the temperature reached 0°C. What integer represents the temperature change from 11:00 A.M. to 4:00 P.M.?

Start at −2. The integer −3 represents the temperature decrease, so move 3 units left. The temperature has a change of −3.

Next, move 5 units right to show the temperature increase to 0°C. The temperature has a change of 5.

At 11:00 A.M. the temperature was −5°C.

At 4:00 P.M. the temperature was 0°C.

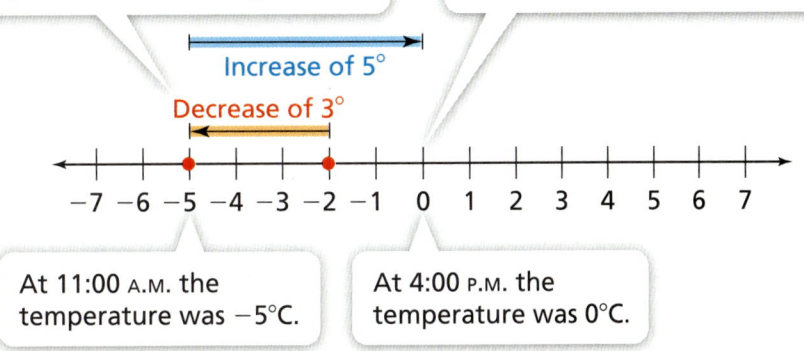

The integer 5 represents the temperature change from 11:00 A.M. to 4:00 P.M.

Try It!

Shaniqua has $45 in her wallet. She spends $4 on snacks and $8 on a movie ticket. What integer represents the change in the amount of money in Shaniqua's wallet? How much money does she have left?

Go Online | PearsonRealize.com

1-1 Relate Integers and Their Opposites

KEY CONCEPT

An integer, n, and its opposite, $-n$, combine to make 0.

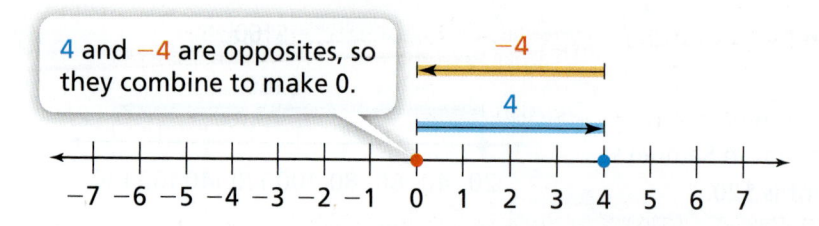

4 and -4 are opposites, so they combine to make 0.

Do You Understand?

1. **Essential Question** How are integers and their opposites related?

2. **Reasoning** In order for an atom to have a zero charge, every proton, which has a charge of $+1$, must be matched with an electron, which has a charge of -1. A helium atom has 2 protons and 2 electrons. Explain why a helium atom has a zero charge.

3. **Model with Math** Explain how to use a number line to show that opposite quantities combine to make 0.

Do You Know How?

4. Marcus dives from the surface of the ocean to a reef 18 meters below sea level. What integer represents Marcus's location relative to the surface? How far does Marcus have to go to return to the surface?

5. The temperature of the water in Emily's fish tank was 78°F on Sunday. The water temperature changed by $-3°$ on Monday, and then by $3°$ on Tuesday. What integer represents the temperature change of the water from Sunday to Tuesday? What was the water temperature on Tuesday?

6. The scores of players on a golf team are shown in the table. The team's combined score was 0. What was Travis's score?

Golfer	Score
CELIA	−3
JANINE	3
SAMI	1
TED	4
TRAVIS	

Name: _____

Practice & Problem Solving

Scan for Multimedia

Leveled Practice In 7–9, write the integer that represents the situation.

7. Max spent $53 and now has no money left. He had $ ☐ before his purchase.

8. The temperature was 8°F. It dropped so that the temperature was 0°F.
   ☐ °F represents the change in temperature.

9. An airplane descended 4,000 feet before landing. The integer that represents how many feet the airplane was above the ground before its descent is ☐.

10. Carolyn says that point A and point B represent opposite integers.

    a. What is the opposite of the integer represented by point A? By point B?

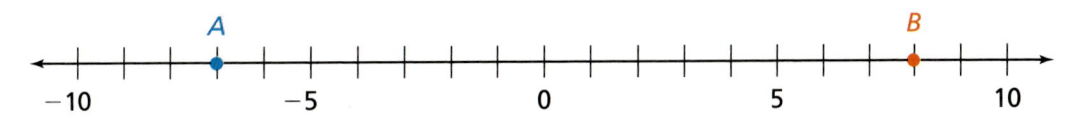

    [Number line from −10 to 10 showing point A near −7 and point B near 7]

    b. **Construct Arguments** Do you agree with Carolyn? Explain.

11. A football team lost 9 yards during a play. The team had a combined gain or loss of 0 yards after the next play. What integer represents the yards gained or lost on the next play? Show this on the number line.

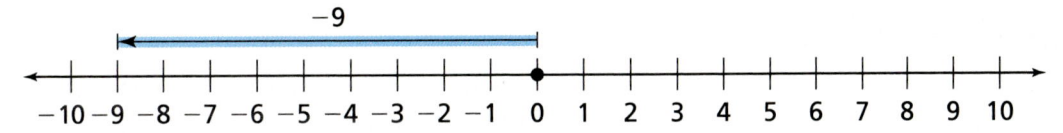

    [Number line from −10 to 10 with arrow showing −9]

12. A roller coaster car goes above and below ground. Use the number line to show its changes in height. What is the height of the car at the end of the ride?

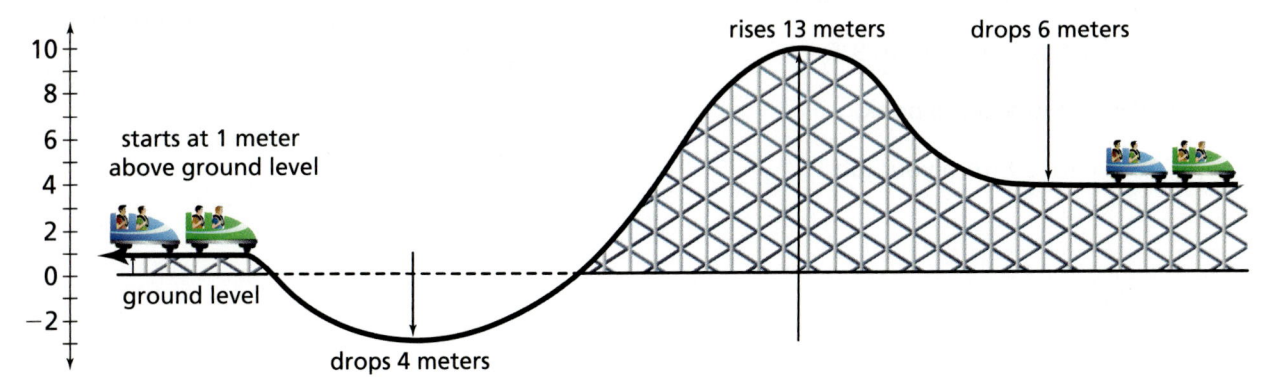

    [Diagram of roller coaster: starts at 1 meter above ground level, drops 4 meters, rises 13 meters, drops 6 meters]

Go Online | PearsonRealize.com   1-1 Relate Integers and Their Opposites

13. Dimitri is buying a car. He chooses Option 1 to add a new sound system to his car. What integer represents the change from the base price of the car to its final price?

Used Car DEALER Price Sticker
Base Price
Sale −$700.00
Opt.1 +$1,400.00
Markdown −$1,100.00
?

14. Make Sense and Persevere What values do x and y have if $|x| = 16$, $|y| = 16$, and when x and y are combined they equal 0? Explain your reasoning.

15. Write a situation that can be represented by the opposite of −42.

16. Higher Order Thinking Three friends all live on the same street that runs west to east. Beth lives 5 blocks from Ann. Carl lives 2 blocks from Beth. If the street is represented by a number line and Ann's house is located at 0, what are the possible locations for Carl's house? Assume that each unit on the number line represents 1 block.

Assessment Practice

17. Which of these situations can be represented with an integer that when combined with −9 makes 0? Select all that apply.

☐ You walk down 9 flights of stairs.
☐ You climb up 9 flights of stairs.
☐ The temperature drops 9°F.
☐ You spend $9 on a book.
☐ You earn $9 from your job.

18. Which of these situations can be represented by the opposite of 80? Select all that apply.

☐ An airplane descends 80 m.
☐ An elevator ascends 80 m.
☐ The cost of a train ticket drops by $80.
☐ You remove 80 songs from an MP3 player.
☐ Suzy's grandmother is 80 years old.

Lesson 1-2
Understand Rational Numbers

Go Online | PearsonRealize.com

I can... recognize rational numbers and write them in decimal form.

Solve & Discuss It!

Calvin wants to customize his surfboard so that it is wider than the 82 model but narrower than the 92 model. What measurement could be the width of his surfboard? Explain.

Be Precise Between which two numbers is the custom width located?

Calvin's Custom SURFBOARDS

Model	82	92	102
	$22\frac{1}{2}$" wide	$23\frac{1}{4}$" wide	24" wide
	$3\frac{1}{4}$" thick	$3\frac{1}{2}$" thick	$3\frac{5}{8}$" thick

Focus on math practices

Use Structure Lindy's surfboard is $23\frac{1}{3}$ inches wide. Between which two surfboard models is her custom surfboard's width? How do you know?

? **Essential Question** How are rational numbers written as decimals?

EXAMPLE 1 Write Rational Numbers in Decimal Form: Terminating Decimals

Juanita is reporting on pitching statistics. Pedro's fastball statistic is $\frac{52}{80}$. How can Juanita write the fastball statistic in decimal form?

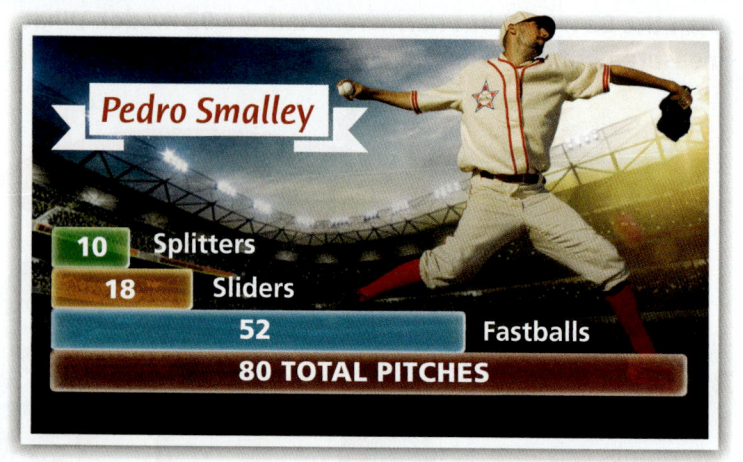

Pedro Smalley
- 10 Splitters
- 18 Sliders
- 52 Fastballs
- 80 TOTAL PITCHES

Make Sense and Persevere
How can you write a rational number as a decimal?

Make a bar diagram to show how the quantities are related.

52 Fastballs
80 TOTAL PITCHES

$\frac{52}{80}$

Divide the numerator by the denominator to convert the rational number $\frac{52}{80}$ to decimal form.

```
      0.65
80) 52.00
    −480
     400
    −400
       0
```

A **terminating decimal** is a decimal that ends in zero.

The remainder is 0, so the decimal form of $\frac{52}{80}$ is a terminating decimal.

Juanita can write $\frac{52}{80}$ as 0.65.

Try It!

In the next several games, the pitcher threw a total of 384 pitches and used a fastball 240 times. What decimal should Juanita use to update her report?

240 Fastballs
384 TOTAL PITCHES

Juanita should use the decimal ☐ to update her report.

```
         ☐ ☐ . ☐ ☐ ☐
384) 2 4 0 . 0 0  ☐
    −2 3 0 4
        9 6 0
       −7 6 8
          ☐ ☐ ☐ ☐
         −1 9 2 0
              ☐
```

Convince Me! How do you know that the answer is a terminating decimal?

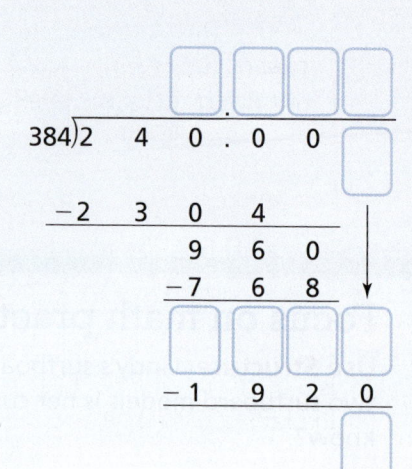

14   1-2 Understand Rational Numbers

EXAMPLE 2 Write Rational Numbers in Decimal Form: Repeating Decimals

A class votes on whether to change their school mascot. How can you express the number of students in favor of a new mascot in decimal form?

In a class of **18** students, **5** voted to change their mascot.

Divide to write $\frac{5}{18}$ in decimal form.

```
      0.277
18)5.000
   −3 6
     1 4 0
    −1 2 6
       1 4 0
      −1 2 6
          1 4
```

A **repeating decimal** has a decimal expansion that repeats the same digit, or block of digits, without end.

The products and differences repeat. The remainder will never be 0.

The decimal form of $\frac{5}{18}$ is 0.277... or $0.2\overline{7}$.

The ... means the decimal does not terminate.

A line over one or more digits indicates that those digits repeat.

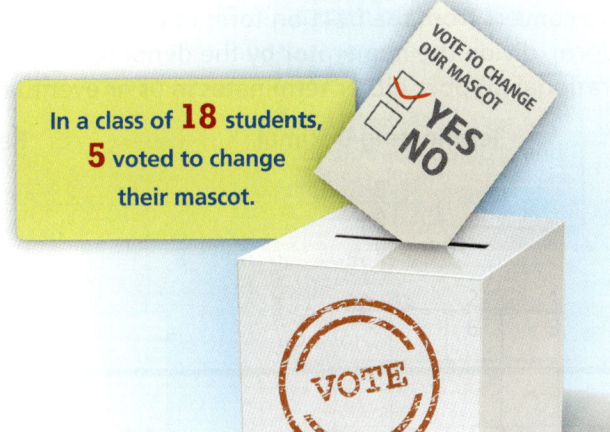

Try It!

What is the decimal form of $\frac{100}{3}$, $\frac{100}{5}$, and $\frac{100}{6}$? Determine whether each decimal repeats or terminates.

EXAMPLE 3 Recognize Rational Numbers in Decimal Form

Explain whether each of the following is a rational number.

a. −6.382

The decimal terminates, so this is a rational number.

b. $1.539\overline{81}$

The digits 8 and 1 repeat infinitely, so this is a rational number.

c. 0.43524982...

The decimal does not terminate and the digits do not repeat, so this is **NOT** a rational number.

Try It!

Is $-0.\overline{3}$ a rational number? Is 3.14144144414444... a rational number? Explain your reasoning.

1-2 Understand Rational Numbers   15

KEY CONCEPT

To convert from the fraction form of a rational number to its decimal form, divide the numerator by the denominator. The decimal form of a rational number either terminates in 0s or eventually repeats.

Terminating Decimal

$$\frac{3}{4}$$

$$4\overline{)3.00}^{0.75}$$

Repeating Decimal

$$\frac{1}{6}$$

$$6\overline{)1.00}^{0.1\overline{6}}$$

Do You Understand?

1. **Essential Question** How are rational numbers written as decimals?

2. **Reasoning** How can you use division to find the decimal equivalent of a rational number?

3. **Be Precise** What is the difference between a terminating decimal and a repeating decimal?

Do You Know How?

4. What is the decimal equivalent of each rational number?

   a. $\frac{7}{20}$

   b. $-\frac{23}{20}$

   c. $\frac{1}{18}$

   d. $-\frac{60}{22}$

5. There are 5,280 feet in a mile. What part of a mile, in decimal form, will you drive until you reach the exit?

   EXIT 1,000 FEET

Practice & Problem Solving

Scan for Multimedia

Leveled Practice In 6–8, write the decimal equivalent for each rational number. Use a bar over any repeating digits.

6. $\frac{2}{3}$

7. $\frac{3}{11}$

8. $8\frac{4}{9}$

9. Is $1.02\overline{27}$ a rational number? Explain.

10. Which should Aaron use to convert a fraction to a decimal?

    Ⓐ numerator$\overline{)}$denominator

    Ⓑ $\frac{denominator}{numerator} \cdot 100$

    Ⓒ denominator$\overline{)}$numerator

    Ⓓ $\frac{numerator}{denominator} \cdot 100$

11. Is the fraction $\frac{1}{3}$ equivalent to a terminating decimal or a decimal that does not terminate?

12. Determine whether the given number belongs to each set.

	Whole Numbers	Integers	Rational Numbers
−34			

13. Ariel incorrectly says that $2\frac{5}{8}$ is the same as 2.58.

    a. Convert $2\frac{5}{8}$ to a decimal.

    b. What was Ariel's likely error?

14. **Use Structure** Consider the rational number $\frac{3}{11}$.

    a. What are the values of a and b in $a\overline{)b}$ when you use division to find the decimal form?

    b. What is the decimal form for $\frac{3}{11}$?

15. At a grocery store, Daniel wants to buy $3\frac{1}{5}$ lb of ham. What decimal should the digital scale show?

    Write $3\frac{1}{5}$ as a fraction and then divide.

    The scale should read ☐ lb.

1-2 Understand Rational Numbers   17

16. **Reasoning** At a butcher shop, Hilda bought beef and pork. She left with $18\frac{8}{25}$ pounds of meat. Express the number of pounds of pork she bought using a decimal.

17. **Be Precise** Is 9.373 a repeating decimal? Is it rational? Explain your reasoning.

18. **Reasoning** Aiden has one box that is $3\frac{3}{11}$ feet tall and a second box that is 3.27 feet tall. If he stacks the boxes, about how tall will the stack be?

19. You are adding air to a tire. The air pressure in the tire should be $32\frac{27}{200}$ pounds per square inch. What decimal should you watch for on the digital pressure gauge?

20. **Higher Order Thinking** Dion has a pizza with a diameter of $10\frac{1}{3}$ in. Is the square box shown big enough to fit the pizza inside? Justify your answer.

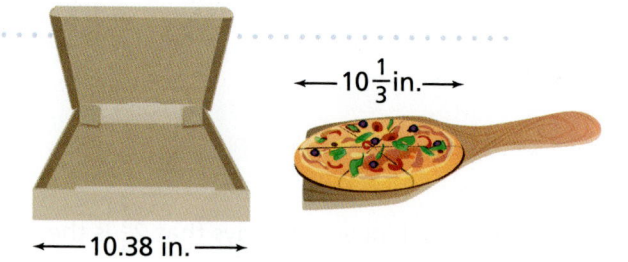

← $10\frac{1}{3}$ in. →

← 10.38 in. →

Assessment Practice

21. Which of the following shows $117\frac{151}{200}$ as a decimal?

    Ⓐ 117.755   Ⓑ $117.\overline{7}$ Ⓒ $117.\overline{5}$ Ⓓ 117.00

22. Use the negative fractions $-\frac{4}{5}$ and $-\frac{5}{6}$.

    PART A
    Find the decimal equivalents for each fraction.

    PART B
    Which is a repeating decimal? Which digit is repeating?

18   1-2 Understand Rational Numbers

Lesson 1-3
Add Integers

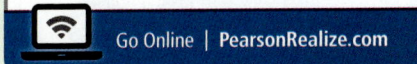

Go Online | PearsonRealize.com

I can... add integers.

Explore It!

Rain increases the height of water in a kiddie pool, while evaporation decreases the height. The pool water level is currently 2 inches above the fill line.

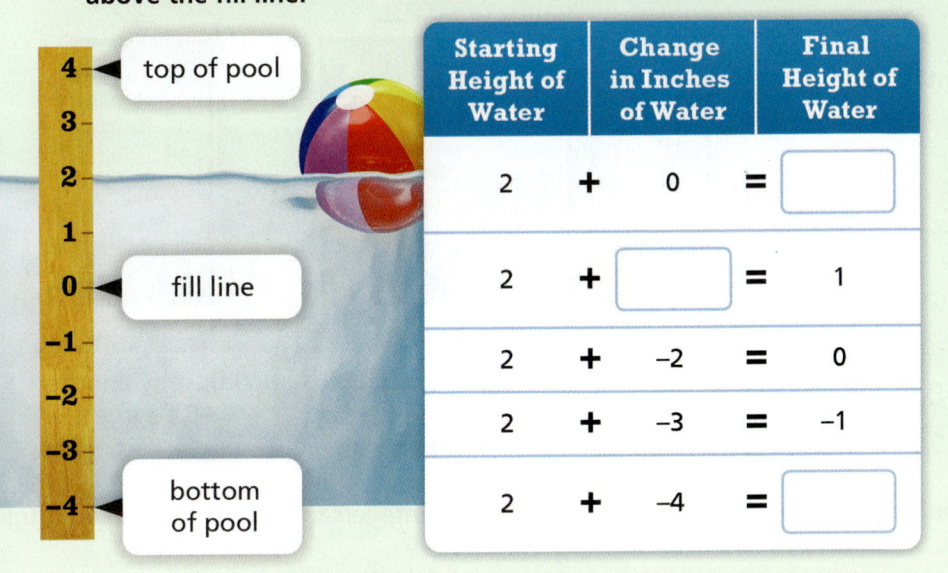

Starting Height of Water	Change in Inches of Water	Final Height of Water
2	+ 0 =	☐
2	+ ☐ =	1
2	+ −2 =	0
2	+ −3 =	−1
2	+ −4 =	☐

A. Look for patterns in the equations in the table so you can fill in the missing numbers. Describe any relationships you notice.

B. Will the sum of 2 and (−6) be a positive or negative number? Explain.

Focus on math practices

Look for Relationships Suppose the water level of the pool started at 2 inches below the fill line. Make a table to show the starting height of the water, the change in inches, and the new final height of the water.

19

Essential Question How do you use what you know about absolute value to add integers?

EXAMPLE 1 Add Two Negative Integers

Nita wants to straighten a photo. She uses an app to adjust the tilt. What was the total tilt adjustment?

Reasoning Why is the total tilt adjustment negative?

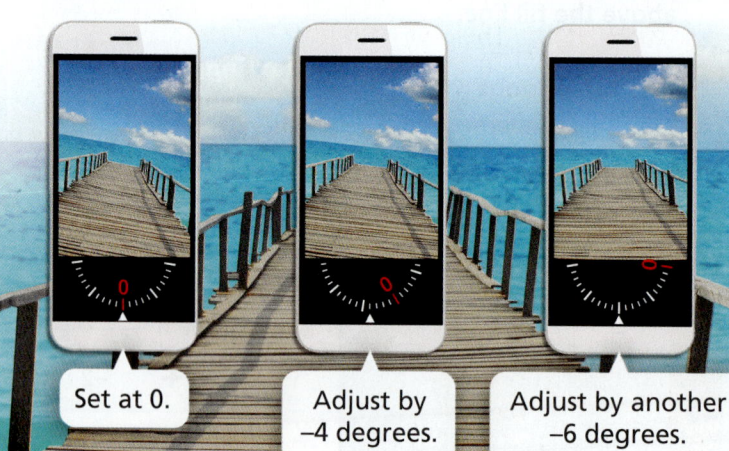

Set at 0. Adjust by −4 degrees. Adjust by another −6 degrees.

Use a number line to represent the total tilt adjustment.

Start at 0. Move 4 units left to show an adjustment of −4.

Then move 6 units left to show an adjustment of −6. The total adjustment was −10.

The sum of −4 and −6 is located 6 units to the left of −4.

The tilt starts at 0 degrees.

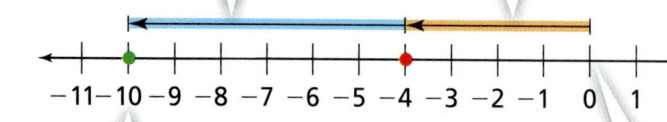

Add integers to find the total tilt adjustment.

$-4 + (-6)$

Because you moved 4 units and then 6 units in the **same direction** on the number line, **add** the absolute values to find the amount of tilt.

$|-4| + |-6|$
$4 + 6 = 10$

10 represents the amount of tilt.

Because you moved to the **left** twice, the sum is negative.

$-4 + (-6) = -10$

Both adjustments are negative, so the tilt is negative.

The total tilt adjustment was −10.

Try It!

Dana recorded a temperature drop of 2° and a second temperature drop of 3°. What is the total change in temperature?

☐ + ☐ = ☐

The sign of the sum is ☐. The total change in temperature is ☐°.

Convince Me! Would the sum of two positive integers be positive or negative? Explain.

20   1-3 Add Integers

EXAMPLE 2 — Add Integers with Different Signs

Kara entered her chili recipe into the neighborhood cook-off. Nine judges rated each recipe with a thumbs up (+1) or thumbs down (−1). What was the final rating for Kara's recipe?

Reasoning There were more thumbs-down votes, so the final rating is negative.

Use a number line to represent Kara's final rating.

Start at 0. Move 5 units left for −5. Move 4 units right for 4. The final rating is −1.

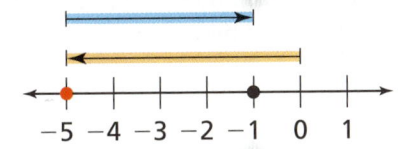

The sum of −5 and 4 is located 4 units to the right of −5.

Add integers to find Kara's final rating.

$-5 + 4$

Because you moved in **different directions** on the number line, **subtract** the absolute values.

$|-5| - |4|$

There is 1 more thumbs down vote than thumbs up.

$5 - 4 = 1$

Because you moved a **greater distance** to the left than to the right, the sum is negative.

$-5 + 4 = -1$

The sum is negative because $|-5|$ is greater than $|4|$.

The final rating for Kara's recipe was −1.

EXAMPLE 3 — Identify Additive Inverses and Opposite Integers

Playing golf, Mike got a +2 on the first hole and −2 on the second hole. What is his combined score for the first two holes?

$2 + (-2)$

$|2| = 2$ and $|-2| = 2$

$2 - 2 = 0$

So, $2 + (-2) = 0$.

When the signs of the addends are different, subtract the absolute values.

Mike's combined score for the first two holes is 0.

Two numbers that have a sum of 0 are called **additive inverses**, or opposites.

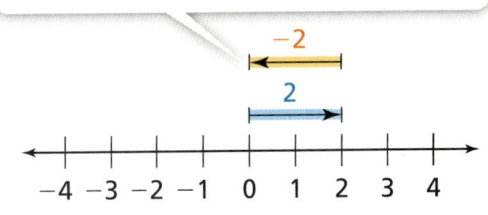

Try It!

Find the sum for each expression.

a. $-66 + 42$

b. $-57 + 57$

c. $29 + (-28)$

1-3 Add Integers

KEY CONCEPT

When adding integers with the **same** sign, find the **sum** of the absolute values.

$(-36) + (-12)$

$|-36| = 36$ and $|-12| = 12$
$36 + 12 = 48$

So, $(-36) + (-12) = -48$ — Use the **same** sign as the addends.

When adding integers with **different** signs, find the **difference** of the absolute values.

$18 + (-14)$

$|18| = 18$ and $|-14| = 14$
$18 - 14 = 4$

So, $18 + (-14) = 4$ — Use the sign of the greater absolute value.

Do You Understand?

1. **Essential Question** How do you use what you know about absolute value to add integers?

2. **Reasoning** How can you tell the sign of the sum of a positive and negative integer without doing any calculations?

3. **Model with Math** How would you use a number line to determine the sum of two negative integers?

Do You Know How?

4. Sarah bought a bike that cost $260. She had a coupon that was worth $55 off the cost of any bike. Use the expression $260 + (-55)$ to find how much Sarah paid for her bike.

5. A shark is swimming 60 feet below the surface of the ocean. There is a fish that is 25 feet deeper in the water. Use the expression $(-60) + (-25)$ to describe the fish's location relative to the surface of the ocean.

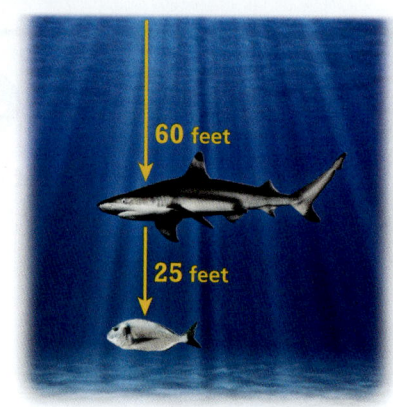

6. The high temperature one day was 30°F. Then the temperature dropped 23 degrees during the night. Does the expression $30 + (-23)$ represent the temperature at night? Explain.

Name: _____

Practice & Problem Solving

Leveled Practice For 7–9, use a number line to help find the sum.

7. 5 + (−3) is ☐ units from 5, in the ☐ direction.

Use the number line to find 5 + (−3).

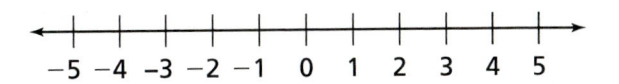

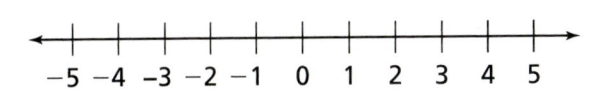

-5 -4 -3 -2 -1 0 1 2 3 4 5

8. −1 + (−3) is ☐ units from −1, in the ☐ direction.

-5 -4 -3 -2 -1 0 1 2 3 4 5

9. In City A, the temperature rises 9° from 8 A.M. to 9 A.M. Then the temperature drops 8° from 9 A.M. to 10 A.M. In City B, the temperature drops 5° from 8 A.M. to 9 A.M. Then the temperature drops 4° from 9 A.M. to 10 A.M.

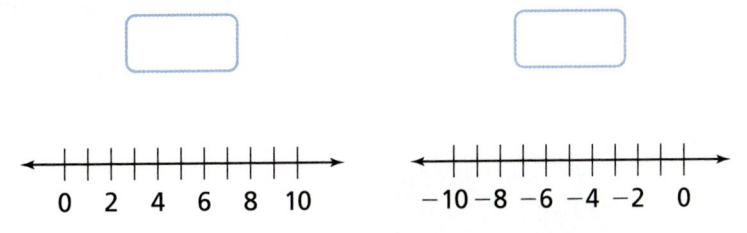

☐   ☐

0 2 4 6 8 10   −10 −8 −6 −4 −2 0

a. What expression represents the change in temperature for City A?

b. What integer represents the change in temperature for City A?

c. What expression represents the change in temperature for City B?

d. What integer represents the change in temperature for City B?

e. Which city has the greater change in temperature from 8 A.M. to 10 A.M.?

10. An airplane flying at an altitude of 30,000 feet flies up to avoid a storm. Immediately after passing the storm, the airplane returns to its original altitude.

a. What integer represents the airplane's change in altitude to avoid the storm?

b. What integer represents the airplane's change in altitude immediately after passing the storm?

c. Use Appropriate Tools Draw a number line to represent the airplane's change in altitude.

The airplane flies up to 38,000 feet to avoid a storm.

30,000   34,000   38,000

Go Online | PearsonRealize.com

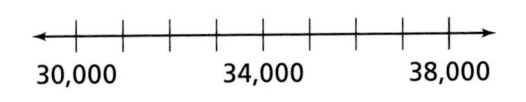

1-3 Add Integers   23

11. A deep-sea diver dives 81 feet from the surface. He then dives 14 more feet. The diver's depth can be represented by $-81 + (-14)$. What is the diver's present location?

12. Rena's rowboat drifts 23 feet from shore, followed by 9 more feet. The rowboat's current position can be represented by $-23 + (-9)$. What integer represents the rowboat's position?

13. Critique Reasoning A submarine traveling 200 meters below the surface of the ocean increases its depth by 45 meters. Adam says that the new location of the submarine is -155 meters. Describe an error Adam could have made that would result in the answer he gave.

14. Kim has $45 to spend for a day at the zoo. She pays $17 for admission, $8 for lunch, and $4 for a snack.

  a. Model with Math Use integers to write an addition expression that represents the amount of money Kim has left.

  b. Kim goes to the gift shop and finds a T-shirt she likes for $19. Does she have enough money to buy the T-shirt? Explain.

15. Higher Order Thinking Samantha has $300 for guitar lessons to learn her favorite song. Mrs. Jones charges $80 per lesson and requires three lessons to teach Samantha the song. Mr. Beliz charges $62 per lesson and will require four lessons to teach Samantha the song. Use integers to represent what each teacher charges. Which is the better deal for Samantha?

Assessment Practice

16. Draw lines to match each situation on the left with its addition expression on the right.

A fish swims at 10 ft below sea level, and then swims another 10 ft deeper to avoid a shark.	$10 + (-10)$
Troy takes 10 steps forward, and then takes 10 steps back.	$-10 + (-10)$
The temperature drops 10 degrees, and then rises 10 degrees.	$-10 + (10)$

24   1-3 Add Integers

Lesson 1-4
Subtract Integers

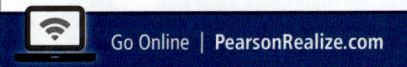

Go Online | PearsonRealize.com

I can... subtract integers.

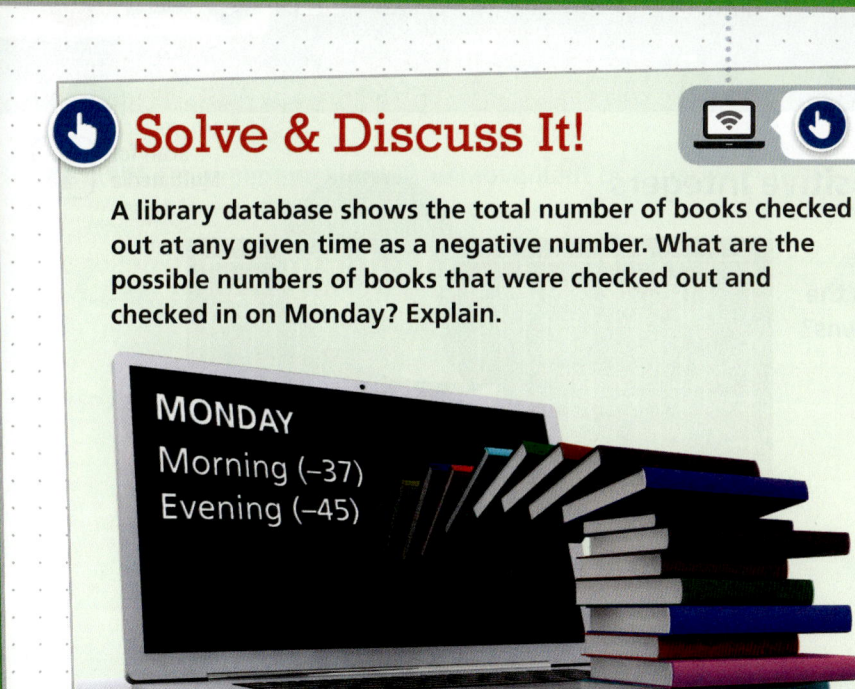

Solve & Discuss It!

A library database shows the total number of books checked out at any given time as a negative number. What are the possible numbers of books that were checked out and checked in on Monday? Explain.

MONDAY
Morning (−37)
Evening (−45)

Make Sense and Persevere How can you use the data to understand what happened during the day?

Focus on math practices

Reasoning Suppose the library database showed 0 for Monday evening. What do you know about the number of books checked out and checked in that day?

? Essential Question How is subtracting integers related to adding integers?

EXAMPLE 1 Subtract Positive Integers

A football team gains 3 yards on first down. On second down, they lose 8 yards. What is the total change in yards after the first two downs?

Look for Relationships You can use what you know about adding integers to subtract integers.

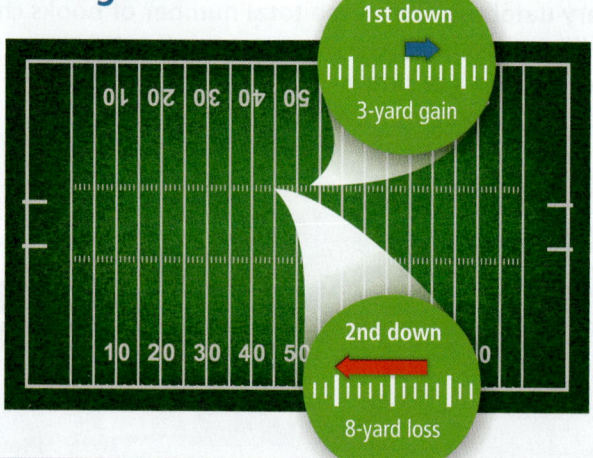

1st down — 3-yard gain
2nd down — 8-yard loss

Use a number line to represent the team's total change in yards.

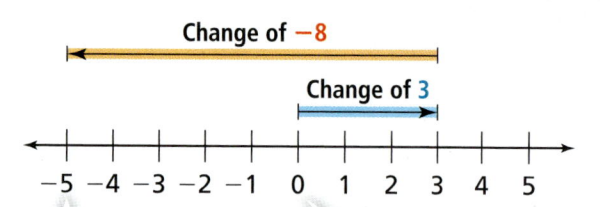

Change of −8
Change of 3

−5 −4 −3 −2 −1 0 1 2 3 4 5

The team's final position represents a 5-yard loss.

0 represents the team's starting position.

Use a subtraction expression to represent the teams' change in yards.

$3 - 8$
$= 3 + (-8)$

Now add.

Subtraction is the same as adding the opposite. To subtract 8, add its opposite, −8.

$|3| = 3$ and $|-8| = 8$
$8 - 3 = 5$
$3 - 8 = -5$

The total change in yards after the first two downs is represented by −5.

✓ Try It!

On the next play, the team gained 5 yards and then lost 6 yards. What is the total change in yards?

$5 - \boxed{}$

$= 5 + \boxed{}$

$= \boxed{}$

☐-yard loss
☐-yard gain

−5 −4 −3 −2 −1 0 1 2 3 4 5

The total change in yards is ☐, so they had a total loss of ☐ yard.

Convince Me! Is the additive inverse of an integer always negative? Explain.

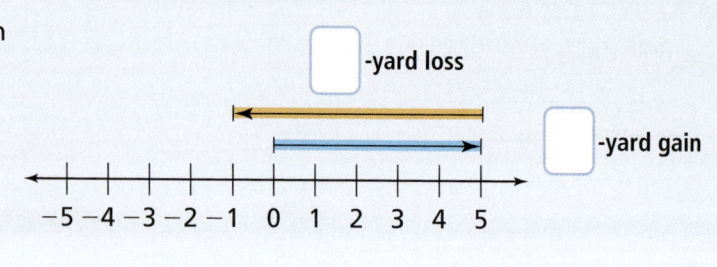

26   1-4 Subtract Integers

EXAMPLE 2: Subtract Integers with Different Signs

Ian's football team lost 2 yards on a running play. Then they received a 5-yard penalty. What is the team's total change in yards?

Write a subtraction expression to represent the change in yards.

$-2 - 5$
$= (-2) + (-5)$ — Write an equivalent addition expression.

Add.

$|-2| = 2$ and $|-5| = 5$
$2 + 5 = 7$
$(-2) + (-5) = -7$
$-2 - 5 = -7$

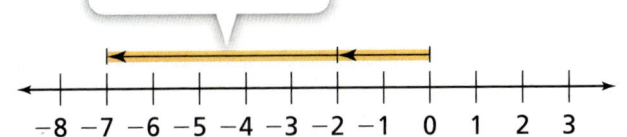

Move 5 units to the left from -2.

The team's total change in yards is represented by -7, so they lost 7 yards.

EXAMPLE 3: Subtract Negative Integers

Find $-7 - (-8)$.

Write $-7 - (-8)$ as an equivalent addition expression. Then add.

$-7 + (8)$
$|-7| = 7$ and $|8| = 8$
$8 - 7 = 1$
$-7 + (8) = 1$
$-7 - (-8) = 1$

The signs of the addends are different, so find the difference of the absolute values. The sum has the same sign as the greater absolute value.

Subtracting -8 is the same as adding the opposite of -8, or $+8$.

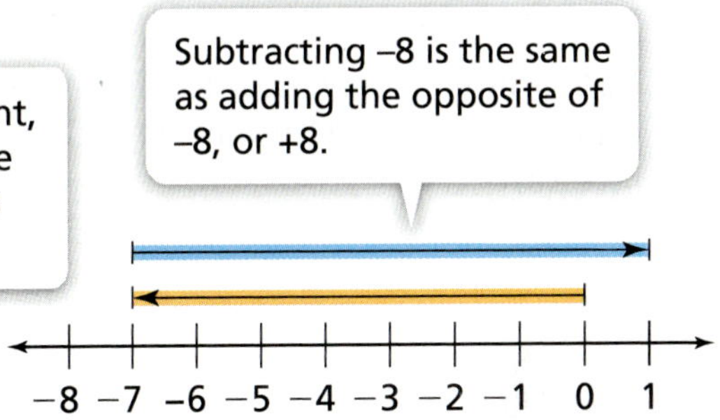

✓ Try It!

Subtract. Use a number line to help you find the answer.

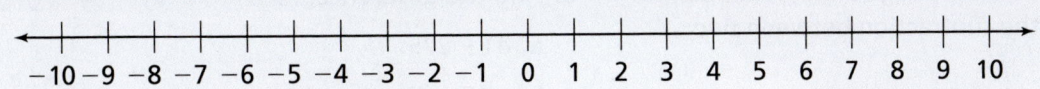

a. $-4 - 6$ **b.** $-6 - (-4)$ **c.** $4 - (-6)$

d. $6 - 4$ **e.** $4 - 6$ **f.** $-4 - (-6)$

1-4 Subtract Integers

KEY CONCEPT

When subtracting integers, such as $a - b$, you can use the additive inverse to write subtraction as an equivalent addition expression.

Subtracting b is the same as adding the opposite of b.

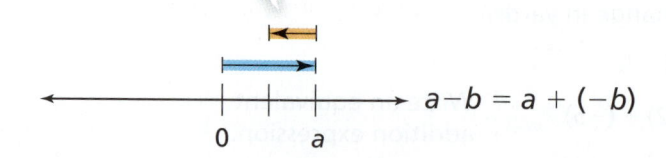

$$a - b = a + (-b)$$

Do You Understand?

1. **Essential Question** How is subtracting integers related to adding integers?

2. **Reasoning** Explain how to simplify the expression $-98 - 31$ using the additive inverse.

3. **Model with Math** How can you use a number line to represent the subtraction between two integers?

Do You Know How?

4. It was 12°C when Preston got home from school. The weather report shows a storm front moving in that will drop the temperature by 17°C. What is the expected temperature?

5. Complete the equation.
   $-67 - \boxed{} = 0$

6. Find the difference.
   a. $41 - 275$
   b. $-15 - 47$
   c. $-72 - (-151)$
   d. $612 - (-144)$

Name: _____

Practice & Problem Solving

Leveled Practice In 7–8, fill in the boxes to solve.

7. What subtraction expression does the number line model show?

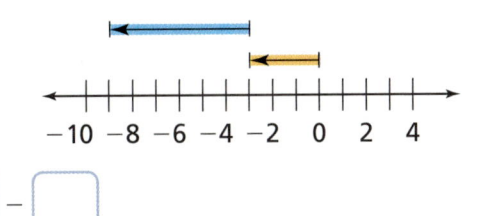

□ − □

8. What is the value of the expression $-9 - (-5)$?

$-9 - (-5)$

$= -9 \;\square\; 5$

$= \square$

9. The temperature at the beginning of the day was 6°F. The temperature dropped 9°F by the end of the day. Use the number line to find the temperature at the end of the day.

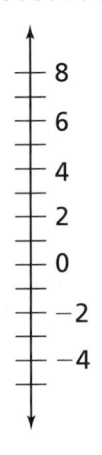

10. Murphy and Naryam do their math homework together. When they find $9 - (-8)$, they get different answers. Murphy claims the difference is 17. Naryam claims the difference is -1.

a. Who is correct?

b. What error likely led to the incorrect answer?

11. The news reports that today's high temperature is 16°F colder than yesterday's high temperature. Yesterday's high temperature was −2°F.

a. Write an expression to represent today's high temperature.

b. **Reasoning** Is today's high temperature positive or negative? Why?

12. Max sprints forward 10 feet and then stops and sprints back 15 feet. Use subtraction to explain where Max is relative to where he started.

Go Online | PearsonRealize.com

1-4 Subtract Integers 29

13. **Higher Order Thinking** Use the number line at the right.

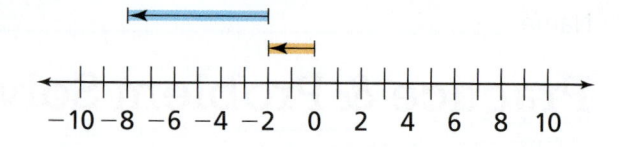

    a. What subtraction equation does the number line represent?

    b. Use the number line to represent a different subtraction equation that has the same difference shown in the number line. Write the subtraction equation.

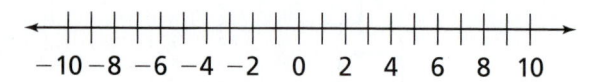

14. A crane lifts a pallet of concrete blocks 8 feet from the back of a truck. The truck drives away and the crane lowers the pallet 13 feet. What is the final position of the pallet relative to where it started in the back of the truck?

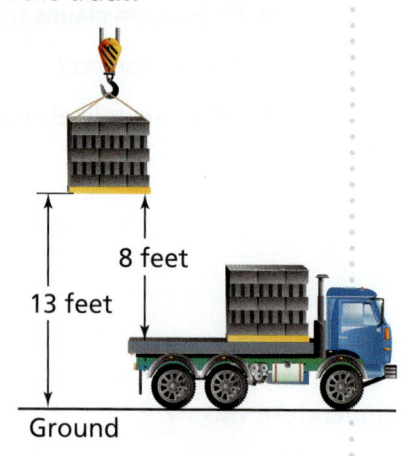

15. **Make Sense and Persevere** At its highest point, the elevation of a county is 5,762 feet above sea level. At its lowest point, the elevation of the county is 9 feet below sea level.

    a. Write an expression using integers to represent the difference between the elevations.

    b. Will the answer be written as a positive or negative integer?

    c. What is the difference between the highest and lowest points of the county?

Assessment Practice

16. Which number line model shows the subtraction $2 - 4$?

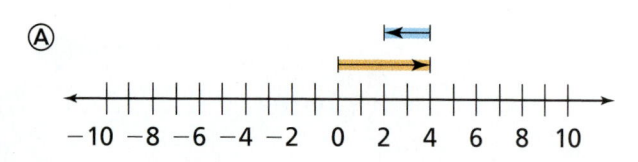

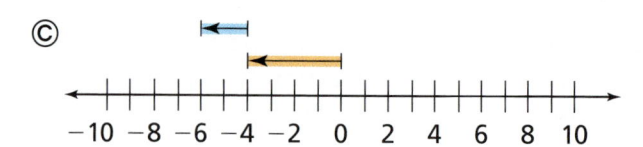

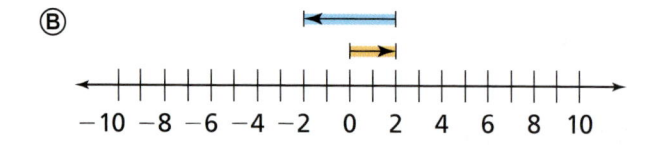

    Ⓐ
    Ⓑ
    Ⓒ
    Ⓓ

30 1-4 Subtract Integers

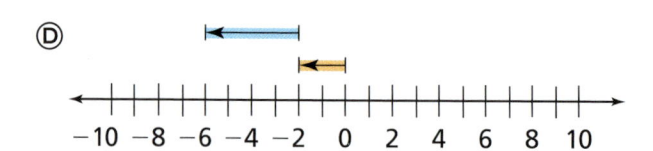

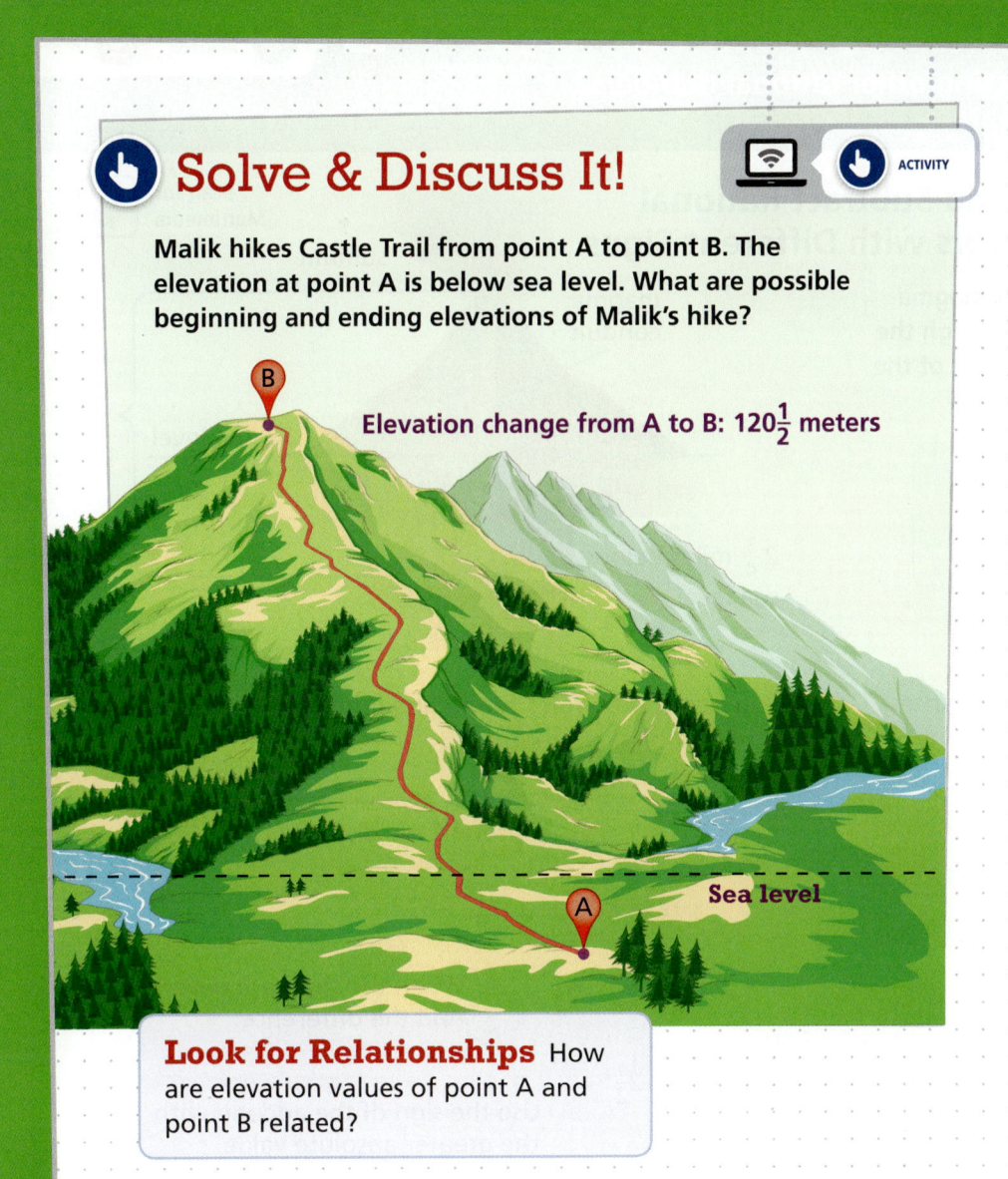

Lesson 1-5
Add and Subtract Rational Numbers

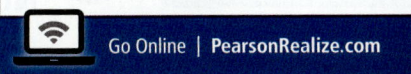

Go Online | PearsonRealize.com

I can... add and subtract rational numbers.

Solve & Discuss It!

Malik hikes Castle Trail from point A to point B. The elevation at point A is below sea level. What are possible beginning and ending elevations of Malik's hike?

Elevation change from A to B: $120\frac{1}{2}$ meters

Sea level

Look for Relationships How are elevation values of point A and point B related?

Focus on math practices

Reasoning What would be different about the hike from point B to point A?

31

Essential Question How are adding and subtracting integers related to adding and subtracting other rational numbers?

EXAMPLE 1 Add and Subtract Rational Numbers with Different Signs

Lava flows from an active volcano's magma reservoir located below sea level through the magma conduit. How far is the summit of the volcano from sea level?

summit

magma conduit

sea level

$5\frac{1}{4}$ miles

$2\frac{3}{4}$ miles below sea level

Generalize You can use the rules for adding integers to add all other rational numbers.

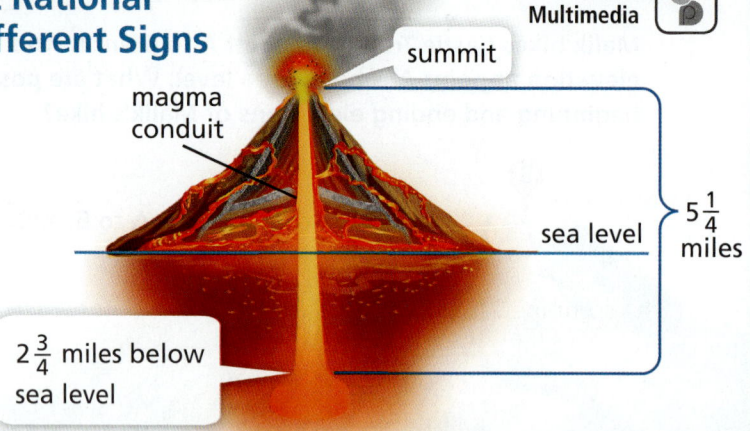

Use a number line to represent the distances.

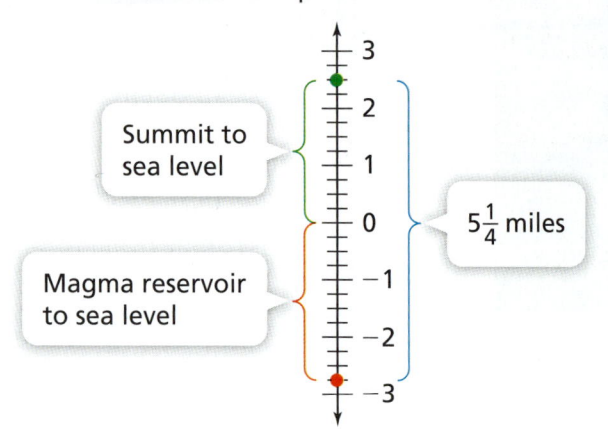

Summit to sea level

Magma reservoir to sea level

$5\frac{1}{4}$ miles

You can use the rules for adding integers to add any other rational numbers.

$\left(-2\frac{3}{4}\right) + 5\frac{1}{4}$ ← Write an expression to represent the distance.

$\left|-2\frac{3}{4}\right| = 2\frac{3}{4}$ and $\left|5\frac{1}{4}\right| = 5\frac{1}{4}$

$5\frac{1}{4} - 2\frac{3}{4} = 2\frac{1}{2}$ ← When the signs are different, find the difference.

$-2\frac{3}{4} + 5\frac{1}{4} = 2\frac{1}{2}$ ← Use the sign of the addend with the greater absolute value.

The summit of the volcano is $2\frac{1}{2}$ miles above sea level.

Try It!

A dolphin is at the surface of the water and then descends to a depth of $4\frac{1}{2}$ feet. Then the dolphin swims down another $2\frac{3}{4}$ feet. What is the location of the dolphin relative to the surface of the water?

$-4\frac{1}{2} - \boxed{}$

$-4\frac{1}{2} + \boxed{} = \boxed{}$

$\boxed{}$ feet

The location of the dolphin relative to the surface of the water is $\boxed{}$ feet.

dolphin's location relative to the surface of the water

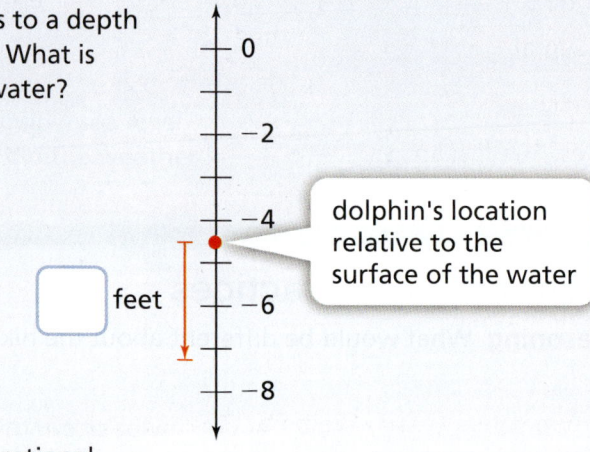

Convince Me! How are adding and subtracting two rational numbers with different signs related to adding and subtracting two integers with different signs?

32 1-5 Add and Subtract Rational Numbers

EXAMPLE 2 — Use Properties of Operations to Add and Subtract

The force of gravity added to the force of thrust is the combined force at work on a model rocket. What is the combined force, in newtons, on the rocket?

$-0.49 + 1\frac{1}{2}$

$= 1\frac{1}{2} + (-0.49)$ — Use the Commutative Property and additive inverses as a strategy to add.

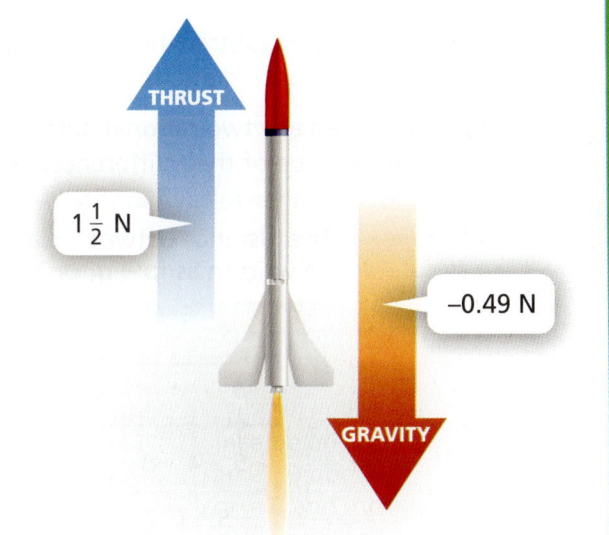

$= 1\frac{1}{2} - 0.49$

$= 1.5 - 0.49$

$= 1.01$

The combined force on the rocket is 1.01 newtons.

THRUST
$1\frac{1}{2}$ N
−0.49 N
GRAVITY

Try It!

Find the sum or difference of the rational numbers.

a. $-2.5 + \left(-5\frac{6}{10}\right)$ **b.** $-4.4 - \left(-1\frac{1}{2}\right)$ **c.** $-135.4 + 78\frac{1}{2}$

EXAMPLE 3 — Find Distances on a Number Line

Ruby looks over the edge of her boat and sees fish 0.4 meter below the surface of the water. If Ruby holds a 1-meter-long net at 0.5 meter above sea level, can she reach the fish? Explain.

ONE WAY

$|0.5 - (-0.4)|$

$= |0.5 + 0.4|$

$= |0.9|$

$= 0.9$

To find the distance between any two points on a number line, find the absolute value of their difference.

ANOTHER WAY

$|-0.4 - 0.5|$

$= |-0.4 + (-0.5)|$

$= |-0.9|$

$= 0.9$

Ruby holds the net — 0.5
0.4
0.3
0.2
0.1
Sea level — 0
−0.1
−0.2
−0.3
Fish — −0.4
−0.5

Yes. The fish are 0.9 meter below where Ruby holds the net, so Ruby can reach the fish with a 1-meter-long net.

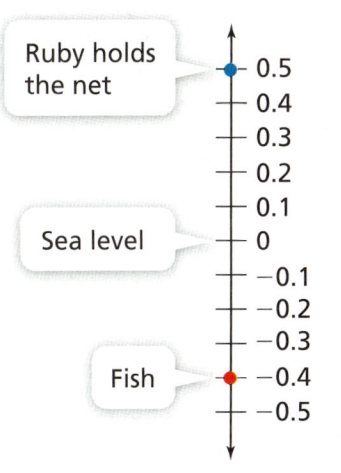

Try It!

Two divers are swimming at different depths below sea level. One diver is at −25.5 feet. The other diver is at −40.75 feet. How much farther below sea level is the diver who is farthest below sea level?

Go Online | PearsonRealize.com   1-5 Add and Subtract Rational Numbers

KEY CONCEPT

The rules for adding and subtracting all rational numbers are the same as those for adding and subtracting integers.

The distance between any two rational numbers p and q on a number line is the absolute value of their difference.

The distance between p and q can be written as $|p - q|$ or $|q - p|$.

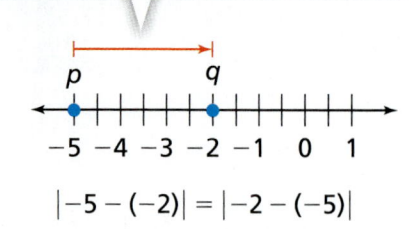

$|-5 - (-2)| = |-2 - (-5)|$

Do You Understand?

1. **Essential Question** How are adding and subtracting integers related to adding and subtracting other rational numbers?

2. **Reasoning** When finding the distance between two rational numbers on a number line, does the order of the numbers you subtract matter? Explain.

3. **Critique Reasoning** Gwen says that the sum of $-1\frac{3}{4}$ and $2\frac{1}{2}$ is the same as the difference between $2\frac{1}{2}$ and $1\frac{3}{4}$. Is Gwen correct? Explain why or why not.

Do You Know How?

4. What is the distance between the top of the fishing pole and the fish?

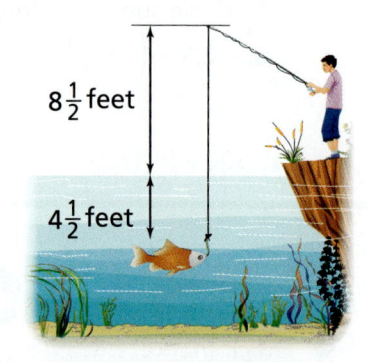

   $8\frac{1}{2}$ feet

   $4\frac{1}{2}$ feet

5. A shark began at 172.5 meters below sea level and then swam up 137.1 meters. Where is the shark's location now in relation to sea level?

6. Find the sum or difference.

   a. $-12\frac{1}{2} + 4\frac{1}{2}$

   b. $-0.35 - (-0.25)$

Name: _____

Practice & Problem Solving

Scan for Multimedia

Leveled Practice In 7–8, complete the expressions to find the sum or difference.

7. $3.2 - (-5.7)$

$= 3.2 + \boxed{}$

$= \boxed{}$

8. $\frac{12}{13} + \left(\frac{-1}{13}\right)$

$= \boxed{} - \boxed{}$

$= \boxed{}$

9. Reasoning When Tom simplified the expression $-2.6 + (-5.4)$, he got 2.8. What mistake did Tom likely make?

10. The temperature in a town is 36.6°F during the day and −12.6°F at night. What is the temperature change from day to night?

11. Simplify each expression.

a. $50\frac{1}{2} + (-12.3)$

b. $-50\frac{1}{2} + (-12.3)$

c. $-50\frac{1}{2} + 12.3$

12. At the beginning of the day, the stock market goes up $30\frac{1}{2}$ points. At the end of the day, the stock market goes down $120\frac{1}{4}$ points. What is the total change in the stock market from the beginning of the day to the end of the day?

13. A dolphin is swimming 18 feet below the surface of the ocean. There is a coast guard helicopter 75.5 feet above the surface of the water that is directly above the dolphin. What is the distance between the dolphin and the helicopter?

14. A bird flies from its nest to the bottom of the canyon. How far did the bird fly?

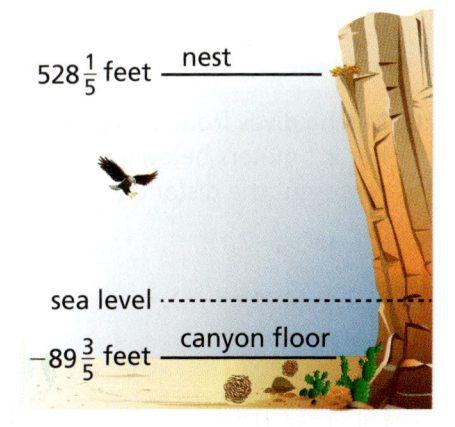

$528\frac{1}{5}$ feet —— nest

sea level

$-89\frac{3}{5}$ feet —— canyon floor

Go Online | PearsonRealize.com

1-5 Add and Subtract Rational Numbers 35

15. A scuba diving instructor takes a group of students to a depth of 54.96 feet. Then they ascend 22.38 feet to see some fish. Where are the fish in relation to the surface?

16. **Model with Math** Write an addition expression that is represented by the number line.

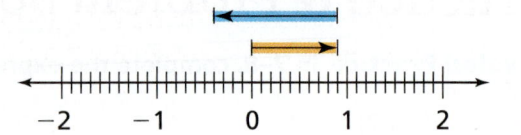

17. The roots of a plant reach down $3\frac{3}{4}$ inches below ground. How many inches is the plant above the ground?

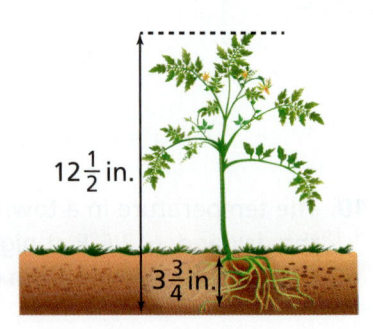

    $12\frac{1}{2}$ in.

    $3\frac{3}{4}$ in.

18. **Higher Order Thinking**

    a. Simplify the expression $(-13.2) + 8.1$.

    b. How are $(-13.2) + 8.1$ and $13.2 + (-8.1)$ related? Explain without computing.

    c. Using a property of operations, what can you say about the sum of the two expressions?

Assessment Practice

19. The temperatures at sunrise and sunset are shown in the table.

	Temperature at Sunrise (°F)	Temperature at Sunset (°F)
Day 1	−11.31	13.49
Day 2	−7.69	25.25

    PART A
    What was the temperature change on Day 1? On Day 2?

    PART B
    On which day did the temperature change more? Explain your reasoning.

20. Mischa dives from a platform that is 5 meters above water. Her dive takes her 2.1 meters below the surface of the water. Which expression could represent the distance, in meters, that Mischa dives? Select all that apply.

    ☐ $|5 - (-2.1)|$
    ☐ $|-(2.1) - (-5)|$
    ☐ $|2.1 - 5|$
    ☐ $|-(2.1) - 5|$
    ☐ $|5 + (-2.1)|$

36 1-5 Add and Subtract Rational Numbers

Name: _____

MID-TOPIC CHECKPOINT
TOPIC 1

1. **Vocabulary** How do you find the additive inverse of a number? Give an example of a number and its additive inverse. *Lesson 1-3*

2. A plastic toy submarine is held 15 centimeters below the water surface in a bath tub. The submarine is let go and rises 15 centimeters. What integer represents the toy submarine's position with respect to the surface of the water? *Lesson 1-1*

3. The temperature in the late afternoon was −7.5°C. It dropped 5 degrees by early evening and then dropped another 8.5 degrees by midnight. What was the temperature at midnight? *Lessons 1-3, 1-4, and 1-5*

4. The floor of an elevator in a building is 30 feet above ground level. It travels down to the lower level of the building, where the floor is 10 feet below ground level. What distance has the elevator's floor traveled? *Lessons 1-4 and 1-5*

5. Greg says that $3.\overline{3}$ is a rational number. Kari says $3.\overline{3}$ is not a terminating decimal. Who is correct and why? *Lesson 1-2*

6. Cece is hiking on a mountain and stops at $15\frac{5}{8}$ feet above sea level. The base of the mountain is 10.2 feet below sea level. What is the vertical distance between Cece and the base of the mountain? *Lesson 1-5*

   Ⓐ 5.425 feet

   Ⓑ 25.825 feet

   Ⓒ $25\frac{3}{8}$ feet

   Ⓓ $5\frac{1}{4}$ feet

How well did you do on the mid-topic checkpoint? Fill in the stars.

TOPIC 1
MID-TOPIC PERFORMANCE TASK

An oceanographer, Dr. Price, is studying the types of sea life at various depths.

Location	Sea Life	Depth Relative to Sea Level (m)
A	Eels	−895.9
B	Eels	$-1{,}098\frac{3}{20}$
C	Shrimp	−2,784.75
D	Shrimp	$-3{,}259\frac{5}{8}$

PART A

Dr. Price uses a table to organize the types of sea life and the positions relative to sea level of each location.

Complete each sentence.

The difference between Location A and Location B is _____ meters.

The difference between Location B and Location C is _____ meters.

The difference between Location C and Location D is _____ meters.

PART B

After observing Location B, Dr. Price returns to Location A before descending to Location C. What is the total distance she travels?

PART C

Dr. Price descends to Location D to observe shrimp. She then ascends and stops to observe sea life that is halfway between Location B and Location C. What is the total distance between Location D and where Dr. Price stopped to observe?

Lesson 1-6
Multiply Integers

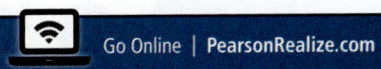

Go Online | PearsonRealize.com

I can... multiply integers.

Explore It!

A popular beach erodes 4 inches per year on average.

A. How many years will it take for the coastline to erode one foot?

B. The number line below shows the expected change in the coastline as years pass. How could you use the number line to show the erosion after 10 years?

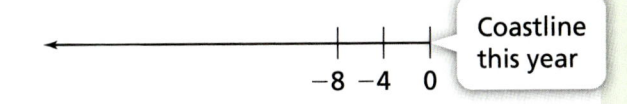

−8 −4 0 ← Coastline this year

Focus on math practices

Be Precise What expression could you use to represent the change in the coastline in 5 years?

? Essential Question How do the signs of factors affect their product?

EXAMPLE 1 — Multiply a Negative Integer by a Positive Integer

While playing a board game, unlucky Lawrence had to move back 2 spaces for 4 turns in a row. What integer represents his change in position?

Model with Math What integer can you use to represent the number of spaces Lawrence had to move back each turn?

Use a number line to represent the change in position on the game board.

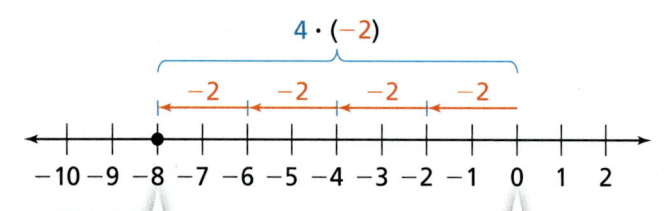

$4 \cdot (-2)$

−8 represents the change in position on the board.

0 represents the starting position.

The total change in position on the board is −8. Lawrence had to move back 8 spaces.

Use multiplication and properties of operations to show why $4 \cdot (-2) = -8$.

$4 \cdot (-2 + 2) = 0$

$4 \cdot (-2) + 4 \cdot 2 = 0$

$4 \cdot (-2) + 8 = 0$

$? + 8 = 0$

So, $4 \cdot (-2) = -8$.

Use additive inverses and the Zero Property of Multiplication to write a multiplication problem.

You know that opposites add to 0, so $-8 + 8 = 0$.

Generalize A rule for multiplication of integers is: positive • negative = negative.

✓ Try It!

A race car game takes 6 points from a player each time the player hits a cone. What integer represents the change in total points if the player hits 10 cones?

10 · ☐ = ☐

The change in total points is ☐.

Convince Me! Could the product of a positive integer and a negative integer be positive? Explain.

40 1-6 Multiply Integers

EXAMPLE 2 — Multiply a Positive Integer by a Negative Integer

What is the balloon's change in elevation in 3 minutes?

$-500 \cdot 3$ — Write an expression to represent the change in elevation.

$= 3 \cdot (-500)$

$= -1,500$

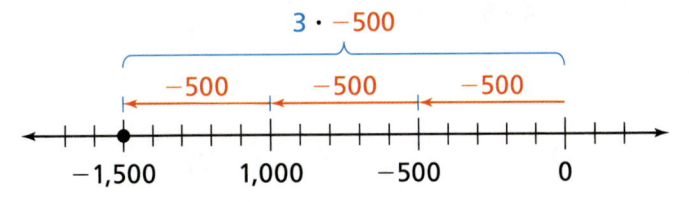

The change in elevation for the balloon is $-1,500$ feet.

Generalize A rule for multiplication of integers is: negative • positive = negative.

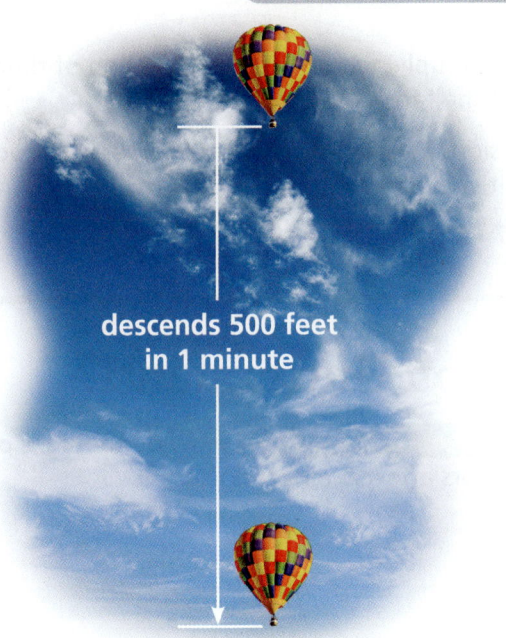

descends 500 feet in 1 minute

EXAMPLE 3 — Multiply a Negative Integer by a Negative Integer

a. Use a number line to represent $-3 \cdot (-10)$.

$3 \cdot (-10) = -30$

$-(3 \cdot (-10))$ is the opposite of $3 \cdot (-10)$. So, $-3 \cdot (-10) = 30$.

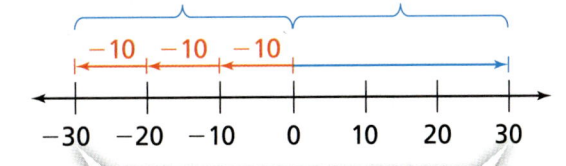

Opposites are the same distance from 0, but on opposite sides of 0.

b. Use multiplication and properties of operations to show why $-3 \cdot (-10) = 30$.

$-3 \cdot (-10 + 10) = 0$

$-3 \cdot (-10) + -3 \cdot 10 = 0$

$-3 \cdot (-10) + (-30) = 0$

$? \quad + (-30) = 0$

So, $-3 \cdot (-10) = 30$.

Use additive inverses and the Zero Property of Multiplication to write a multiplication problem.

You know that opposites add to 0, so $30 + (-30) = 0$.

Generalize A rule for multiplication of integers is: negative • negative = positive.

Try It!

Find each product.

a. $-7 \cdot (-2)$ b. $7 \cdot (-13)$ c. $-6 \cdot 8$ d. $(-1) \cdot (-1)$

Go Online | PearsonRealize.com

1-6 Multiply Integers

KEY CONCEPT

When multiplying two integers, the sign of the product depends on the sign of the factors.

If the signs of the factors are the *same*, the product is positive.

$7 \cdot 3 = 21$ $-7 \cdot (-3) = 21$

If the signs of the factors are *different*, the product is negative.

$-4 \cdot 5 = -20$ $4 \cdot (-5) = -20$

Do You Understand?

1. **Essential Question** How do the signs of factors affect their product?

2. **Construct Arguments** What is the sign of the product if you multiplied three negative integers? Explain your answer.

3. **Reasoning** Explain why the product of two negative integers is not negative. Use $(-1)(-1)$ as an example.

4. **Use Structure** Is the product the same when multiplying $22 \times (-5)$ and multiplying $(-5) \times 22$? Explain.

Do You Know How?

5. Represent $2 \cdot (-3)$ on the number line.

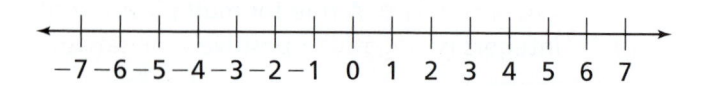

6. Which of these products is negative? Select all that apply.

   ☐ $-8 \cdot (-3)$
   ☐ $-2 \cdot 8$
   ☐ $0 \cdot (-2)$
   ☐ $15 \cdot (-5)$
   ☐ $-8 \cdot (-9)$

7. Find each product.

   a. $-9 \cdot (-4)$ b. $-7 \cdot 12$
   c. $8 \cdot (-8)$ d. $9 \cdot 15$

8. A game show contestant starts a game by answering two questions incorrectly. Each incorrect answer costs the contestant $600. Use a product of two integers to show the point total that would appear for the contestant.

42   1-6 Multiply Integers   Go Online | PearsonRealize.com

Name: _____

Practice & Problem Solving

In 9–14, multiply.

9. $(-6) \cdot (-2)$

10. $4 \cdot (-8)$

11. $7 \cdot (-5)$

12. $-5 \cdot 2$

13. $-1 \cdot (-24)$

14. $(5) \cdot (-9) \cdot (-2)$

15. A football team lost the same number of yards on each of 3 consecutive plays. What is the total change in yards from where the team started?

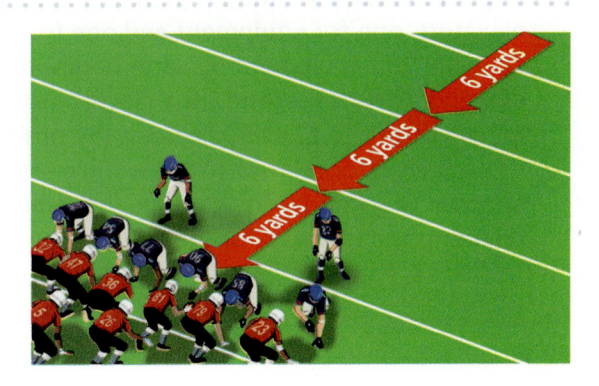

16. a. Find the product.

$-41 \cdot (-1)$

b. Construct Arguments Describe how you use the properties of multiplication to find the product.

17. Alex is working to simplify $5 \cdot (-8) \cdot 2$.

a. What is the product?

b. Suppose Alex found the opposite of the correct product. Describe an error he could have made that resulted in that product.

Go Online | PearsonRealize.com

1-6 Multiply Integers

18. Which product is greater, (−4) · (−6) or (−7) · (−8)? Explain.

19. **Make Sense and Persevere** While playing a board game, Cecilia had to move back 6 spaces 9 times. What integer represents Cecilia's movement on the board for those 9 turns?

20. Anya makes withdrawals from and deposits into her bank account.

    a. What integer represents the change in the amount in her account if Anya withdraws $12 once each day for four days?

    b. What integer represents the change in the amount in her account if Anya deposits $12 once each day for four days?

    c. **Look for Relationships** Explain the difference between the integer for the withdrawals and the integer for the deposits.

21. **Higher Order Thinking** A gold mine has two elevators, one for equipment and one for miners. One day, the equipment elevator begins to descend. After 28 seconds, the elevator for the miners begins to descend. What is the position of each elevator relative to the surface after another 14 seconds? At that time, how much deeper is the elevator for the miners?

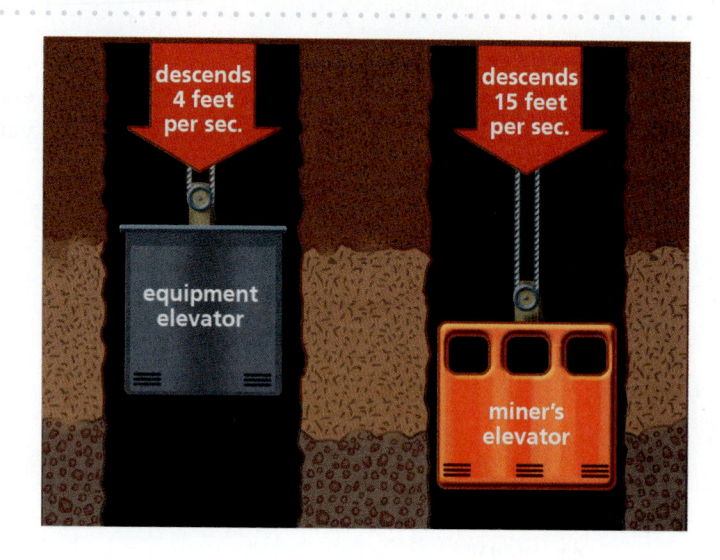

    descends 4 feet per sec.
    equipment elevator

    descends 15 feet per sec.
    miner's elevator

Assessment Practice

22. Use the number line to find −35 · 2.

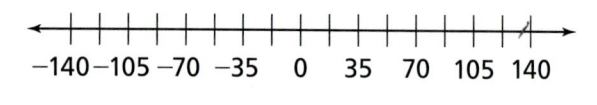

    −140 −105 −70 −35 0 35 70 105 140

    −35 · 2 = ☐

23. Which of these expressions has the same product as (−6) · 7? Select all that apply.

    ☐ (−3) · 14
    ☐ 16 · (−3)
    ☐ −6 · (−7)
    ☐ 7 · (−6)
    ☐ 14 · (−3)

44   1-6 Multiply Integers

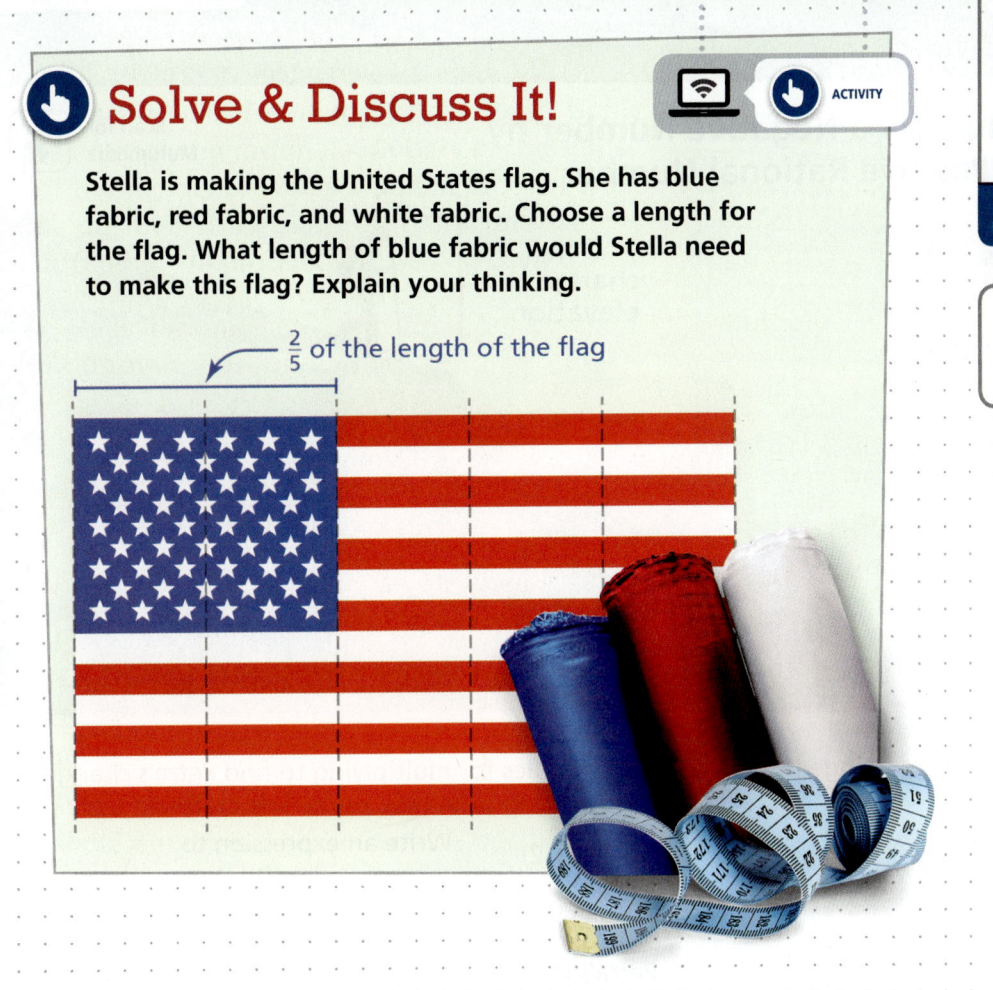

Lesson 1-7
Multiply Rational Numbers

Go Online | PearsonRealize.com

I can...
multiply rational numbers.

Solve & Discuss It!

Stella is making the United States flag. She has blue fabric, red fabric, and white fabric. Choose a length for the flag. What length of blue fabric would Stella need to make this flag? Explain your thinking.

$\frac{2}{5}$ of the length of the flag

Focus on math practices

Be Precise The blue region of the flag is $\frac{7}{13}$ the width and $\frac{2}{5}$ the length of the flag. What part of the total area is the blue region of the flag?

45

? Essential Question How is multiplying rational numbers like multiplying integers?

EXAMPLE 1 Multiply a Negative Number by a Positive Rational Number

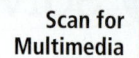

Two hikers descend from the summit of a mountain. What is Petra's change in elevation?

Petra's change in elevation is 3.5 times as great as Ben's change in elevation.

−1.2 m change in elevation — Ben

Petra

Use a number line to represent Petra's change in elevation.

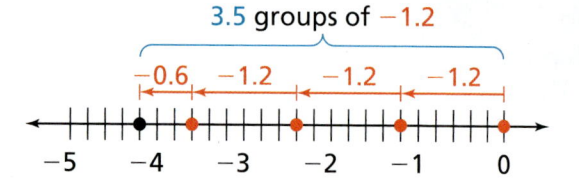

3.5 groups of −1.2

−0.6 −1.2 −1.2 −1.2

Petra's change in elevation is −4.2 meters.

Use the rules for multiplying to find Petra's change in elevation.

$3.5 \cdot (-1.2)$ Write an expression to represent the situation.

$= -4.2$

Petra's change in elevation is −4.2 meters.

Generalize The rules for multiplying integers apply to all rational numbers.

positive • negative = negative

✓ Try It!

Meghan's bank account is charged $9.95 per month for an online newspaper subscription. How could you represent the change in her account balance after three months of charges?

☐ groups of ☐

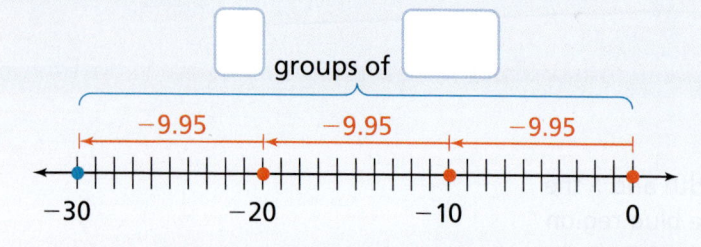

−9.95 −9.95 −9.95

☐ • −9.95 = ☐

After three months, the change in her account balance is $ ☐ .

Convince Me! Meghan's bank account is charged 3 times. Without calculating, how can you determine whether this is a negative or positive change to her account? Explain.

46 1-7 Multiply Rational Numbers

EXAMPLE 2 — Multiply a Positive Number by a Negative Rational Number

Find the product of $-\frac{5}{6}$ and $\frac{2}{5}$.

$-\frac{5}{6} \cdot \frac{2}{5}$

$= \frac{-5 \cdot 2}{6 \cdot 5}$

$= \frac{-10}{30} = -\frac{1}{3}$ — Multiply the numerators and the denominators and then simplify.

So, $-\frac{5}{6} \cdot \frac{2}{5} = -\frac{1}{3}$.

Plot the negative value and then find $\frac{2}{5}$ of that length.

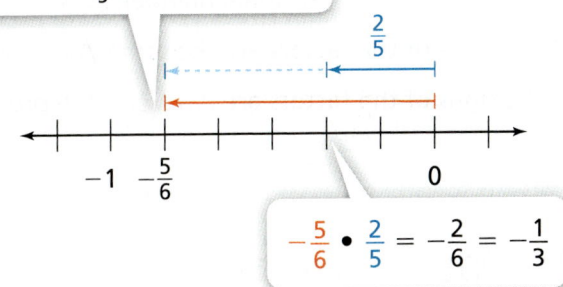

$-\frac{5}{6} \cdot \frac{2}{5} = -\frac{2}{6} = -\frac{1}{3}$

EXAMPLE 3 — Multiply a Negative Number by a Negative Rational Number

Find the product of -0.3 and $-\frac{11}{30}$.

$-0.30 \cdot \left(-\frac{11}{30}\right)$

$= \frac{-3}{10} \cdot \left(-\frac{11}{30}\right)$ — Convert one of the rational numbers so that they are both fractions or both decimals.

$= \frac{-3 \cdot (-11)}{10 \cdot 30}$

$= \frac{33}{300}$ or 0.11

So, $-0.3 \cdot \left(-\frac{11}{30}\right) = 0.11$ or $\frac{11}{100}$.

Generalize The rules for multiplying integers apply to all rational numbers.

negative • negative = positive

✅ Try It!

Find each product.

a. $-5.3 \cdot (-2.6)$

b. $-\frac{3}{5} \cdot 4\frac{1}{6}$

c. $0.2 \cdot (-1.78)$

d. $-2.5 \cdot \left(-\frac{7}{10}\right)$

Go Online | PearsonRealize.com

1-7 Multiply Rational Numbers   47

KEY CONCEPT

The same rules for multiplying integers apply to multiplying all rational numbers.

When multiplying two rational numbers:

- If the signs of the factors are the *same*, the product is *positive*.
- If the signs of the factors are *different*, the product is *negative*.

Do You Understand?

1. **Essential Question** How is multiplying rational numbers like multiplying integers?

2. How do you multiply a decimal greater than 0 and a fraction less than 0?

3. **Model with Math** How does this number line represent multiplication of a negative number by a positive number? Explain.

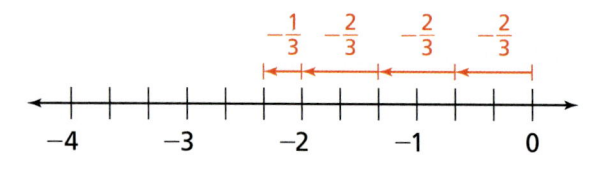

Do You Know How?

4. Use the number line to find the product $3 \cdot \left(-1\frac{1}{2}\right)$.

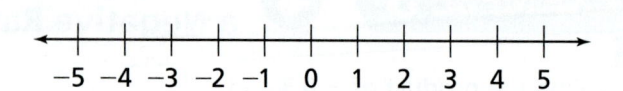

5. Which of these products is positive? Select all that apply.

   ☐ $-0.2 \cdot (12.5)$

   ☐ $-\frac{1}{12} \cdot \left(-6\frac{1}{2}\right)$

   ☐ $3.2 \cdot \left(-\frac{1}{900}\right)$

   ☐ $-3\frac{1}{2} \cdot 0$

   ☐ $-4.7 \cdot (-1)$

6. Find the product.

   a. $-3.1 \cdot (-2.9)$

   b. $1\frac{1}{2} \cdot \left(-\frac{5}{3}\right)$

   c. $-3\frac{1}{2} \cdot 0.5$

   d. $-\frac{4}{5} \cdot -\frac{1}{8}$

Practice & Problem Solving

In 7–14, multiply.

7. $(-2.655) \cdot (18.44)$

8. $-1\frac{5}{6} \cdot 6\frac{1}{2}$

9. $-2\frac{1}{2} \cdot \left(-1\frac{2}{3}\right)$

10. $-3\frac{7}{8} \cdot \left(-5\frac{3}{4}\right)$

11. $-7.5 \cdot -2\frac{3}{4}$

12. $-0.6 \cdot (-0.62)$

13. $-0.2 \cdot -\frac{5}{6}$

14. $-\frac{5}{6} \cdot \frac{1}{8}$

15. At the beginning of the season, Jamie pays full price for a ticket to see the Panthers, her favorite baseball team.

The Panthers currently have 33 wins and 31 losses.

a. Represent the total change in the cost of a ticket given their losses.

b. What is the cost of a ticket for the next game they play?

Ticket prices decrease $0.41 for every game the Panthers lose this season!

Standard Price $49.64

1-7 Multiply Rational Numbers 49

16. The price per share of ENVX stock is dropping at a rate of $1.45 each hour.

    a. Write the rate as a negative number.

    b. What rational number represents the change in the price per share after 5 hours?

    c. What is the price per share after 5 hours?

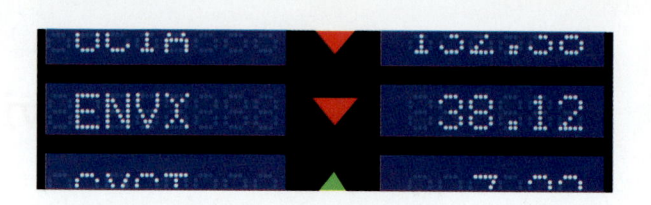

17. Ming incorrectly says that this product is $\frac{4}{63}$.

    $$-\left(-\frac{4}{9}\right) \cdot \left(-\frac{1}{7}\right)$$

    a. What is the correct product?

    b. What error could Ming have made?

18. **Higher Order Thinking** Place the products in order from least to greatest.

    $4\frac{4}{7} \cdot 4\frac{4}{7}$

    $5\frac{6}{7} \cdot \left(-6\frac{6}{7}\right)$

    $-5\frac{1}{8} \cdot \left(-2\frac{1}{4}\right)$

Assessment Practice

19. Multiply $-2\frac{1}{4} \cdot (16.4)$.

20. Suppose there is a 1.3°F drop in temperature for every thousand feet that an airplane climbs into the sky. The temperature on the ground is −2.8°F.

    PART A

    Write a multiplication expression to represent the change in temperature after the plane ascends 10,000 feet.

    PART B

    What will the temperature be when the plane reaches an altitude of 10,000 feet?

Lesson 1-8
Divide Integers

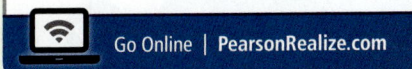

Go Online | PearsonRealize.com

I can... divide integers.

Explain It!

The shapes below are used to show the relationship between each of the four equations in the same fact family.

$8 \times 3 = 24$ $\blacksquare \times \bullet = \bigstar$
$3 \times 8 = 24$ $\bullet \times \blacksquare = \bigstar$
$24 \div 3 = 8$ $\bigstar \div \bullet = \blacksquare$
$24 \div 8 = 3$ $\bigstar \div \blacksquare = \bullet$

A. Suppose the star represents -24. What values could the other shapes represent?

B. What do you know about the square and circle if the star represents a negative number?

C. What do you know about the star if the square and circle both represent a negative number?

Focus on math practices

Use Structure Suppose the square represents -8 and the circle represents 3. Use what you know about integer multiplication and the relationship between multiplication and division to write the complete fact family.

51

Essential Question How does dividing integers relate to multiplying integers?

EXAMPLE 1 Divide Integers with Different Signs

A machine drill is used to access water under the ground. If the machine drills the same distance each day, what is the change in the location of the bottom of the hole each day?

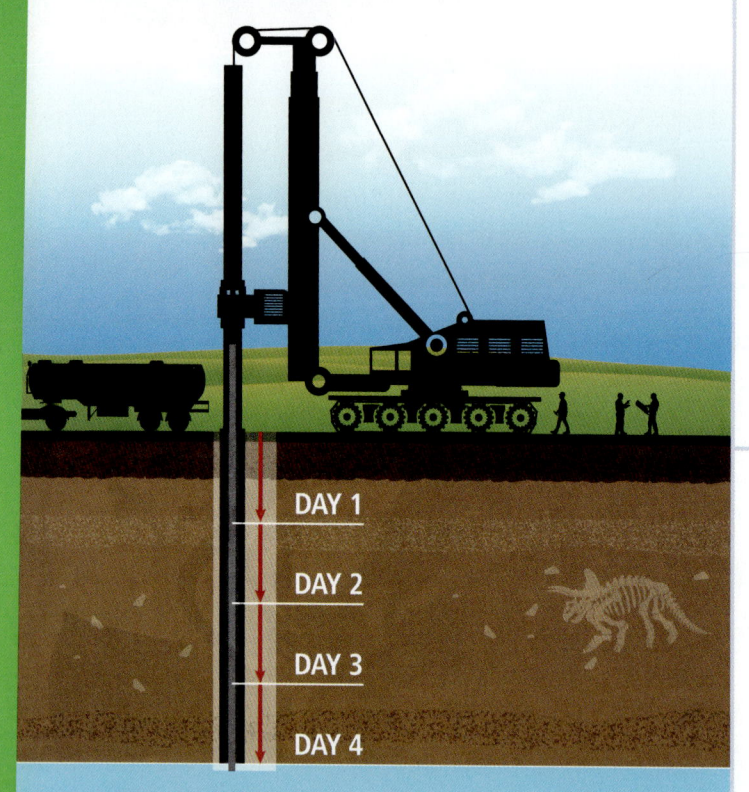

water at 160 feet below ground level

Use a number line to represent the change each day.

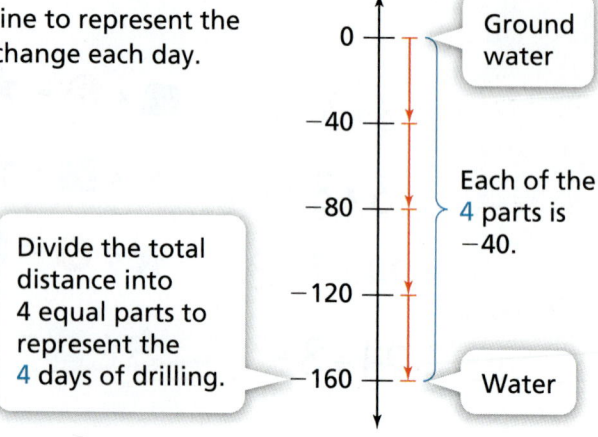

- 0 — Ground water
- −40
- −80 — Each of the 4 parts is −40.
- −120
- −160 — Water

Divide the total distance into 4 equal parts to represent the 4 days of drilling.

The location of the bottom of the hole changed −40 feet, or 40 feet lower each day.

Use the inverse relationship between multiplication and division.

$-160 \div 4 = ?$

$4 \cdot ? = -160$ — Write a related multiplication equation.

$4 \cdot (-40) = -160$

So, $-160 \div 4 = -40$.

When dividing integers with different signs, the quotient will be negative.

The location of the bottom of the hole changed by −40 feet, or decreased by 40 feet, each day.

Try It!

Suppose the machine drilled the same distance into the ground for 3 days and reached water at 84 feet below ground level. What was the change in the location of the bottom of the hole each day?

Each day, the location of the bottom of the hole changed by ☐ feet, or decreased by ☐ feet.

☐ ÷ 3 = ?

3 · ? = ☐

3 · ☐ = −84

So, ☐ ÷ 3 = ☐.

0

−84

Convince Me! Explain why the quotient of two integers with different signs is negative.

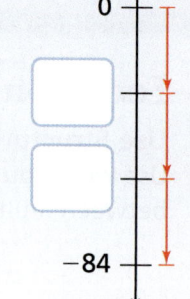

52 1-8 Divide Integers

EXAMPLE 2 — Divide Integers with the Same Sign

Simplify $-27 \div (-3)$.

ONE WAY Use a related multiplication fact.

$-27 \div (-3) = ?$

$-3 \cdot ? = -27$ — Write division as a product with a missing factor.

$-3 \cdot 9 = -27$

So, $-27 \div (-3) = 9$.

When dividing integers with the same sign, the quotient will be positive.

ANOTHER WAY Write the division expression as a fraction and use properties of operations.

$\dfrac{-27}{-3}$

$= \dfrac{-1 \cdot 27}{-1 \cdot 3}$ — Write negative numbers as a product, and then write as a product of fractions.

$= \dfrac{-1}{-1} \cdot \dfrac{27}{3}$

$= 1 \cdot 9$

$= 9$

So, $-27 \div (-3) = 9$.

Try It!

Simplify.

a. $-40 \div (-5)$

b. $40 \div (-5)$

c. $0 \div -40$

EXAMPLE 3 — Write Equivalent Quotients of Integers

Are the following quotients equivalent? Justify your answer.

$-\left(\dfrac{18}{4}\right) \qquad \dfrac{-18}{4} \qquad \dfrac{18}{-4}$

$-\left(\dfrac{18}{4}\right) = -(18 \div 4)$
$= -(4.5)$
$= -4.5$

$\dfrac{-18}{4} = -18 \div 4$
$= -4.5$

$\dfrac{18}{-4} = 18 \div -4$
$= -4.5$

Yes, each expression is equivalent to -4.5.

Generalize The value of $-\left(\dfrac{p}{q}\right)$ is equivalent to $\dfrac{-p}{q}$ and $\dfrac{p}{-q}$.

Try It!

Which of the following are equivalent to -5?

$\dfrac{55}{11} \qquad -\left(\dfrac{55}{11}\right) \qquad \dfrac{-55}{11} \qquad \dfrac{-55}{-11} \qquad \dfrac{55}{-11} \qquad -\left(\dfrac{-55}{-11}\right)$

1-8 Divide Integers

KEY CONCEPT

The rules for dividing integers are related to the rules for multiplying integers.

If the signs of the dividend and the divisor are the same, the quotient is positive.

$24 \div 4 = 6$ $-24 \div (-4) = 6$

If the signs of the dividend and the divisor are different, the quotient is negative.

$-15 \div 3 = -5$ $15 \div (-3) = -5$

Do You Understand?

1. **Essential Question** How does dividing integers relate to multiplying integers?

2. **Reasoning** Why is the quotient of two negative integers positive?

3. Helen wrote the following facts to try to show that division by 0 results in 0. Explain her error.

   $0 \times (-7) = 0$
   So, $(-7) \div 0 = 0$ ✗

Do You Know How?

4. Find each quotient.

   a. $-\frac{18}{3}$
   b. $\frac{-5}{-1}$
   c. $\frac{24}{-6}$
   d. $\frac{-10}{-1}$
   e. $\frac{-25}{5}$
   f. $-\frac{8}{2}$

5. A scuba diver descends 63 feet in 18 seconds. What integer represents the change in the diver's position in feet per second?

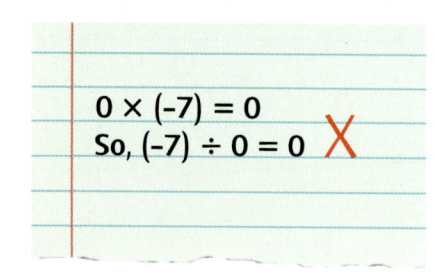

6. Which of the following are equivalent to -7?

   ☐ $\frac{-49}{-7}$
   ☐ $\frac{0}{-7}$
   ☐ $\frac{49}{-7}$
   ☐ $\frac{-21}{3}$
   ☐ $\frac{21}{3}$

1-8 Divide Integers

Name: _____

Practice & Problem Solving

Scan for Multimedia

Leveled Practice In 7–8, fill in the boxes to find each quotient.

7. $-16 \div 4 = ?$

   $4 \cdot ? = \boxed{}$

   $4 \cdot \boxed{} = \boxed{}$

   So, $-16 \div 4 = \boxed{}$.

8. $-56 \div -7 = ?$

   $\boxed{} \cdot ? = \boxed{}$

   $\boxed{} \cdot \boxed{} = \boxed{}$

   So, $-56 \div -7 = \boxed{}$.

9. Classify the quotient $-50 \div 5$ as positive, negative, zero, or undefined.

10. Is the expression $\frac{42}{-7}$ undefined? If not, find the quotient.

11. A company loses $780 as a result of a shipping delay. The 6 owners of the company must share the loss equally.

    a. Write an expression to show the change in profit for each owner.

    b. Evaluate the expression.

12. Which of the quotients are equivalent to 2.5? Select all that apply.

    ☐ $\frac{10}{-4}$ ☐ $\frac{-5}{-2}$

    ☐ $\frac{10}{4}$ ☐ $\frac{-5}{2}$

    ☐ $\frac{-10}{-4}$ ☐ $\frac{5}{2}$

13. **Use Structure** The price of a stock steadily decreased by a total of $127 over 15 months. Which expression shows the change in the stock's value?

    Ⓐ $\frac{-\$127}{-15 \text{ months}}$ Ⓒ $\frac{-\$127}{15 \text{ months}}$

    Ⓑ $\frac{\$127}{15 \text{ months}}$ Ⓓ $\frac{\$15}{127 \text{ months}}$

14. Zak goes parachuting and descends at the rate shown. If he maintains a steady descent, what integer represents Zak's change in elevation in feet per second?

    24 feet in 2 seconds

15. **Model with Math** Find each quotient and plot it on the number line. Which of the expressions are undefined?

    $-8 \div 4$ $\frac{-21}{-7}$ $-4 \div 0$ $-25 \div (-5)$ $\frac{36}{-9}$ $\frac{9}{0}$ $0 \div (-8)$

    ←|—|—|—|—|—|—|—|—|—|—|→
    −5 −4 −3 −2 −1 0 1 2 3 4 5

Go Online | PearsonRealize.com

1-8 Divide Integers 55

16. **Use Structure** The temperature in a town increased 16°F in 5 hours. The temperature decreased 31°F in the next 8 hours. Which of the expressions shows the rate of the total change in temperature?

Ⓐ $\frac{-15°F}{13 \text{ hours}}$

Ⓑ $\frac{47°F}{13 \text{ hours}}$

Ⓒ $\frac{15°F}{10 \text{ minutes}}$

Ⓓ $\frac{47°F}{-13 \text{ hours}}$

17. Camille takes a rock-climbing class. On her first outing, she rappels down the side of a boulder in three equal descents. What integer represents Camille's change in altitude in feet each time she descends?

Elevation 165 Feet

18. **Higher Order Thinking** If the fraction $\frac{396}{x-10}$ is equivalent to -22, find the value of x. Show your work.

Assessment Practice

19. Which of the quotients is equivalent to $-\frac{5}{8}$? Select all that apply.

☐ $\frac{-5}{8}$

☐ $\frac{5}{8}$

☐ $\frac{5}{-8}$

☐ $-\left(\frac{5}{-8}\right)$

☐ $\frac{-5}{-8}$

20. Eva incorrectly classifies the quotient $-\left(\frac{-81}{-9}\right)$ as positive.

PART A

What is the correct quotient? Explain how you found your answer.

PART B

Explain what could have caused Eva's error.

56 1-8 Divide Integers

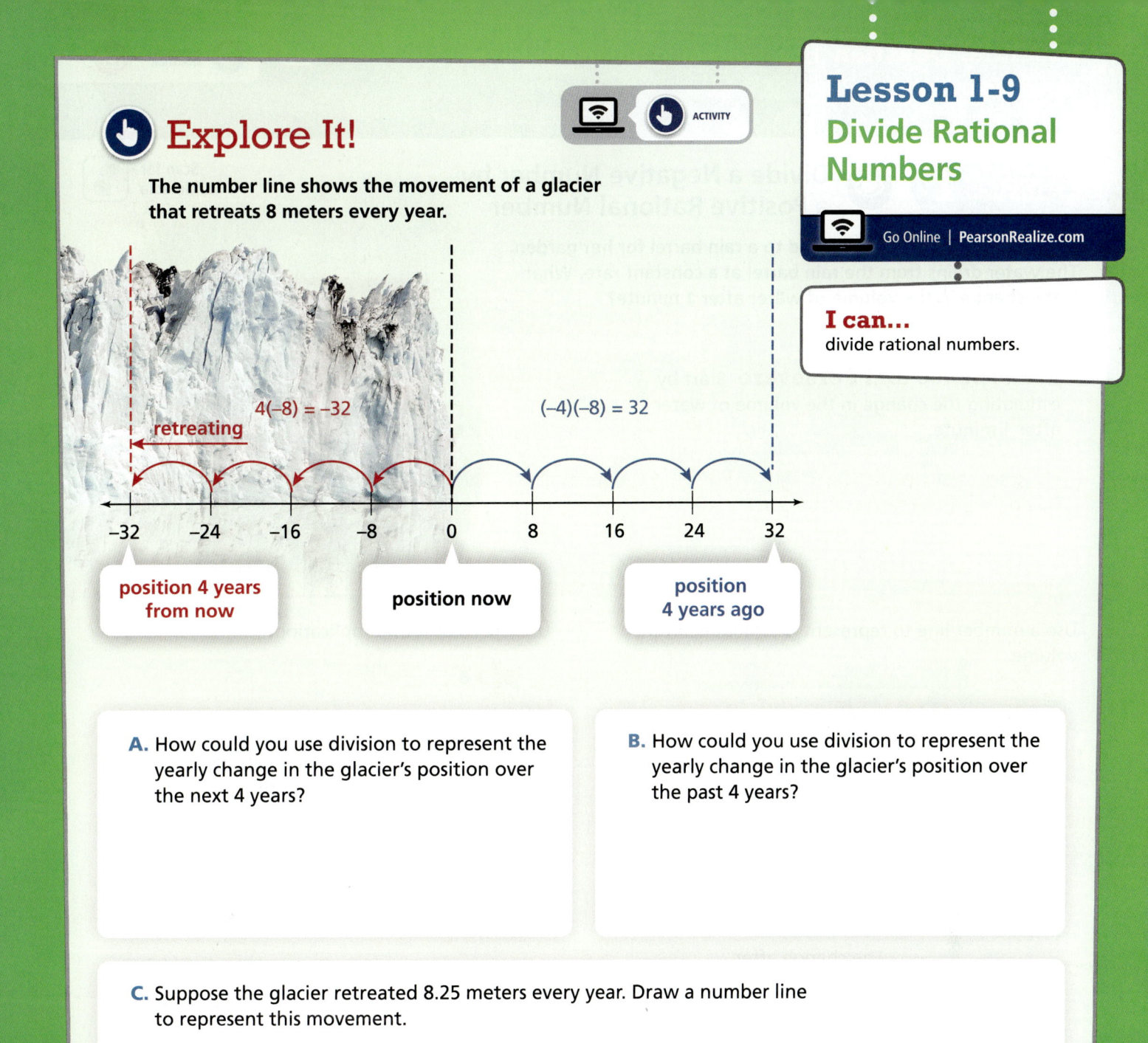

Lesson 1-9
Divide Rational Numbers

Go Online | PearsonRealize.com

I can... divide rational numbers.

Explore It!

The number line shows the movement of a glacier that retreats 8 meters every year.

$4(-8) = -32$
retreating
$(-4)(-8) = 32$

−32 −24 −16 −8 0 8 16 24 32

position 4 years from now

position now

position 4 years ago

A. How could you use division to represent the yearly change in the glacier's position over the next 4 years?

B. How could you use division to represent the yearly change in the glacier's position over the past 4 years?

C. Suppose the glacier retreated 8.25 meters every year. Draw a number line to represent this movement.

Focus on math practices

Reasoning If the number of meters the glacier retreats each year changes, does it affect the signs of each part of the division statement in Part A? Explain.

57

? Essential Question How is dividing rational numbers like dividing integers?

EXAMPLE 1 — Divide a Negative Number by a Positive Rational Number

Yumiko has a drip hose attached to a rain barrel for her garden. The water drains from the rain barrel at a constant rate. What is the change in the volume of water after 1 minute?

$-3\frac{3}{5}$ gallons in 6 minutes

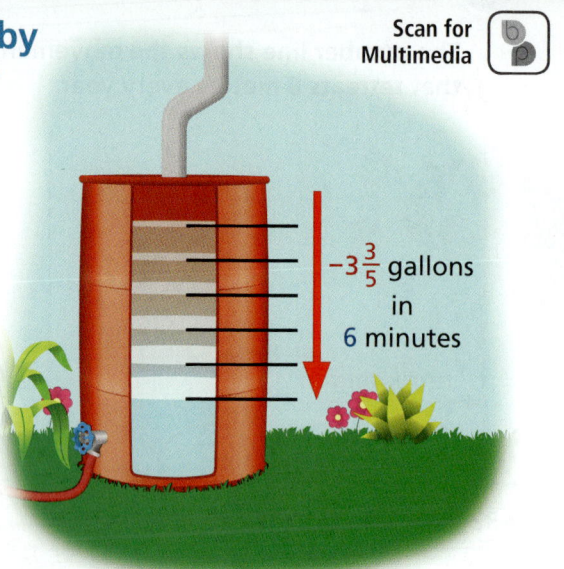

Make Sense and Persevere Start by estimating the change in the volume of water after 1 minute.

Use a number line to represent the change in the volume.

Divide the given change in volume into 6 equal parts.

$-3\frac{3}{5} \div 6$

The change after 1 minute is $-\frac{3}{5}$ gallon.

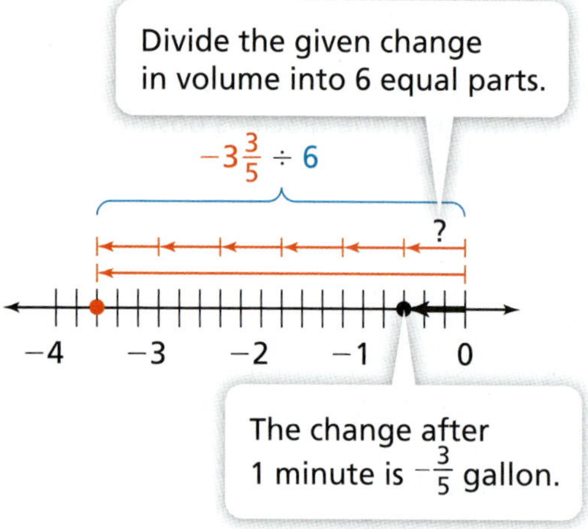

Use the rules for multiplication.

$-3\frac{3}{5} \div 6$

$= -\frac{18}{5} \div \frac{6}{1}$

$= -\frac{18}{5} \cdot \frac{1}{6}$

Two numbers whose product is 1 are **multiplicative inverses**, or reciprocals.

$= -\frac{18}{30} = -\frac{3}{5}$

So, the change in the volume of water after 1 minute is $-\frac{3}{5}$ gallon.

Generalize You can extend what you know about multiplying rational numbers and dividing integers to division of rational numbers.

✓ Try It!

Suppose that the volume of water in the rain barrel decreased by $4\frac{5}{8}$ gallons in 4 minutes. What will be the change in the volume of water after 1 minute?

The rain barrel will lose ☐ gallons in 1 minute.

$-\frac{\square}{8} \div \frac{4}{1}$

$= -\frac{\square}{8} \cdot \frac{\square}{\square}$

$= -\frac{\square}{32}$, or $-1\frac{\square}{32}$

Convince Me! How are multiplicative inverses used in division with rational numbers?

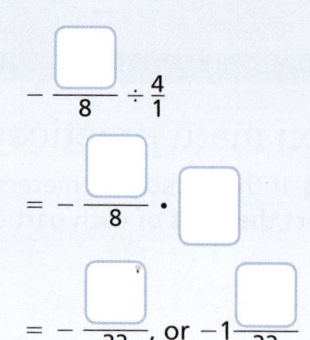

EXAMPLE 2 — Divide a Positive Number by a Negative Rational Number

Simplify $\dfrac{3\frac{2}{3}}{-\frac{2}{3}}$.

A complex fraction has a fraction in the numerator, the denominator, or both.

$3\frac{2}{3} \div \left(-\frac{2}{3}\right)$

$= \dfrac{11}{3} \div \left(-\dfrac{2}{3}\right)$

$= \dfrac{11}{3} \cdot \left(-\dfrac{3}{2}\right)$

The multiplicative inverse of $-\frac{2}{3}$ is $-\frac{3}{2}$ because $-\frac{3}{2} \cdot -\frac{2}{3} = 1$.

$= \dfrac{11 \cdot (-3)}{3 \cdot 2}$

$= -\dfrac{33}{6} = -\dfrac{11}{2}$

$= -5\dfrac{1}{2}$

Try It!

Find each quotient.

a. $\dfrac{1\frac{2}{5}}{-\frac{1}{5}}$

b. $-0.4 \div 0.25$

c. $\dfrac{7}{8} \div -\dfrac{3}{4}$

d. $0.7 \div -1\dfrac{1}{6}$

EXAMPLE 3 — Divide Rational Numbers with the Same Sign

The location of a submarine changes by -0.06 kilometer each minute. How much time does it take to get to the sea bottom?

$-\dfrac{3}{4} \div (-0.06)$ ········ *Divide the location of the sea bottom by the change in the location of the submarine.*

$= -0.75 \div (-0.06)$

$= 12.5$ ← *The rules for dividing integers apply to all rational numbers.*
negative ÷ negative = positive

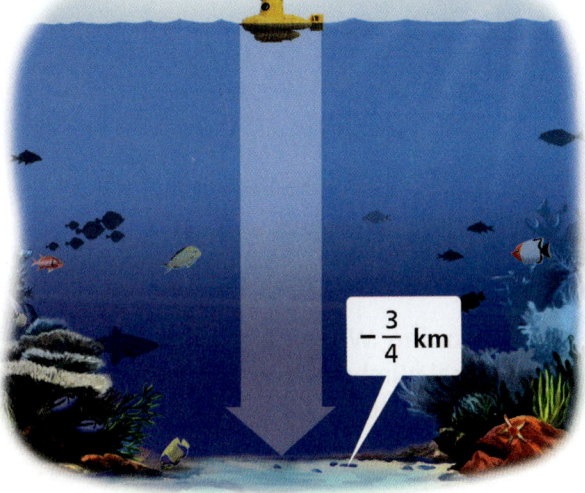

$-\frac{3}{4}$ km

It takes 12.5 minutes to reach the sea bottom.

Try It!

Find each quotient.

a. $-1\dfrac{1}{3} \div (-1.6)$

b. $\dfrac{-\frac{2}{3}}{-\frac{1}{4}}$

c. $-\dfrac{9}{10} \div \left(-\dfrac{3}{10}\right)$

d. $-0.5 \div \left(-\dfrac{3}{13}\right)$

1-9 Divide Rational Numbers

KEY CONCEPT

The same rules for dividing integers apply to dividing rational numbers. When dividing two rational numbers:

- If the signs of the dividend and divisor are the same, the quotient is positive.

- If the signs of the dividend and divisor are different, the quotient is negative.

Do You Understand?

1. **Essential Question** How is dividing rational numbers like dividing integers?

2. **Use Structure** How do you know the sign of the quotient $-\frac{4}{5} \div \frac{1}{6}$?

3. **Reasoning** When −4 is divided by a rational number between 0 and 1, where would the quotient be located on the number line? Why?

Do You Know How?

4. Find each quotient.

   a. $-\frac{7}{12} \div \frac{1}{7}$

   b. $-0.05 \div \left(-\frac{5}{8}\right)$

   c. $6\frac{1}{4} \div \left(-\frac{5}{16}\right)$

   d. $-1 \div \left(-\frac{10}{13}\right)$

5. Simplify the complex fraction.

   a. $\dfrac{-\frac{2}{7}}{1\frac{1}{3}}$

   b. $\dfrac{-\frac{3}{5}}{2\frac{1}{4}}$

   c. $\dfrac{-\frac{9}{10}}{1\frac{3}{5}}$

60   1-9 Divide Rational Numbers

Practice & Problem Solving

Leveled Practice In 6–7, fill in the boxes to find the quotient.

6. Find the quotient $\frac{5}{7} \div \left(-\frac{11}{5}\right)$.

$\frac{5}{7} \div \left(-\frac{11}{5}\right) = \frac{5}{7} \cdot \boxed{}$

$= -\frac{\boxed{}}{\boxed{}}$

7. Simplify the complex fraction $\dfrac{-\frac{4}{5}}{\frac{3}{10}}$.

Rewrite the complex fraction: $\boxed{} \div \boxed{}$

Write the division as multiplication: $\boxed{} \cdot \boxed{}$

The product is $\boxed{}$.

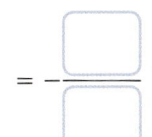

8. Which multiplication expression is equivalent to the division expression $-\frac{7}{17} \div \frac{13}{34}$?

Ⓐ $-\frac{17}{7} \times \frac{13}{34}$
Ⓑ $-\frac{7}{17} \times \frac{13}{34}$
Ⓒ $-\frac{17}{7} \times \frac{34}{13}$
Ⓓ $-\frac{7}{17} \times \frac{34}{13}$

9. Derek says that the quotient $-\frac{2}{7} \div \left(-\frac{2}{21}\right)$ is $-\frac{1}{3}$.

a. What is the correct quotient?

b. What mistake did Derek likely make?

10. The water level of a lake fell by $1\frac{1}{2}$ inches during a $1\frac{2}{3}$-week-long dry spell. Simplify the complex fraction below to find the average rate at which the water level changed every week.

$\dfrac{-1\frac{1}{2}}{1\frac{2}{3}}$ inches/week

Water level dropped $1\frac{1}{2}$ inches

11. Complete the table. Simplify expressions.

	Dividend	Divisor	Quotient
a.	$-\frac{3}{4}$	$\frac{2}{5}$	
b.	-0.75	0.4	
c.	$\frac{3}{4}$	$-\frac{2}{5}$	

12. a. Find the reciprocal of $-1\frac{1}{17}$.

b. Find the reciprocal of $-\frac{17}{18}$.

c. **Reasoning** Explain why the answer for part a is the multiplicative inverse of the answer for part b.

1-9 Divide Rational Numbers

13. Use numbers $-\frac{7}{13}, 1\frac{6}{7}, -1\frac{6}{7}, \frac{7}{13}$

    a. Which is the reciprocal of $1\frac{6}{7}$?

    b. Which is the reciprocal of $\frac{7}{13}$?

    c. **Reasoning** What do you notice about the reciprocals of $1\frac{6}{7}$ and $\frac{7}{13}$?

14. A water tank in Stewart's home had a small, steady leak.

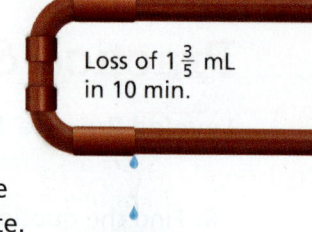

    Loss of $1\frac{3}{5}$ mL in 10 min.

    a. Use a complex fraction to represent the change in the volume of water in 1 minute.

    $\frac{\Box}{10 \text{ minutes}}$ milliliters

    b. Simplify the complex fraction to find the change in the volume of water in the tank in 1 minute.

15. Find the quotient. Express your answer as a simplified fraction.

    $\frac{3}{10} \div 3.8$

16. **Higher Order Thinking** Between 10 P.M. and 7:45 A.M., the water level in a swimming pool decreased by $\frac{13}{16}$ inch.

    Assuming that the water level decreased at a constant rate, how much did it drop each hour?

    The water level decreased by $\Box$ inch each hour.

17. **Critique Reasoning** Kayla wants to find $2\frac{2}{3} \div \left(-1\frac{3}{7}\right)$. She first rewrites the division as $\left(2\frac{2}{3}\right)\left(-1\frac{7}{3}\right)$. What is wrong with Kayla's reasoning?

Assessment Practice

18. Which is an equivalent multiplication expression for $\frac{-\frac{3}{8}}{\left(-\frac{7}{54}\right)}$?

    Ⓐ $-\frac{3}{8} \cdot \left(\frac{7}{54}\right)$

    Ⓑ $-\frac{3}{8} \cdot \left(-\frac{54}{7}\right)$

    Ⓒ $-\frac{3}{8} \cdot \left(\frac{54}{7}\right)$

    Ⓓ $-\frac{8}{3} \cdot \left(-\frac{7}{54}\right)$

19. Divide $-2\frac{1}{8} \div 6\frac{4}{5}$. Explain each step you used to find the quotient.

62 1-9 Divide Rational Numbers   Go Online | PearsonRealize.com

Lesson 1-10
Solve Problems with Rational Numbers

Go Online | PearsonRealize.com

I can... solve problems with rational numbers.

Solve & Discuss It!

Stefan estimates the income and expenses for renting a phone accessory store in the mall. He enters the amounts in the table below. Should Stefan rent a phone accessory store? Explain.

Estimated Income and Expenses

Type	Amount	Frequency
Sales	$950	Each week
Services	$2,875	Each month
Rent	−$4,500	Each month
Travel	−$7.50	Each day
Merchandise	−$1,650	Each month

Focus on math practices

Reasoning How can you assess the reasonableness of your solution using mental math or estimation strategies?

? Essential Question How do you decide which rational number operations to use to solve problems?

EXAMPLE 1 — Decide Which Operations to Use to Solve Problems

Water drains steadily out of a lock to lower a boat from one level to another. What is the boat's change in position each minute?

The boat lowers 3 ft.

$4\frac{1}{2}$ minutes to lower the boat

Reasoning Which operation can you use to find the boat's change in position in 1 minute?

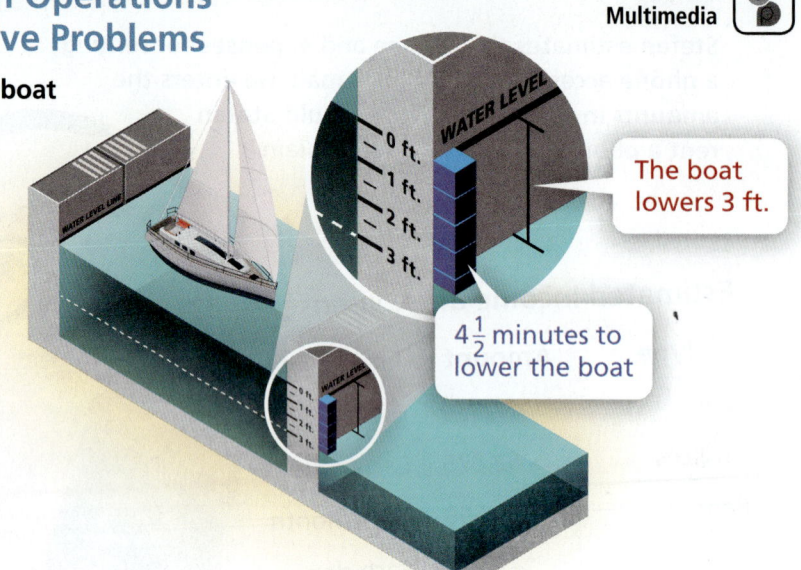

STEP 1 Use a bar diagram to represent the time it takes the boat to lower 3 feet in the lock.

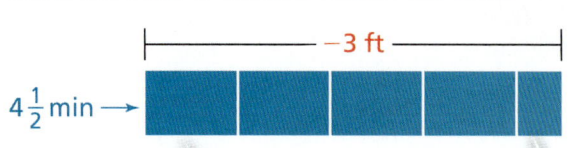

−3 ft

$4\frac{1}{2}$ min →

Each whole box represents the boat's change in position in 1 minute.

This $\frac{1}{2}$ box represents the boat's change in position in $\frac{1}{2}$ minute.

STEP 2 Decide which operation to use to find the boat's change in position in 1 minute.

$\dfrac{-3}{4\frac{1}{2}}$ Divide to find the boat's change in position in 1 minute.

$= -3 \div \frac{9}{2}$

$= -3 \cdot \frac{2}{9}$

$= -\frac{6}{9} = -\frac{2}{3}$

So, the boat's change in position each minute is $-\frac{2}{3}$ feet. The boat lowers $\frac{2}{3}$ feet each minute.

✓ Try It!

A weather balloon ascended from an elevation of 18 feet below sea level to an elevation of $19\frac{1}{2}$ feet above sea level. What distance did the weather balloon rise?

The distance between two points is the absolute value of their ☐.

So, $|-18 \bigcirc 19\frac{1}{2}| =$ ☐.

The weather balloon rose a distance of ☐ feet.

Convince Me! How can you decide which operation to use to solve a problem?

64 1-10 Solve Problems with Rational Numbers

EXAMPLE 2   Use Properties of Operations with Rational Numbers

Kevin played a trivia game. Each correct answer is worth $2\frac{1}{4}$ points, and each incorrect answer is worth $-\frac{1}{2}$ point. What was Kevin's score?

Use Structure How are the two methods of solving the problem alike? How are they different?

ONE WAY

$(15)2\frac{1}{4} + (15)\left(-\frac{1}{2}\right)$

$= \frac{9}{4}(15) + \left(-\frac{1}{2}\right)(15)$ *Multiply first. Then add.*

$= \frac{135}{4} + \left(-\frac{15}{2}\right)$

$= \frac{135}{4} + \left(-\frac{30}{4}\right)$

$= \frac{105}{4} = 26\frac{1}{4}$

Kevin's score was $26\frac{1}{4}$ points.

ANOTHER WAY

$(15)2\frac{1}{4} + (15)\left(-\frac{1}{2}\right)$

$= 15\left[2\frac{1}{4} + \left(-\frac{1}{2}\right)\right]$

$= 15\left(1\frac{3}{4}\right)$

$= 15\left(\frac{7}{4}\right)$

$= \frac{105}{4} = 26\frac{1}{4}$

Kevin's score was $26\frac{1}{4}$ points.

Since Kevin had the same number of correct and incorrect answers, use the Distributive Property.

Try It!

Rashida had 18 correct answers and 12 incorrect answers. What was Rashida's score?

EXAMPLE 3   Solve Multi-Step Problems with Rational Numbers

The temperature at 4:00 P.M. was 2.5°F. It dropped 0.75°F each hour for the next 4 hours. What was the temperature at 8:00 P.M.?

STEP 1 Multiply to find the total change in temperature.

$-0.75 \times 4 = -3$

The total change in temperature was −3 degrees.

STEP 2 Add the total change in temperature to the initial temperature.

$2.5 + (-3) = -0.5$

The temperature at 8:00 P.M. was −0.5°F.

Reasoning Use multiplication if a value is given per hour and you need to find the value after several hours.

Try It!

The temperature at 10:00 A.M. was −3°F and increased 2.25°F each hour for the next 5 hours. What was the temperature at 3:00 P.M.?

Go Online | PearsonRealize.com   1-10 Solve Problems with Rational Numbers

KEY CONCEPT

You can solve a problem with rational numbers by making sense of the problem and deciding which operations to use.

Do You Understand?

1. **Essential Question** How do you decide which rational number operations to use to solve problems?

2. **Reasoning** A truck's position relative to a car's position is −60 feet. The car and the truck move in the same direction, but the car moves 5 feet per second faster for 8 seconds. What operations could be used to find the truck's relative position after 8 seconds? Explain.

3. **Construct Arguments** Emilio used addition of two rational numbers to solve a problem. Jim used subtraction to solve the same problem. Is it possible that they both solved the problem correctly? Use a specific example to explain.

Do You Know How?

4. Kara had a savings account balance of $153 on Monday. On Tuesday, she had six withdrawals of $15.72 and a deposit of $235.15. What was her account balance after these transactions?

5. A scuba diver is swimming at the depth shown, and then swims 0.5 foot toward the surface every 3 seconds. What is the location of the scuba diver, relative to the surface, after 15 seconds?

−46 feet

6. The temperature of a cup of coffee changed by −54°F over $22\frac{1}{2}$ minutes. What was the change in temperature each minute?

Practice & Problem Solving

7. Suppose there is a 1.1°F drop in temperature for every thousand feet that an airplane climbs into the sky. If the temperature on the ground is 59.7°F, what will be the temperature at an altitude of 11,000 ft?

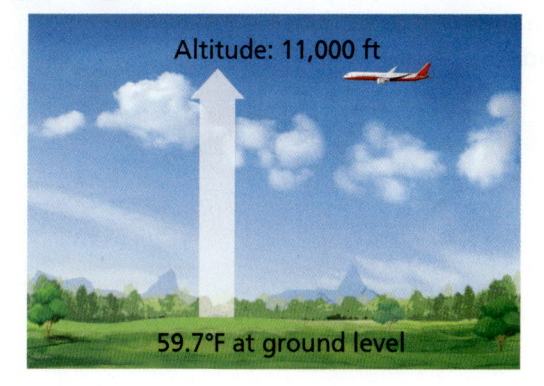

8. A farmer sells an average of $15\frac{3}{5}$ bushels of corn each day. What integer represents the change in bushels of corn in his inventory after 6 days?

9. A certain plant grows $1\frac{1}{6}$ inches every week. How long will it take the plant to grow $6\frac{1}{6}$ inches?

10. An object is traveling at a steady speed of $8\frac{2}{3}$ miles per hour. How long will it take the object to travel $5\frac{1}{5}$ miles?

11. Brianna works as a customer service representative. She knows that the amount of her yearly bonus is $155, but $2.50 is taken away for each customer complaint about her during the year. What is her bonus if there are 12 complaints about her in the year?

12. Make Sense and Persevere There are ten birdbaths in a park. On the first day of spring, the birdbaths are filled. Several weeks later, the overall change in the water level is found. The results are shown in the table. What is the range of the data?

Changes in Water Level (inches)
2.4	1.4	−2.3	2.9	2.3	−1.2	−1.4	−1.8	2.5	0.9

1-10 Solve Problems with Rational Numbers 67

13. **Model with Math** Marcelo played a carnival game 6 times. He spent 3 tokens to play each game, and he won 7 tokens each game. Write two different expressions that can be used to find the total profit in tokens that Marcelo made.

14. The temperature of a pot of water is shown. The temperature of the water changed −2.5°F per minute.

    a. What was the temperature after 20 minutes?

    b. **Make Sense and Persevere** How many minutes did it take to cool to 100.3°F?

15. **Higher Order Thinking** The table shows the relationship between a hedgehog's change in weight and the number of days of hibernation.

    a. What number represents the change in weight for each day of hibernation?

    b. What number represents the change in weight in ounces for the hedgehog in 115 days of hibernation?

Weight Loss of Hedgehog

Days of Hibernation	Change in Weight (oz)
8	−0.24
28	−0.84
75	−2.25
93	−2.79

Assessment Practice

16. A basketball team played six games. In those games, the team won by 7 points, lost by 20, won by 8, won by 11, lost by 3, and won by 9. Which was the mean amount by which the team won or lost over the six games?

    Ⓐ −3 points

    Ⓑ 2 points

    Ⓒ 3 points

    Ⓓ 6 points

17. In digging a hole, the construction crew records the location of the bottom of the hole relative to ground level. After 3 hours the hole is 8.25 feet deep.

    PART A
    What number represents the change in location in feet after 1 hour?

    PART B
    If the crew were to continue digging at the same rate, what number would they record for the location in feet after 8 hours?

1-10 Solve Problems with Rational Numbers

3-ACT MATH ▶ ▶ ▶

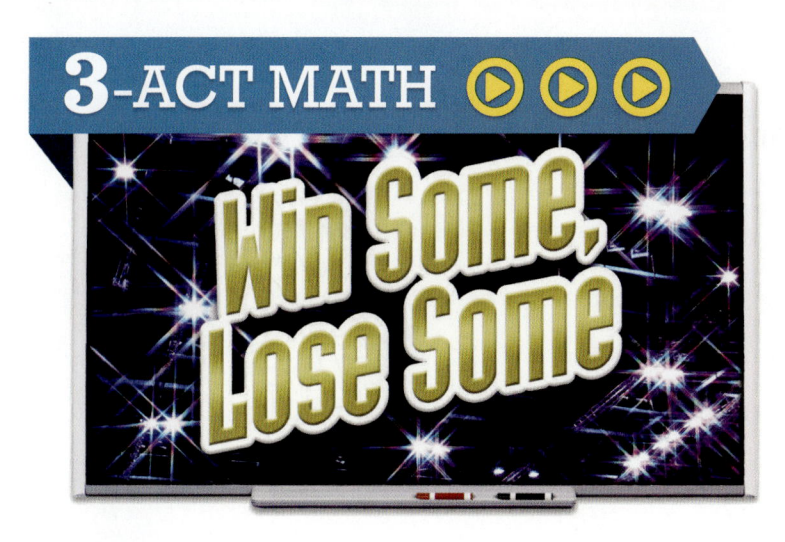

3-Act Mathematical Modeling: Win Some, Lose Some

Go Online | PearsonRealize.com

ACT 1

1. After watching the video, what is the first question that comes to mind?

2. Write the Main Question you will answer.

3. Make a prediction to answer this Main Question.

   The person who will win is ☐.

4. **Construct Arguments** Explain how you arrived at your prediction.

Go Online | PearsonRealize.com   Topic 1 3-Act Mathematical Modeling   69

ACT 2

5. What information in this situation would be helpful to know? How would you use that information?

6. Use Appropriate Tools What tools can you use to get the information you need? Record the information as you find it.

7. Model with Math Represent the situation using the mathematical content, concepts, and skills from this topic. Use your representation to answer the Main Question.

8. What is your answer to the Main Question? Does it differ from your prediction? Explain.

ACT 3

9. Write the answer you saw in the video.

10. Reasoning Does your answer match the answer in the video? If not, what are some reasons that would explain the difference?

11. Make Sense and Persevere Would you change your model now that you know the answer? Explain.

ACT 3 Extension

Reflect

12. Model with Math Explain how you used a mathematical model to represent the situation. How did the model help you answer the Main Question?

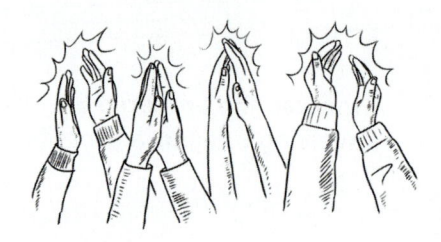

13. Reasoning How is each person's starting score related to their final score?

SEQUEL

14. Construct Arguments If there were one final round where each contestant chooses how much to wager, how much should each person wager? Explain your reasoning.

72 Topic 1 3-Act Mathematical Modeling

REVIEW — TOPIC 1

? Topic Essential Question

How can the properties of operations be used to solve problems involving integers and rational numbers?

Vocabulary Review

Complete each definition and then provide an example of each vocabulary word.

Vocabulary: additive inverses   complex fraction   terminating decimal   repeating decimal

Definition	Example
1. A _____ is a fraction $\frac{a}{b}$ where a and/or b are fractions and b is not equal to 0.	
2. A decimal that ends is a(n) _____.	
3. Two numbers that have a sum of 0 are _____.	

Use Vocabulary in Writing

Explain how you could determine whether $\frac{\frac{21}{3}}{\frac{120}{12}}$ and $\frac{7}{9}$ have the same decimal equivalent. Use vocabulary words in your explanation.

Concepts and Skills Review

LESSON 1-1 Relate Integers and Their Opposites

Quick Review

Integers are the counting numbers, their opposites, and 0. Opposite integers are the same distance from 0 in opposite directions. Opposite quantities combine to make 0.

Example

A climber descends 3 miles into a canyon. What integer represents the descent of her climb? How far does she have to climb to return to her starting point?

The descent of her climb is represented by −3. She has to climb 3 miles to return to her starting point.

Practice

1. On a cold winter morning, the temperature was −4°F. By noon, the temperature increased 4°. What was the temperature at noon?

2. Audrey deposits $27 in her account. Then she makes two withdrawals, one for $15 and one for $12. What is the total change to the balance of Audrey's account? Explain.

LESSON 1-2 Understand Rational Numbers

Quick Review

All rational numbers have an equivalent decimal form. The decimal equivalent will be either a terminating decimal or a repeating decimal. A **terminating decimal** ends in repeating zeros. A **repeating decimal** has a never-ending pattern of the same digits.

Example

Write the decimal equivalents for $\frac{5}{8}$ and $\frac{8}{11}$. Are the decimals terminating or repeating?

The decimal equivalent for $\frac{5}{8} = 0.625$, which is a terminating decimal.

The decimal equivalent for $\frac{8}{11} = 0.7272... = 0.\overline{72}$, which is a repeating decimal.

Practice

1. Which fractions have a decimal equivalent that is a repeating decimal? Select all that apply.
   - ☐ $\frac{13}{65}$
   - ☐ $\frac{141}{47}$
   - ☐ $\frac{11}{12}$
   - ☐ $\frac{19}{3}$

2. Greg bought $19\frac{11}{16}$ gallons of gas. What decimal should the meter on the gas pump read?

3. What is the decimal equivalent of each rational number?
   a. $\frac{9}{11}$
   b. $\frac{4}{5}$
   c. $-\frac{17}{5}$
   d. $\frac{5}{9}$

74 Topic 1 Topic Review

LESSON 1-3 Add Integers

Quick Review

To add integers with the same sign, add the absolute value of each integer. The sign of the sum will be the same as the sign of the addends. To add integers with different signs, find the difference of the absolute value of each integer. The sign of the sum will be the same as the sign of the greater addend.

Example

Find the sum of $(-28) + (-19)$.

$|-28| + |-19| = 28 + 19 = 47$

The sum of $(-28) + (-19) = -47$.

Find the sum of $(-28) + 19$.

$|-28| - |19| = 28 - 19 = 9$

The sum of $(-28) + 19 = -9$, because $|-28| > |19|$.

Practice

1. Jonah's cell phone came with 64 GB of memory. He has used 15 GB. He then uses 5 GB of memory to record photos and videos from a trip. Use the addition expression $64 + (-15) + (-5)$ to find how much memory is left on his phone.

2. Stella walks down a flight of stairs to the basement. Then she walks back up the stairs and up another flight of stairs to the second floor of her house. Each flight of stairs represents a change of 12 feet in height. How far is Stella above the ground?

3. Find the sum.
   a. $64 + (-15)$
   b. $-121 + (-34)$
   c. $-86 + 92$
   d. $109 + (-162)$

LESSON 1-4 Subtract Integers

Quick Review

To subtract integers, use the additive inverse to write an equivalent addition expression. Then follow the rules for addition. When the signs are the same, find the sum of the absolute values. When the signs are different, find the difference. Use the sign of the number with the greater absolute value.

Example

Find $-7 - (8)$.

$-7 + (-8) = -15$

The signs are the same, so the sum has the same sign as the addends.

Find $-7 - (-8)$.

$-7 + 8 = 1$

The signs are different, so the sign of the difference is the same sign as the integer (8) with the greater absolute value, which is positive.

Practice

1. The temperature is 1°F at dusk. It is 8 degrees colder at dawn. What is the temperature at dawn?

2. Kyle and Nadim are on the same space on a board game they are playing. Kyle moves back 2 spaces in one turn and moves back 3 more spaces in his second turn. Nadim has remained in the same place. What integer represents Kyle's location relative to Nadim's location on the game board?

3. Find the difference.
   a. $82 - (-14)$
   b. $-18 - (-55)$
   c. $-17 - 44$
   d. $70 - (-101)$

LESSON 1-5 Add and Subtract Rational Numbers

Quick Review
Positive and negative rational numbers and decimals can be added and subtracted following the same rules as adding and subtracting integers.

Example
Find $-5\frac{1}{2} - 1.75$.

Convert 1.75 to an equivalent fraction, $1\frac{3}{4}$.

$-5\frac{1}{2} - 1\frac{3}{4}$

$= -5\frac{2}{4} + (-1\frac{3}{4})$

$= -6\frac{5}{4}$

$= -7\frac{1}{4}$

Practice
1. Doug digs a hole that is 1.7 feet below ground level. He plants a bush that is $3\frac{2}{10}$ feet tall from the bottom of the root to the top branch. How much of the bush is above the ground?

2. Penelope has a birdhouse that is $4\frac{9}{10}$ feet above the roof of her garage. She has a second birdhouse that is 5.36 feet below the roof of her garage. What is the distance between the birdhouses?

3. Find the sum or difference.

   a. $-2.63 + 3\frac{1}{4}$ b. $-4\frac{1}{2} - (-1.07)$

   c. $0.74 + \left(-\frac{3}{5}\right)$ d. $-\frac{1}{8} - 0.356$

LESSON 1-6 Multiply Integers

Quick Review
Multiply integers the same way you multiply whole numbers. If the signs of the factors are the same, the product is positive. If the signs of the factors are different, the product is negative.

Example
$-9 \cdot -8 = 72$
$-9 \cdot 8 = -72$

Practice
1. Marisa buys 4 books at $13 per book. What integer represents the total change in the amount of money Marisa has?

2. Which expressions have a product of -18? Select all that apply.

   ☐ $-2 \cdot -9$ ☐ $-6 \cdot 3$

   ☐ $-3 \cdot 6$ ☐ $-9 \cdot 2$

3. Find the product.

   a. $-7 \cdot -14$ b. $-15 \cdot 12$

   c. $9 \cdot -20$ d. $-11 \cdot -16$

LESSON 1-7 Multiply Rational Numbers

Quick Review
The same rules for multiplying integers apply to multiplying rational numbers. If the signs of the factors are the same, the product will be positive. If the signs of the factors are different, the product will be negative.

Example
$-9.6 \cdot 1.8 = -17.28$
$-9.6 \cdot -1.8 = 17.28$

Practice
1. Jason spends $2.35 to buy lunch at school. If he buys a lunch on 9 days, what number represents the total change in the amount of money Jason has?

Multiply.

2. $-2\frac{2}{3} \cdot -4\frac{3}{7}$

3. $-3\frac{4}{9} \cdot 5\frac{2}{5}$

4. $6\frac{2}{3} \cdot -4\frac{1}{5}$

LESSON 1-8 Divide Integers

Quick Review
Divide integers the same way you divide whole numbers. The quotient is positive if the signs of the dividend and divisor are the same. The quotient is negative if the signs of the dividend and divisor are different.

Example
$-39 \div 3 = -13$
$-39 \div -3 = 13$

Practice
1. Which expressions have a quotient of -4? Select all that apply.

☐ $\frac{-24}{6}$ ☐ $-36 \div -9$

☐ $-72 \div 18$ ☐ $\frac{84}{-21}$

2. Whitney rolls a ball down a ramp that is 18 feet long. If the ball rolls down 2 feet each second, what integer represents the amount of time, in seconds, the ball takes to reach the end of the ramp?

3. Find the quotient.

a. $\frac{81}{-9}$ b. $-123 \div -4$

c. $-\frac{94}{4}$ d. $65 \div (-5)$

LESSON 1-9 Divide Rational Numbers

Quick Review

The same rules for dividing integers apply to dividing all rational numbers. The quotient is positive when the numbers being divided have the same signs. The quotient is negative when the numbers being divided have different signs. **Complex fractions** have a fraction in the numerator, the denominator, or both. To divide by a fraction, rewrite as multiplication by its **multiplicative inverse**, or reciprocal.

Example

Simplify $\dfrac{-\frac{3}{4}}{\frac{15}{24}}$.

$-\dfrac{3}{4} \div \dfrac{15}{24} = -\dfrac{3}{4} \cdot \dfrac{24}{15} = -\dfrac{72}{60} = -\dfrac{6}{5} = -1\dfrac{1}{5}$

Practice

Find the quotient.

1. $\dfrac{8}{9} \div -1\dfrac{4}{15}$

2. $-3.6 \div 2\dfrac{1}{7}$

3. A boat drops an anchor 17.5 feet to the bottom of a lake. If the anchor falls at a rate of 0.07 feet each second, how long will it take the anchor to reach the bottom of the lake?

LESSON 1-10 Solve Problems with Rational Numbers

Quick Review

You can use rational numbers to solve problems in the same way that you use whole numbers. Be sure to make sense of the problem you are solving to help you choose the correct operations and determine which values will be positive and which will be negative.

Example

During a 15-day dry spell, the water level in a lake changed by $-2\dfrac{3}{8}$ inches. What rational number represents the average change in the water level per day?

$-2\dfrac{3}{8} \div 15$

$= -\dfrac{19}{8} \cdot \dfrac{1}{15}$

$= -\dfrac{19}{120}$ inch

Practice

1. In 5 rounds of a game, Jill scored −3, 8, 9 −7, and 13. What integer represents her average score for the 5 rounds?

2. Peter signed up for a program that costs $10.50 per month to stream movies to his computer. He decided to cancel his service after $\dfrac{5}{6}$ month. He only has to pay for the amount of time he used the service. What number represents the total change in the amount of money Peter has after paying for the service?

3. Maggie spent $4.05 on cheese and fruit at the farmer's market. She bought $\dfrac{1}{8}$ pound of apples, $\dfrac{1}{4}$ pound of pears, and 1.25 pounds of bananas. If fruit cost $0.80 per pound, how much did Maggie spend on cheese?

Crisscrossed

Fluency Practice — Topic 1

Find each sum, difference, product, or quotient. Write your answers in the cross-number puzzle below. Each digit and negative sign in your answers goes in its own box.

I can... add, subtract, multiply, and divide integers.

Across

2. $248 + (-1{,}027)$
5. $818 - (-1{,}021)$
6. $-516 + 774$
8. $242 + (-656)$
9. $2{,}087 + (-1{,}359)$
10. $631 - 897$
11. $-342 + 199$
12. $-49 \cdot -27$
13. $-321 - 987$
14. $2{,}988 \div -3$
15. $2{,}580 \div 6$
16. $4{,}592 \div -82$
17. $48 \cdot -27$
18. $-24 \cdot 83$
21. $-118 + 1{,}201$
22. $-45 \cdot -59$

Down

1. $246 + 173$
2. $22 \cdot -22$
3. $726 - (-219)$
4. $501 - 699$
7. $-10{,}740 \div 15$
8. $6{,}327 \div -9$
10. $144 \cdot -16$
11. $15 \cdot -67$
12. $7{,}164 \div 4$
13. $-33 \cdot 63$
14. $-2{,}695 \div 55$
17. $-1{,}032 - (-285)$
18. $512 - 720$
19. $-729 + 951$
20. $-17 \cdot -25$

Topic 1 Integers and Rational Numbers

TOPIC 2
ANALYZE AND USE PROPORTIONAL RELATIONSHIPS

? Topic Essential Question

How can you recognize and represent proportional relationships and use them to solve problems?

Topic Overview

2-1 Connect Ratios, Rates, and Unit Rates

2-2 Determine Unit Rates with Ratios of Fractions

2-3 Understand Proportional Relationships: Equivalent Ratios

2-4 Describe Proportional Relationships: Constant of Proportionality

3-Act Mathematical Modeling: Mixin' It Up

2-5 Graph Proportional Relationships

2-6 Apply Proportional Reasoning to Solve Problems

Topic Vocabulary

- constant of proportionality
- proportion
- proportional relationship

Lesson Digital Resources

INTERACTIVE ANIMATION Interact with visual learning animations.

ACTIVITY Use with *Solve & Discuss It, Explore It*, and *Explain It* activities, and to explore Examples.

VIDEOS Watch clips to support *3-Act Mathematical Modeling Lessons* and *STEM Projects*.

PRACTICE Practice what you've learned.

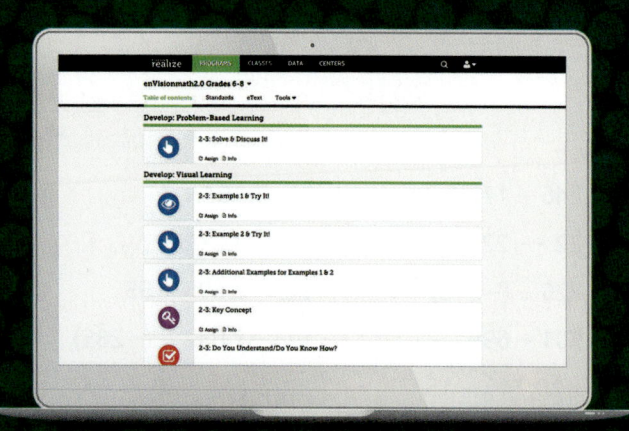

Go online | PearsonRealize.com

3-ACT MATH

Mixin' It Up

▶ Mixin' It Up

Drinking plenty of water each day is important. Water is necessary for everything your body does. Not drinking enough water can lead to health problems. It's even easier to drink enough water if you like the taste.

There are many ways to make water more exciting. You can drink seltzer or filtered water. You can add fruit, vegetables, herbs, or flavor enhancers. You can add more or less based on what you like. Think about this during the 3-Act Mathematical Modeling lesson.

TUTORIALS Get help from *Virtual Nerd*, right when you need it.

KEY CONCEPT Review important lesson content.

GLOSSARY Read and listen to English/Spanish definitions.

ASSESSMENT Show what you've learned.

Additional Digital Resources

MATH TOOLS Explore math with digital tools.

GAMES Play Math Games to help you learn.

ETEXT Interact with your Student's Edition online.

Topic 2 Analyze and Use Proportional Relationships

TOPIC 2 STEM Project

Did You Know?

There are more than **326 million trillion gallons** of water on Earth.

Only a small percentage of all this water is fresh water…

…and **much of that fresh water** is locked up in ice caps and glaciers.

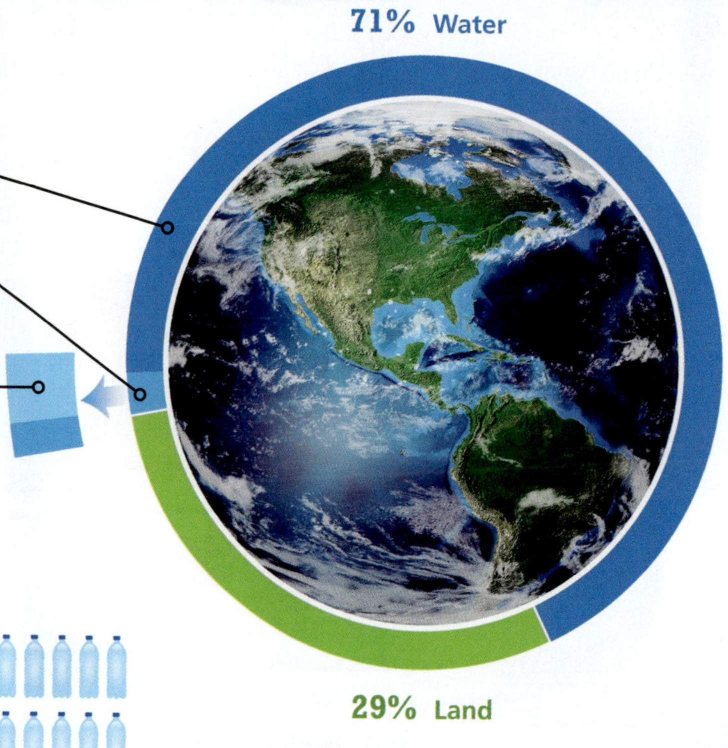

71% Water

29% Land

The United Nations says that each person needs about **50 liters** of water each day.

Each person in Africa has access to less than **20 liters** of water each day.

Many doctors recommend that each person drinks eight 8-ounce glasses of water each day.

Each person in the United States uses on average about **35–40 gallons** of water each day.

Your Task: An Essential Resource

Access to fresh, clean water is important for human survival. You and your classmates will determine how much fresh water is available on Earth for people to use. You will also explore ways in which people have developed access to clean water.

Review What You Know!

GET READY!

TOPIC 2

Vocabulary

Choose the best term from the box to complete each definition.

complex fraction
equivalent ratios
rate
ratio
terms

1. The quantities x and y in the ratio $\frac{x}{y}$ are called _____.

2. $\frac{2 \text{ dogs}}{3 \text{ cats}}$ and $\frac{10 \text{ dogs}}{15 \text{ cats}}$ are an example of _____.

3. A(n) _____ is a type of ratio that has both terms expressed in different units.

4. A(n) _____ has a fraction in its numerator, denominator, or both.

Equivalent Ratios

Complete each equivalent ratio.

5. $\frac{4 \text{ boys}}{7 \text{ girls}} = \frac{8 \text{ boys}}{\square \text{ girls}}$

6. $\frac{16 \text{ tires}}{4 \text{ cars}} = \frac{\square \text{ tires}}{1 \text{ car}}$

7. $\frac{8 \text{ correct}}{10 \text{ total}} = \frac{\square \text{ correct}}{50 \text{ total}}$

8. $\frac{16 \text{ pearls}}{20 \text{ opals}} = \frac{8 \text{ pearls}}{\square \text{ opals}}$

9. $\frac{32 \text{ pencils}}{8 \text{ erasers}} = \frac{8 \text{ pencils}}{\square \text{ erasers}}$

10. $\frac{7 \text{ balls}}{9 \text{ bats}} = \frac{\square \text{ balls}}{27 \text{ bats}}$

Rates

Write each situation as a rate.

11. John travels 150 miles in 3 hours.

12. Cameron ate 5 apples in 2 days.

Equations

Write an equation that represents the pattern in the table.

13.
x	4	5	6	7	8
y	12	15	18	21	24

Build Vocabulary

Use the graphic organizer to help you understand new vocabulary terms.

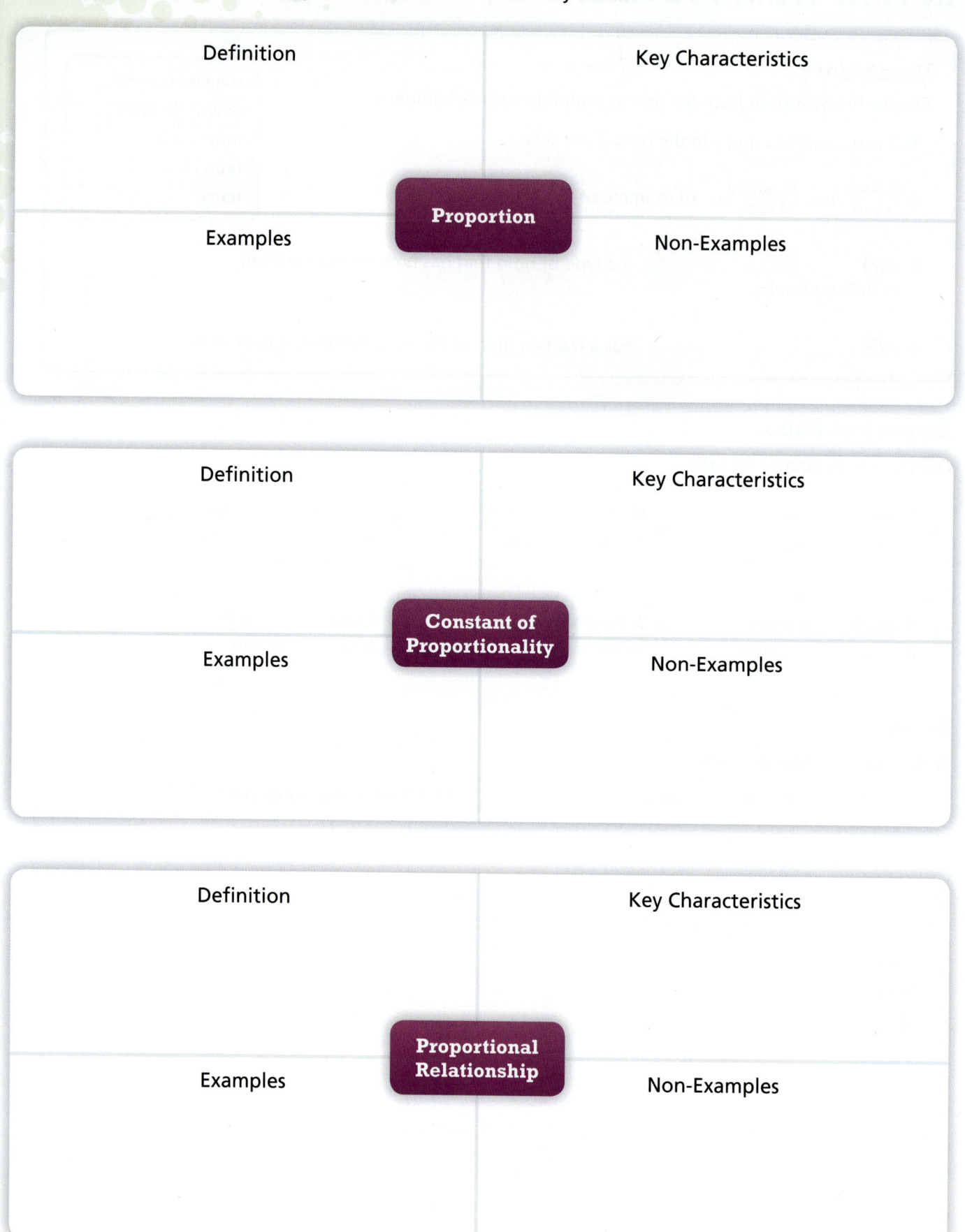

Definition	Key Characteristics
Examples	Non-Examples

Proportion

Definition	Key Characteristics
Examples	Non-Examples

Constant of Proportionality

Definition	Key Characteristics
Examples	Non-Examples

Proportional Relationship

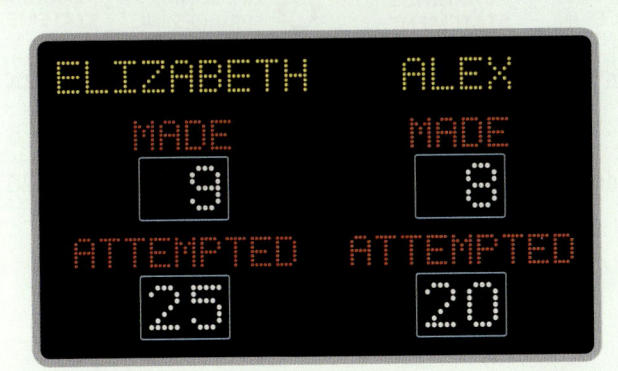

Lesson 2-1
Connect Ratios, Rates, and Unit Rates

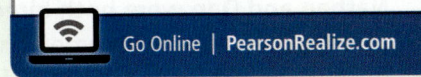

Go Online | PearsonRealize.com

I can... use ratio concepts and reasoning to solve multi-step problems.

Explain It!

In a basketball contest, Elizabeth made 9 out of 25 free throw attempts. Alex made 8 out of 20 free throw attempts. Janie said that Elizabeth had a better free-throw record because she made more free throws than Alex.

ELIZABETH
MADE 9
ATTEMPTED 25

ALEX
MADE 8
ATTEMPTED 20

A. Critique Reasoning Do you agree with Janie's reasoning? Explain.

B. Construct Arguments Decide who had the better free-throw record. Justify your reasoning using mathematical arguments.

Focus on math practices
Construct Arguments What mathematical model did you use to justify your reasoning? Are there other models you could use to represent the situation?

? Essential Question How are ratios, rates, and unit rates used to solve problems?

EXAMPLE 1 Find Unit Rates

Nathan and Dan were both hired as lifeguards for the summer. They receive their paychecks for the first week. Who earns more per hour?

LIFEGUARD SERVICES INC. EARNINGS STATEMENT
EMPLOYEE: Dan Jones
HOURS: 9
TOTAL EARNINGS: $78.75

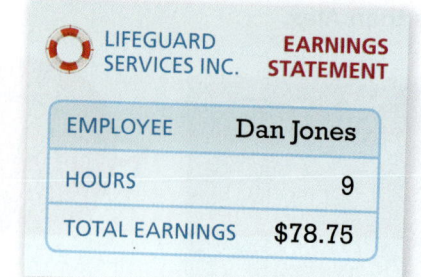

LIFEGUARD SERVICES INC. EARNINGS STATEMENT
EMPLOYEE: Nathan Smith
HOURS: 5
TOTAL EARNINGS: $46.25

Make Sense and Persevere
You can use a ratio to relate the number of hours worked and the amount earned.

Draw a model to show how the quantities are related.

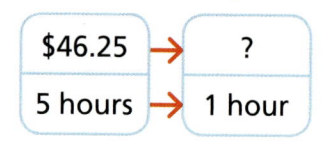

Nathan's Pay
| $46.25 → ? |
| 5 hours → 1 hour |

Dan's Pay
| $78.75 → ? |
| 9 hours → 1 hour |

Find unit rates to determine how much each lifeguard earns each hour.

$$\frac{46.25}{5} = \frac{9.25}{1}$$ (÷ 5)

$$\frac{78.75}{9} = \frac{8.75}{1}$$ (÷ 9)

Nathan earns 50¢ more per hour.

✓ Try It!

Jennifer is a lifeguard at the same pool. She earns $137.25 for 15 hours of lifeguarding. How much does Jennifer earn per hour?

Jennifer earns $ ____ per hour.

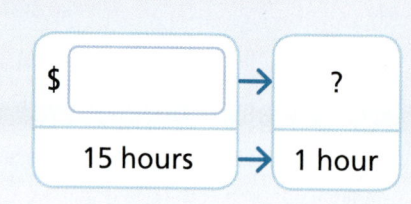

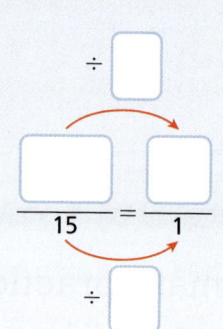

| $ ____ → ? |
| 15 hours → 1 hour |

$$\frac{\Box}{15} = \frac{\Box}{1}$$

Convince Me! What do you notice about the models used to find how much each lifeguard earns per hour?

86 2-1 Connect Ratios, Rates, and Unit Rates

EXAMPLE 2 Use Unit Rates

Brian agrees to watch his neighbor's dogs for 7 days. His neighbor provided a 128-ounce bag of dog food. Does Brian have enough food to feed the dogs all 7 days? Explain.

20.5 ounces in **2** days (Buster)

22.5 ounces in **3** days (Roxy)

STEP 1 Use unit rates to find how much each dog eats in 7 days.

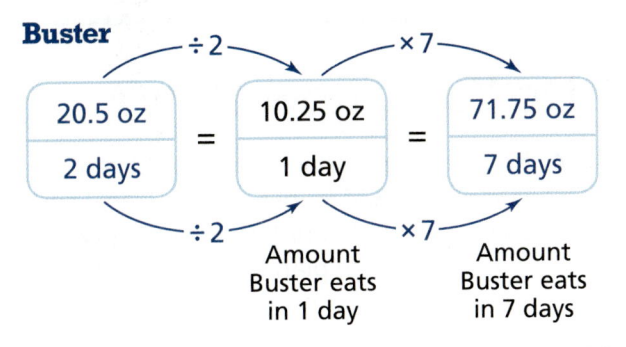

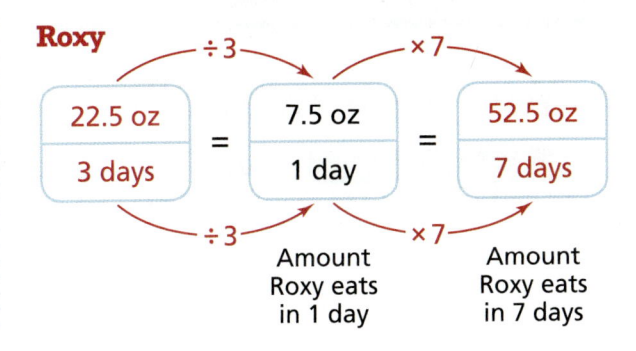

Buster

$$\frac{20.5 \text{ oz}}{2 \text{ days}} \xrightarrow{\div 2} \frac{10.25 \text{ oz}}{1 \text{ day}} \xrightarrow{\times 7} \frac{71.75 \text{ oz}}{7 \text{ days}}$$

Amount Buster eats in 1 day — Amount Buster eats in 7 days

Roxy

$$\frac{22.5 \text{ oz}}{3 \text{ days}} \xrightarrow{\div 3} \frac{7.5 \text{ oz}}{1 \text{ day}} \xrightarrow{\times 7} \frac{52.5 \text{ oz}}{7 \text{ days}}$$

Amount Roxy eats in 1 day — Amount Roxy eats in 7 days

STEP 2 Find the total amount of dog food needed for 7 days. Then compare.

$71.75 + 52.5 = 124.25$ and $124.25 < 128$, so Brian has enough dog food.

EXAMPLE 3 Compare Using Rates

Suppose that each jump covers the same distance. How many jumps does it take each animal to cover the same distance?

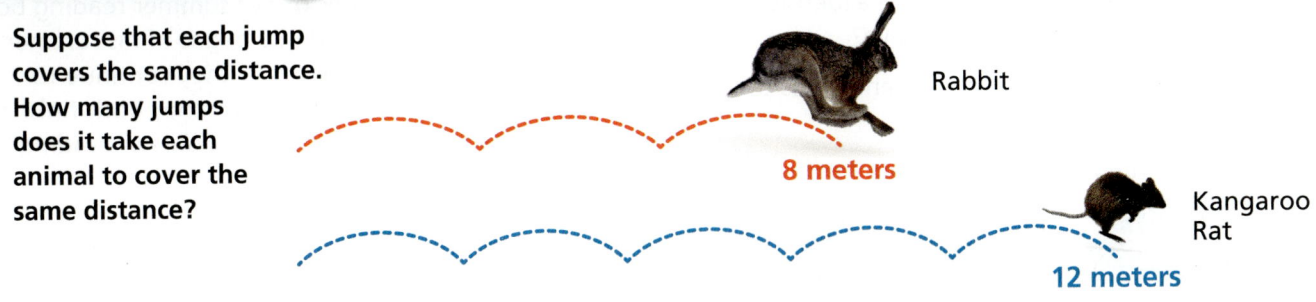

Rabbit — 8 meters

Kangaroo Rat — 12 meters

Make tables of equivalent ratios until the distance jumped is the same.

Rabbit

Jumps	Meters
3	8
6	16
9	24

×3

Kangaroo Rat

Jumps	Meters
5	12
10	24

×2

The rabbit jumps 24 meters in **9** jumps.

The kangaroo rat jumps 24 meters in **10** jumps.

✓ Try It!

A kitchen sink faucet streams 0.5 gallon of water in 10 seconds. A bathroom sink faucet streams 0.75 gallon of water in 18 seconds. Which faucet will fill a 3-gallon container faster?

2-1 Connect Ratios, Rates, and Unit Rates

KEY CONCEPT

You can use equivalent ratios and rates, including unit rates, to compare ratios and to solve problems.

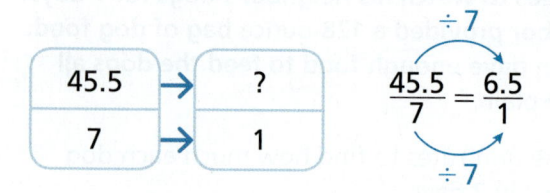

45.5	→	?
7	→	1

$$\frac{45.5}{7} = \frac{6.5}{1}$$

(÷ 7)

Do You Understand?

1. **Essential Question** How are ratios, rates, and unit rates used to solve problems?

2. **Use Structure** Dorian buys 2 pounds of almonds for $21.98 and 3 pounds of dried apricots for $26.25. Which is less expensive per pound? How much less expensive?

   Complete the tables of equivalent ratios to help you solve.

   Almonds

Cost	Weight (lb)
	2

   Dried Apricots

Cost	Weight (lb)
$26.25	

3. **Generalize** How are unit rates and equivalent ratios related?

Do You Know How?

4. Krystal is comparing two Internet service plans. Plan 1 costs $34.99 per month. Plan 2 costs $134.97 every 3 months. If Krystal plans to stay with one service plan for 1 year, which should she choose? How much will she save?

5. Pam read 126 pages of her summer reading book in 3 hours. Zack read 180 pages of his summer reading book in 4 hours. If they continue to read at the same speeds, will they both finish the 215-page book after 5 total hours of reading? Explain.

6. Nora and Eli are making homemade spring rolls for a party. Nora can make 8 spring rolls in 10 minutes. Eli can make 10 spring rolls in 12 minutes. If they each make 40 spring rolls, who will finish first?

Practice & Problem Solving

Leveled Practice In 7–8, complete the tables of equivalent ratios to solve.

7. After Megan walked 5 miles, her activity tracker had counted 9,780 steps. David's activity tracker had counted 11,928 steps after he walked 6 miles. Suppose each person's step covers about the same distance. Who takes more steps to walk 1 mile? How many more steps?

☐ takes more steps to walk 1 mile.

☐ − ☐ = ☐ more steps for 1 mile

Meghan's Steps

Steps	Miles
9,780	☐
☐	1

David's Steps

Steps	Miles
☐	6
☐	1

8. A package of 5 pairs of insulated gloves costs $29.45. What is the cost of a single pair of gloves?

One pair of gloves costs ☐.

Price	Pairs of Gloves
☐	5
☐	1

9. Which package has the lowest cost per ounce of rice?

$6.30 WHITE RICE 18 OUNCES
WHITE Rice 12 ounces $4.56
WHITE RICE 7 OUNCES $2.59

10. A nursery owner buys 5 panes of glass to fix some damage to her greenhouse. The 5 panes cost $14.25. Unfortunately, she breaks 2 more panes while repairing the damage. What is the cost of another 2 panes of glass?

11. Be Precise An arts academy requires there to be 3 teachers for every 75 students and 6 tutors for every 72 students. How many tutors does the academy need if it has 120 students?

12. Make Sense and Persevere In large cities, people often take taxis to get from one place to another. What is the cost per mile of a taxi ride? How much is a 47-mile taxi ride?

FARE $25.20   MILES 36

2-1 Connect Ratios, Rates, and Unit Rates

13. The track team needs new uniforms. The students plan to sell plush toy tigers (the school mascot) for $5. The students find three companies online that sell stuffed mascots.

    Company A
    12 tigers for $33.24

    Company B
    16 tigers for $44.80

    Company C
    15 tigers for $41.10

    a. Which company has the lowest cost per tiger?

    b. If they use that company, how much profit will the students make for each tiger sold?

14. A contractor purchases 7 dozen pairs of padded work gloves for $103.32. He incorrectly calculates the unit price at $14.76 per pair.

    a. What is the correct unit price?

    b. **Critique Reasoning** What error did the contractor likely make?

15. **Higher Order Thinking** A warehouse store sells 5.5-ounce cans of tuna in packages of 6. A package of 6 cans costs $9.24. The store also sells 6.5-ounce cans of the same tuna in packages of 3 cans for $4.68. It also sells 3.5-ounce cans in packages of 4 cans for $4.48. Which package has the lowest cost per ounce of tuna?

Assessment Practice

16. Lena is making two dishes for an event. Each batch of her mac-and-cheese recipe calls for 6 ounces of cheese and 2 tablespoons of basil. For every two pizzas, she needs 16 ounces of cheese and 5 tablespoons of basil.

    PART A
    Lena buys a 32-oz package of cheese. Does she have enough cheese to make 2 batches of mac-and-cheese and 3 pizzas? Explain.

    PART B
    Lena decides to make 1 batch of mac-and-cheese and 3 pizzas. How many tablespoons of basil does she need? Explain your answer.

17. Irene's car had 6 gallons of gas in its 15-gallon tank. Irene wants to fill it at least half way. If gas costs $3.80 per gallon, which of the following statements is true? Select all that apply.

    ☐ Irene needs to add more than 1.5 gallons of gas to the car's gas tank.

    ☐ If Irene adds $3.80 worth of gas, her tank will be more than half full.

    ☐ If Irene adds $7.60 worth of gas, her tank will be more than half full.

    ☐ If Irene filled her tank, it would cost $34.20.

Lesson 2-2
Determine Unit Rates with Ratios of Fractions

Go Online | PearsonRealize.com

I can... find unit rates with ratios of fractions and use them to solve problems.

Solve & Discuss It!

ACTIVITY

Allison and her classmates planted bean seeds at the same time as Yuki and her classmates in Tokyo did. Allison is video-chatting with Yuki about their class seedlings. Assume that both plants will continue to grow at the same rate. Who should expect to have the taller plant at the end of the school year?

Allison's Class
2.5 inches in **5 days**

Yuki's Class
5.5 centimeters in **4 days**

Look for Relationships
How can you compare the growth rates of the seedlings?

Focus on math practices

Be Precise What must the students do before they can compare the heights of the plants?

91

? **Essential Question** Why is it useful to write a ratio of fractions as a unit rate?

EXAMPLE 1 Find a Unit Rate Involving Unit Fractions

Sergio is training for a triathlon. His target speed is 25 miles per hour. Did he achieve his target speed for the first 7 miles of his ride?

Reasoning You can use a unit rate to describe Sergio's cycling speed.

7 miles
15 minutes

You know that 15 minutes is equal to $\frac{1}{4}$ hour. Draw a diagram to show how the distance Sergio bikes is related to the time he bikes.

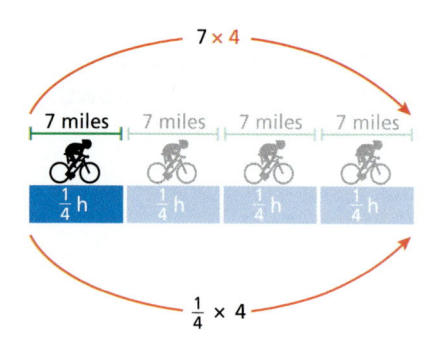

7 × 4

7 miles | 7 miles | 7 miles | 7 miles
$\frac{1}{4}$ h | $\frac{1}{4}$ h | $\frac{1}{4}$ h | $\frac{1}{4}$ h

$\frac{1}{4}$ × 4

Make a table of equivalent ratios to find the unit rate.

× 4

Miles	7	28
Hour	$\frac{1}{4}$	1

× 4

Sergio bikes $\frac{28 \text{ miles}}{1 \text{ hour}}$, or 28 miles per hour, so he has achieved, and exceeded, his target speed.

✓ Try It!

Sergio increases his target speed to 30 miles per hour. How many more miles does Sergio need to ride in $\frac{1}{4}$ hour to achieve this target speed?

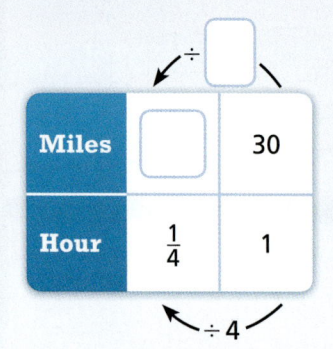

÷ ☐

Miles	☐	30
Hour	$\frac{1}{4}$	1

÷ 4

Sergio must ride ☐ miles in $\frac{1}{4}$ hour to achieve this target speed, so he needs to ride an additional ☐ mile per $\frac{1}{4}$ hour.

Convince Me! How does the unit rate describe Sergio's cycling speed? How is the unit rate helpful in determining how much farther Sergio must cycle in a given amount of time each time he increases his target speed?

EXAMPLE 2 — Find and Apply a Unit Rate Involving Fractions

Bronwyn mows the lawn every other weekend. She can mow 12,000 ft² in $\frac{2}{3}$ hour. The lawn is 36,000 ft².

How long does it take her to mow the entire lawn?

$$\frac{12{,}000}{\frac{2}{3}} = \frac{12{,}000 \times \frac{3}{2}}{\frac{2}{3} \times \frac{3}{2}} = \frac{18{,}000 \text{ ft}^2}{1 \text{ h}}$$

$$\frac{18{,}000 \times 2}{1 \times 2} = \frac{36{,}000}{2}$$

Multiply each term by 2 for the area of the entire lawn.

Bronwyn mows at a rate of 18,000 ft² per hour. It takes her 2 hours to mow the entire lawn.

Look for Relationships How do the operations used in the table relate to the operations used in the equations at the left?

Area (ft²)	12,000	18,000	36,000
Time (h)	$\frac{2}{3}$	$\frac{6}{6}$ or 1	2

($\times \frac{3}{2}$, $\times 2$)

Try It!

Every other weekend, Bronwyn's brother Daniel mows the lawn. He can mow 15,000 ft² in $\frac{3}{4}$ hour. Who mows the lawn in less time? Explain.

EXAMPLE 3 — Solve Problems Using Unit Rates

Omar knows that his friend Chris lives $\frac{3}{5}$ mile away. **How far is the school from his house?**

$$\frac{\frac{3}{5} \text{ mi}}{\frac{3}{4} \text{ in.}} = \frac{\frac{3}{5} \times \frac{4}{3}}{\frac{3}{4} \times \frac{4}{3}} = \frac{\frac{4}{5} \text{ mi}}{1 \text{ in.}}$$

Divide both terms by $\frac{3}{4}$ to find the unit rate.

$$\frac{\frac{4}{5} \text{ mi} \times 2}{1 \text{ in.} \times 2} = \frac{\frac{8}{5} \text{ mi}}{2 \text{ in.}} = \frac{1\frac{3}{5} \text{ mi}}{2 \text{ in.}}$$

Multiply both terms of the unit rate by 2 to find an equivalent rate.

Omar's school is $1\frac{3}{5}$ miles from his house.

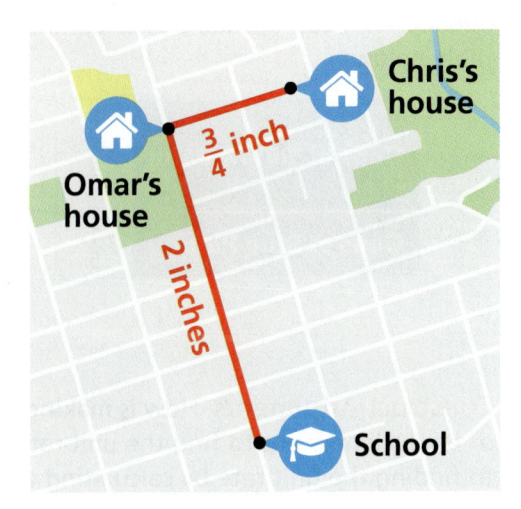

Map shows Omar's house to Chris's house is $\frac{3}{4}$ inch, and Omar's house to School is 2 inches.

Try It!

Sonoma bikes 5 miles to Paige's house. On a map, they measure that distance as $\frac{5}{6}$ cm. The same map shows that the mall is $3\frac{1}{2}$ cm from Paige's house. What is the actual distance between Paige's house and the mall?

Go Online | PearsonRealize.com

2-2 Determine Unit Rates with Ratios of Fractions

KEY CONCEPT

You can use what you know about equivalent ratios and operations with fractions to write a ratio of fractions as a unit rate.

Tia skateboards $\frac{2}{3}$ mile for every $\frac{1}{6}$ hour.

$$\frac{\frac{2}{3}}{\frac{1}{6}} = \frac{\frac{2}{3} \times \frac{6}{1}}{\frac{1}{6} \times \frac{6}{1}} = \frac{4}{1} = 4$$

		$\times \frac{6}{1}$	
Miles	$\frac{2}{3}$		4
Hours	$\frac{1}{6}$		1
		$\times \frac{6}{1}$	

She skateboards 4 miles per hour.

Do You Understand?

1. **Essential Question** Why is it useful to write a ratio of fractions as a unit rate?

2. **Use Structure** Jacob mixes $\frac{1}{3}$ cup of yellow paint for every $\frac{1}{5}$ cup of blue paint to make green paint. How many cups of yellow paint are needed for 1 cup of blue paint? Complete the table below.

Cups of Yellow Paint	$\frac{1}{3}$	
Cups of Blue Paint	$\frac{1}{5}$	1

3. **Construct Arguments** How is making a table of equivalent ratios to find the unit rate similar to finding the unit rate by calculating with fractions? Use a specific example to explain your reasoning.

Do You Know How?

4. Claire boarded an airplane in Richmond, VA, and flew 414 miles directly to Charleston, SC. The total flight time was $\frac{3}{4}$ hour. How fast did Claire's airplane fly, in miles per hour?

5. Brad buys two packages of mushrooms. Which mushrooms cost less per pound? Explain.

   Cremini
   $11.25 for $\frac{2}{3}$ lb

   Chanterelle
   $7.99 for $\frac{1}{2}$ lb

6. Jed is baking shortbread for a bake sale. The recipe calls for $1\frac{1}{4}$ cups of flour and $\frac{1}{2}$ stick of butter. How many cups of flour will Jed need if he uses 3 sticks of butter?

Practice & Problem Solving

Leveled Practice In 7–10, fill in the boxes to find the unit rate.

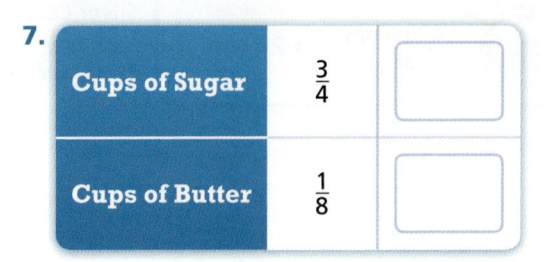

7.

Cups of Sugar	$\frac{3}{4}$	☐
Cups of Butter	$\frac{1}{8}$	☐

☐ cups of sugar for each cup of butter

8.

Miles	$\frac{3}{5}$	☐
Hours	$\frac{1}{3}$	☐

☐ miles in 1 hour

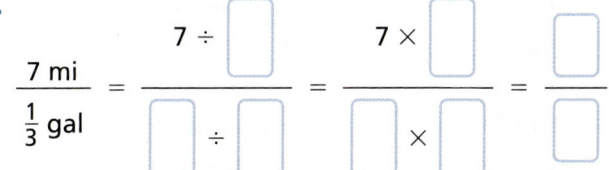

9.

$$\frac{7 \text{ mi}}{\frac{1}{3} \text{ gal}} = \frac{7 \div \Box}{\Box \div \Box} = \frac{7 \times \Box}{\Box \times \Box} = \frac{\Box}{\Box}$$

☐ miles per gallon

10. $\frac{\frac{3}{4} \text{ page}}{2 \text{ minutes}}$

☐ page in 1 minute

11. Hadley paddled a canoe $\frac{2}{3}$ mile in $\frac{1}{4}$ hour. How fast did Hadley paddle, in miles per hour?

12. A box of cereal states that there are 90 Calories in a $\frac{3}{4}$-cup serving. How many Calories are there in 4 cups of the cereal?

13. A robot can complete 8 tasks in $\frac{5}{6}$ hour. Each task takes the same amount of time.

  a. How long does it take the robot to complete one task?

  b. How many tasks can the robot complete in one hour?

14. You are running a fuel economy study. You want to find out which car can travel a greater distance on 1 gallon of gas.

    Blue Car: $1\frac{1}{2}$ gallons of gas → $35\frac{1}{2}$ miles

    Silver Car: $\frac{4}{5}$ gallons of gas → $27\frac{1}{5}$ miles

    a. What is the gas mileage, in miles per gallon, for the blue car?

    b. What is the gas mileage, in miles per gallon, for the silver car?

    c. Which car could travel the greater distance on 1 gallon of gas?

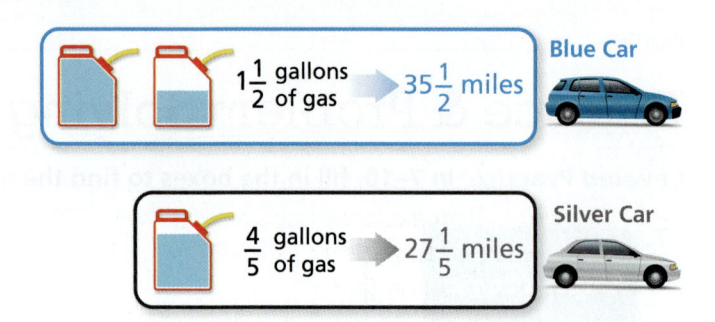

15. Henry incorrectly said the rate $\dfrac{\frac{1}{5} \text{ pound}}{\frac{1}{20} \text{ quart}}$ can be written as the unit rate $\frac{1}{100}$ pound per quart.

    a. What is the correct unit rate?

    b. **Critique Reasoning** What error did Henry likely make?

16. **Higher Order Thinking** Ari walked $2\frac{3}{4}$ miles at a constant speed of $2\frac{1}{2}$ miles per hour. Beth walked $1\frac{3}{4}$ miles at a constant speed of $1\frac{1}{4}$ miles per hour. Cindy walked for 1 hour and 21 minutes at a constant speed of $1\frac{1}{8}$ miles per hour. List the three people in order of the times they spent walking from least time to greatest time.

Assessment Practice

17. A blueprint shows a house with two fences. Fence A is $1\frac{4}{5}$ inches long on the blueprint and is to be $1\frac{1}{2}$ feet long. How long is Fence B on the blueprint?

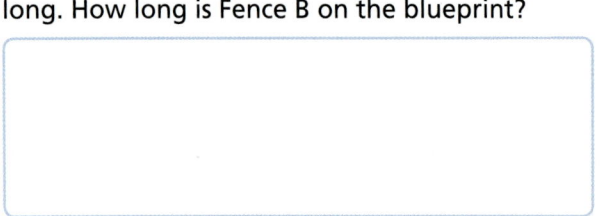

    Fence B: 5 feet

18. Leo reads 13 pages in $\frac{1}{3}$ hour. Use the table to find how many pages he reads in one hour.

    Leo reads ☐ pages in one hour.

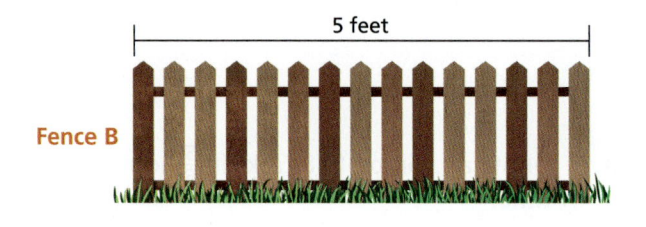

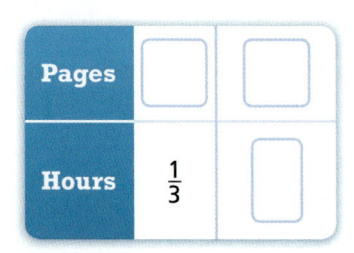

Pages		
Hours	$\frac{1}{3}$	

96 2-2 Determine Unit Rates with Ratios of Fractions

Lesson 2-3
Understand Proportional Relationships: Equivalent Ratios

Go Online | PearsonRealize.com

I can…
test for equivalent ratios to decide whether quantities are in a proportional relationship.

Solve & Discuss It!

Weight is a measure of force affected by gravity. The Moon's gravity is less than Earth's gravity, so objects weigh less on the Moon than on Earth.

Using the information provided, how much do you think a cat will weigh on the Moon? Explain your reasoning.

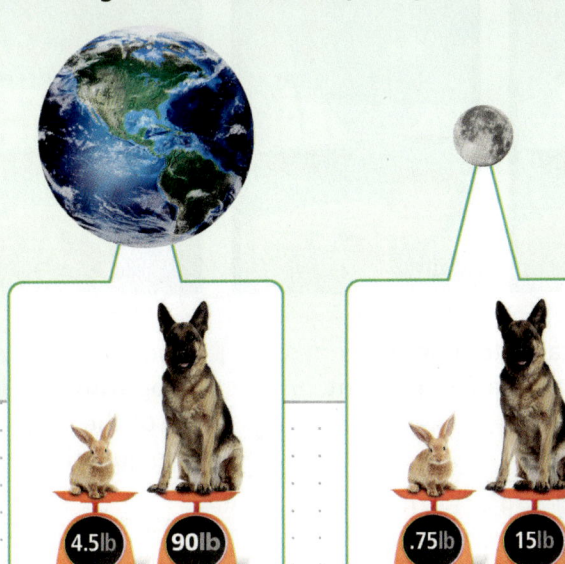

4.5 lb   90 lb   .75 lb   15 lb

Make Sense and Persevere
About how much does a cat weigh on Earth?

Focus on math practices

Generalize How could you find the approximate weight of any object on the Moon? Explain your reasoning.

97

? **Essential Question** How are proportional quantities described by equivalent ratios?

EXAMPLE 1 Recognize a Proportional Relationship

On Sarah's favorite mobile game, she is awarded game lives when she finds gold coins. How is the number of game lives awarded related to the number of gold coins found? Explain.

Write ratios that relate the gold coins found and the game lives awarded.

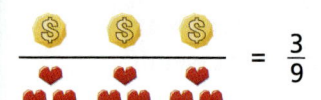

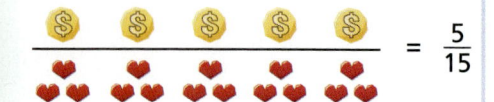

$$\frac{\text{3 coins}}{\text{9 hearts}} = \frac{3}{9}$$

$$\frac{\text{2 coins}}{\text{6 hearts}} = \frac{2}{6}$$

$$\frac{\text{5 coins}}{\text{15 hearts}} = \frac{5}{15}$$

Make a ratio table to determine whether the ratios are equivalent.

Coins	3	2	5
Game Lives	9	6	15
Coins/Game Lives	$\frac{3}{9} = \frac{1}{3}$	$\frac{2}{6} = \frac{1}{3}$	$\frac{5}{15} = \frac{1}{3}$

Two quantities are in a **proportional relationship** if all of the ratios that relate the quantities are equivalent.

Each ratio $\frac{\text{coins}}{\text{game lives}}$ is equivalent to $\frac{1}{3}$. The number of game lives awarded is proportional to the number of gold coins found.

✓ Try It!

Miles records the time it takes to download a variety of file types. How is the download time related to the file size? Explain.

The ratios for each pair of data are ☐, so the download time and the file size are ☐.

Type of Media	File Size (MB)	Download Time (s)	Download Time / File Size
Document	1.25	25	$\frac{25}{\square} = 20$
Song	3.6	72	$\frac{\square}{3.6} = 20$
Video	6.25	125	$\frac{125}{6.25} = \square$

Convince Me! How can you show that two quantities have a proportional relationship?

98   2-3 Understand Proportional Relationships: Equivalent Ratios

EXAMPLE 2 — Decide Whether Quantities are Proportional

Is the relationship between the area and the side length of the squares proportional? Explain your reasoning.

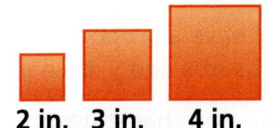

2 in. 3 in. 4 in.

STEP 1 Make a table to organize the data. Find the ratio of area to side length for each data pair.

STEP 2 Compare the ratios by finding the unit rates.

$\frac{2}{1} \neq \frac{3}{1} \neq \frac{4}{1}$

The ratios are not equivalent so the relationship between the area and side length is NOT proportional.

Side Length (x)	Area (y)	$\frac{Area\ (y)}{Side\ Length\ (x)}$
2	4	$\frac{4}{2} = \frac{2}{1}$
3	9	$\frac{9}{3} = \frac{3}{1}$
4	16	$\frac{16}{4} = \frac{4}{1}$

Try It!

The table at the right shows information about regular hexagons. Is the relationship between the perimeter and the side length of the hexagons proportional? Explain.

Side Length (x)	Perimeter (y)
2	12
3	18

EXAMPLE 3 — Use Proportions to Solve Problems

A **proportion** is an equation that represents equal ratios. Use the table at the right. How many times will a hummingbird beat its wings in 60 seconds?

Hummingbird Wing Beats

Seconds (x)	2	7	10
Wing Beats (y)	160	560	800

STEP 1 Verify that the quantities are proportional.

$\frac{160}{2} = \frac{80}{1}$ $\frac{560}{7} = \frac{80}{1}$ $\frac{800}{10} = \frac{80}{1}$

The ratios are equivalent, so the quantities are proportional.

STEP 2 Write and solve a proportion.

$\frac{80}{1} = \frac{y}{60}$

$\frac{80}{1} \cdot 60 = \frac{y}{60} \cdot 60$ Multiply both sides by 60 to solve for y.

$4{,}800 = y$

A hummingbird beats its wings 4,800 times in 60 seconds.

Try It!

Ginny's favorite cookie recipe requires $1\frac{1}{2}$ cups of sugar to make 24 cookies. How much sugar does Ginny need to make 36 of these cookies?

KEY CONCEPT

Two quantities x and y have a proportional relationship if all the ratios $\frac{y}{x}$ for related pairs of x and y are equivalent.

A proportion is an equation that states that two ratios are equivalent.

$$\frac{3}{120} = \frac{5}{200}$$

x	y	$\frac{y}{x}$
120	3	$\frac{3}{120} = 0.025$
200	5	$\frac{5}{200} = 0.025$

Do You Understand?

1. **Essential Question** How are proportional quantities described by equivalent ratios?

2. **Look for Relationships** How do you know if a relationship between two quantities is NOT proportional?

3. **Reasoning** If the ratio $\frac{y}{x}$ is the same for all related pairs of x and y, what does that mean about the relationship between x and y?

Do You Know How?

4. Use the table below. Do x and y have a proportional relationship? Explain.

x	2	3	5	8
y	5	7.5	12.5	18

5. Each triangle is equilateral. Is the relationship between the perimeter and the side length of the equilateral triangles proportional? Explain.

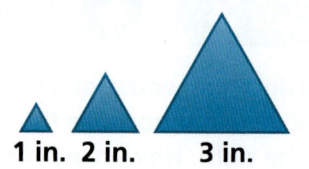

1 in.   2 in.   3 in.

6. Is the relationship between the number of tickets sold and the number of hours proportional? If so, how many tickets were sold in 8 hours?

Hours (h)	Tickets Sold (t)
3	240
5	400
9	720

100   2-3 Understand Proportional Relationships: Equivalent Ratios

Practice & Problem Solving

7. The amount of seed a landscaper uses and the area of lawn covered have a proportional relationship. Complete the table.

Lawn Seed

Seed (oz)	2	3	4
Area Covered (ft²)	50	75	100
Area Covered / Seed	$\frac{50}{2} = \frac{25}{1}$		

8. Construct Arguments Is the relationship between the number of slices of salami in a sandwich and the number of Calories proportional? Explain.

Calories in a Sandwich

Slices of Salami	Calories
1	66
2	96
3	126
4	156

9. Look for Relationships A wholesale club sells eggs by the dozen. Does the table show a proportional relationship between the number of dozens of eggs and the cost? Explain.

Cost of Dozens of Eggs

Dozen	Cost ($)
6	21
8	28
10	35
14	49

10. Does the table show a proportional relationship? If so, what is the value of y when x is 11?

x	4	5	6	10
y	64	125	216	1,000

11. Does the table show a proportional relationship? If so, what is the value of y when x is 10?

x	5	6	7	8
y	$1\frac{2}{3}$	2	$2\frac{1}{3}$	$2\frac{2}{3}$

2-3 Understand Proportional Relationships: Equivalent Ratios

12. The height of a building is proportional to the number of floors. The figure shows the height of a building with 9 floors.

    h = 135 feet

    a. **Reasoning** Write the ratio of height of the building to the number of floors. Then find the unit rate, and explain what it means in this situation.

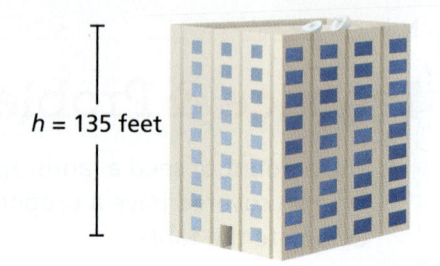

    b. How tall would the building be if it had 15 floors?

13. **Higher Order Thinking** Do the two tables show the same proportional relationship between x and y? Explain how you know.

x	160	500	1,200
y	360	1,125	2,700

x	2	5	7
y	4.5	11.25	15.75

✅ Assessment Practice

14. The table shows the number of cell phone towers a company will build as the number of its customers increases.

    PART A

    Is the relationship between number of towers and number of customers proportional? Explain.

    Cell Phone Towers

Customers (thousands)	Towers
5.25	252
6.25	300
7.25	348
9.25	444

    PART B

    If there are 576 towers, how many customers does the company have? Write a proportion you can use to solve.

15. Which of the following statements about the table is true? Select all that apply.

x	12	18	22	26
y	1.5	2.25	2.75	3.25

    ☐ The table shows a proportional relationship.

    ☐ When x is 20, y is 2.55.

    ☐ All the ratios $\frac{y}{x}$ for related pairs of x and y are equivalent to 8.

    ☐ The unit rate of $\frac{y}{x}$ for related pairs of x and y is $\frac{1}{8}$.

102   2-3 Understand Proportional Relationships: Equivalent Ratios

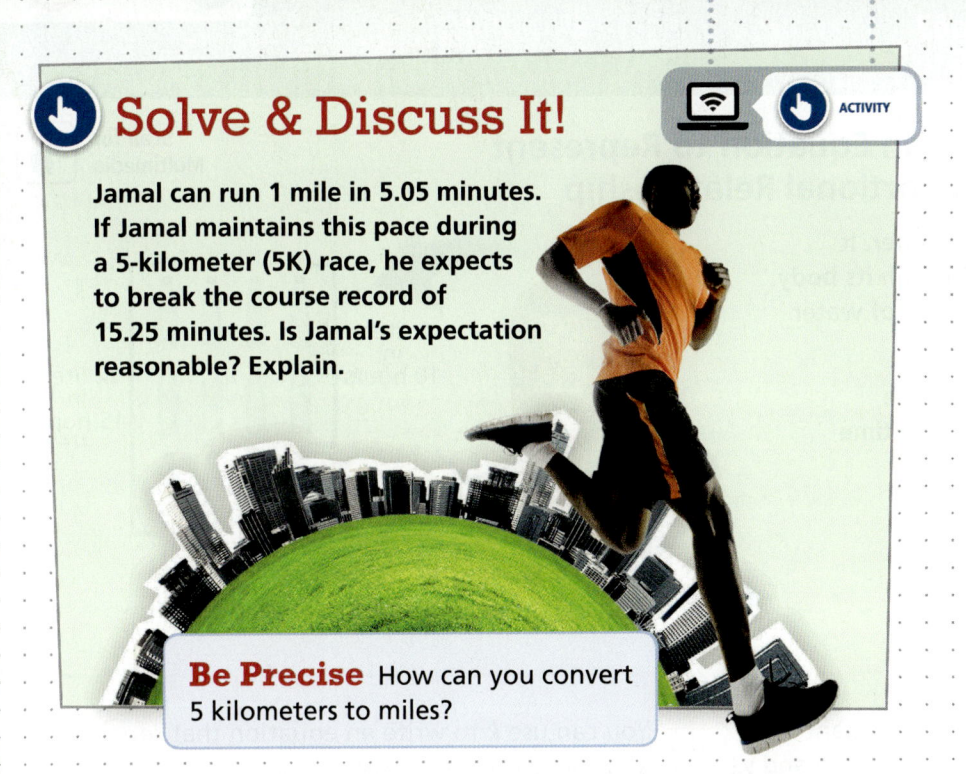

Lesson 2-4
Describe Proportional Relationships: Constant of Proportionality

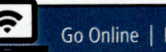

Go Online | PearsonRealize.com

I can… use the constant of proportionality in an equation to represent a proportional relationship.

Solve & Discuss It!

Jamal can run 1 mile in 5.05 minutes. If Jamal maintains this pace during a 5-kilometer (5K) race, he expects to break the course record of 15.25 minutes. Is Jamal's expectation reasonable? Explain.

Be Precise How can you convert 5 kilometers to miles?

Focus on math practices

Reasoning Assuming that Jamal runs at a constant rate, how does his pace describe the time it takes him to finish a race of any length?

Essential Question How can you represent a proportional relationship with an equation?

EXAMPLE 1: Write an Equation to Represent a Proportional Relationship

A sponge is an example of a *filter feeder*. It takes in food by filtering water through its body. The sponge maintains a constant flow of water through its body.

What is an equation that represents the proportional relationship between the time and the amount of water filtered?

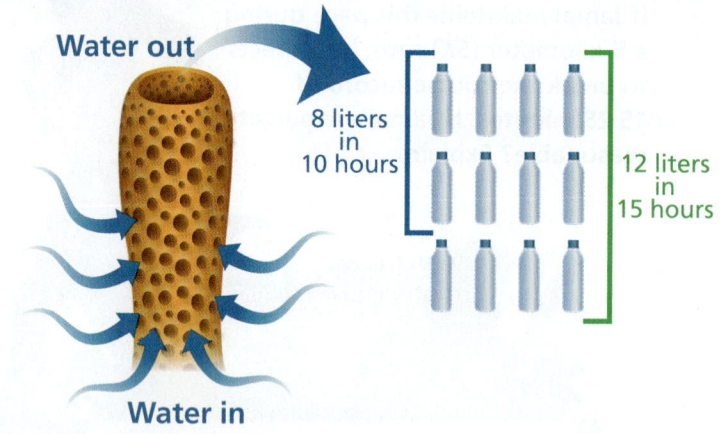

- 8 liters in 10 hours
- 12 liters in 15 hours

The **constant of proportionality** is the constant multiple that relates proportional quantities x and y. It is the value of the ratio $\frac{y}{x}$ and is represented by k.

Make a table to find the constant of proportionality.

Hours (x)	Liters (y)	$\frac{\text{Liters}}{\text{Hours}}\left(\frac{y}{x}\right)$
10	8	$\frac{8}{10} = 0.8$
15	12	$\frac{12}{15} = 0.8$

The constant of proportionality, k, is 0.8.

You can use k to write an equation that represents a proportional relationship.

$$k = \frac{y}{x}$$
$$kx = y$$
$$y = kx$$

You can use an equation in the form $y = kx$ to represent any proportional relationship.

Use the equation to represent the relationship between time and the amount of water filtered.

$$y = 0.8x$$

✓ Try It!

Maria made two batches of fruit punch. The table at the right shows how many quarts of juice she used for each batch. Write an equation that relates the proportional quantities.

Apple Juice (x)	Grape Juice (y)	$\frac{\text{Grape Juice}}{\text{Apple Juice}}\left(\frac{y}{x}\right)$
5	8	
10	16	

The constant of proportionality is ☐.

An equation that represents this proportional relationship is $y =$ ☐ x.

Convince Me! How does the equation change if the amount of grape juice is the independent variable, x, and the amount of apple juice is the dependent variable, y?

2-4 Describe Proportional Relationships: Constant of Proportionality

EXAMPLE 2 — Solve Problems Using an Equation

1 inch = 2.54 centimeters. How many centimeters long is an 18-inch ruler?

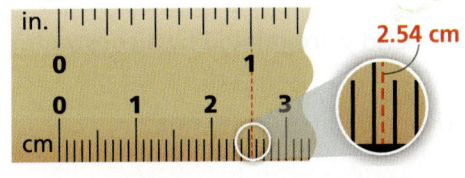

STEP 1 Write an equation to represent this relationship.

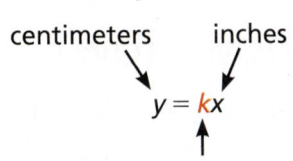

centimeters — inches

$y = kx$

↑ constant multiple or constant of proportionality

$y = 2.54x$

STEP 2 Use the equation to find the length of the ruler in centimeters.

$y = 2.54x$

$y = 2.54(18)$

$y = 45.72$

The ruler is 45.72 centimeters long.

Try It!

A florist sells a dozen roses for $35.40. She sells individual roses for the same unit cost. Write an equation to represent the relationship between the number of roses, x, and the total cost of the roses, y. How much would 18 roses cost?

EXAMPLE 3 — Determine Whether $y = kx$ Describes a Situation

Can you represent the total cost, y, for admission and x rides at the amusement park using an equation in the form $y = kx$? Explain.

WELCOME TO FUN FAIR
ADMISSION: $20
EACH RIDE: $5

STEP 1 Make a table that shows the total cost.

Rides	Cost
1	$25
2	$30
3	$35

STEP 2 Compare the ratios to determine whether the relationship is proportional.

$\frac{\$25}{1} = \$25$

$\frac{\$30}{2} = \$15$

$\frac{\$35}{3} = \$11.67$

This relationship is not proportional, so it cannot be represented with an equation of the form $y = kx$.

Try It!

Balloon A is released 5 feet above the ground. Balloon B is released at ground level. Both balloons rise at a constant rate.

Which situation can you represent using an equation of the form $y = kx$? Explain.

Balloon A

Time (s)	Height (ft)
1	9
2	13
3	17

Balloon B

Time (s)	Height (ft)
1	4
2	8
3	12

KEY CONCEPT

Two proportional quantities x and y are related by a constant multiple, or the constant of proportionality, k.

You can represent a proportional relationship using the equation $y = kx$.

Do You Understand?

1. **Essential Question** How can you represent a proportional relationship with an equation?

2. **Generalize** How can you use an equation to find an unknown value in a proportional relationship?

3. **Reasoning** Why does the equation $y = 3x + 5$ NOT represent a proportional relationship?

Do You Know How?

4. Determine whether each equation represents a proportional relationship. If it does, identify the constant of proportionality.

   a. $y = 0.5x - 2$

   b. $y = 1,000x$

   c. $y = x + 1$

5. The manager of a concession stand estimates that she needs 3 hot dogs for every 5 people who attend a baseball game. If 1,200 people attend the game, how many hot dogs should the manager order?

6. A half dozen cupcakes cost $15. What constant of proportionality relates the number of cupcakes and total cost? Write an equation that represents this relationship.

Practice & Problem Solving

7. What is the constant of proportionality in the equation $y = 5x$?

8. What is the constant of proportionality in the equation $y = 0.41x$?

9. The equation $P = 3s$ represents the perimeter P of an equilateral triangle with side length s. Is there a proportional relationship between the perimeter and the side length of an equilateral triangle? Explain.

10. Model with Math In a chemical compound, there are 3 parts zinc for every 16 parts copper, by mass. A piece of the compound contains 320 grams of copper. Write and solve an equation to determine the amount of zinc in the chemical compound.

11. The weight of 3 eggs is shown. Assuming the three eggs are all the same weight, find the constant of proportionality.

12. The height of a stack of DVD cases is proportional to the number of cases in the stack. The height of 6 DVD cases is 114 mm.

   a. Write an equation that relates the height, y, of a stack of DVD cases and the number of cases, x, in the stack.

   b. What would be the height of 13 DVD cases?

13. Ann's car can travel 228 miles on 6 gallons of gas.

   a. Write an equation to represent the distance, y, in miles Ann's car can travel on x gallons of gas.

   b. Ann's car used 7 gallons of gas during a trip. How far did Ann drive?

14. The value of a baseball player's rookie card began to increase once the player retired in 1996. The value has increased by $2.52 each year since then.

   a. How much was the baseball card worth in 1997? In 1998? In 1999?

   b. **Construct Arguments** Why is there not a proportional relationship between the years since the player retired and the card value? Explain.

   1996
   Value: $7.46

15. **Higher Order Thinking** A car travels $2\frac{1}{3}$ miles in $3\frac{1}{2}$ minutes at a constant speed.

   a. Write an equation to represent the distance the car travels, d, in miles for m minutes.

   b. Write an equation to represent the distance the car travels, d, in miles for h hours.

Assessment Practice

16. For every ten sheets of stickers you buy at a craft store, the total cost increases $20.50.

    An equation that relates the number of sheets purchased, x, and the total cost, y, of the stickers is $y = \boxed{} x$.

    Use the equation you wrote to complete the table.

    Cost of Stickers

Number of Sheets (x)	3			19
Total Cost (y)		$10.25	$26.65	

17. 600,000 gallons of water pass through a given point along a river every minute. Which equation represents the amount of water, y, that passes through the point in x minutes?

    Ⓐ $x = 10,000y$

    Ⓑ $y = 600,000x$

    Ⓒ $y = 10,000x$

    Ⓓ $y = 600,000 + x$

108   2-4 Describe Proportional Relationships: Constant of Proportionality

Name: _____

MID-TOPIC CHECKPOINT
TOPIC 2

1. **Vocabulary** How can you show that a situation represents a proportional relationship? *Lessons 2-3 and 2-4*

2. Ana runs $\frac{3}{4}$ mile in 6 minutes, or $\frac{1}{10}$ hour. Assuming she runs at a constant rate, what is her speed, in miles per hour? *Lessons 2-1 and 2-2*

Miles	$\frac{3}{4}$	
Hour	$\frac{1}{10}$	

3. A trail mix recipe includes granola, oats, and almonds. There are 135 Calories in a $\frac{1}{4}$-cup serving of the trail mix. How many Calories are in 2 cups of trail mix? *Lesson 2-2*

4. Does this table show a proportional relationship? If so, what is the constant of proportionality? *Lessons 2-3 and 2-4*

x	40	50	60	70
y	8	10	12	14

   Ⓐ Yes; $\frac{1}{5}$

   Ⓑ Yes; 5

   Ⓒ Yes; 10

   Ⓓ The quantities are not proportional.

5. Janet, Rosi, and Tanya buy postcards from their favorite souvenir shop. Janet buys 3 postcards for $1.05. Rosi buys 5 postcards for $1.75. Tanya buys 8 postcards for $2.80. Are the cost, *y*, in dollars and the number of postcards, *x*, proportional? Explain. Write an equation to represent this relationship. *Lesson 2-4*

6. Four movie tickets cost $30.00. Five concert tickets cost $36.50. Do the movies or the concert cost less per ticket? How much less? *Lesson 2-1*

How well did you do on the mid-topic checkpoint? Fill in the stars.

Go Online | PearsonRealize.com   Topic 2 Analyze and Use Proportional Relationships

TOPIC 2: MID-TOPIC PERFORMANCE TASK

The school's theater club is building sets that will make ordinary students look like giants. The actors need a door, a table, and a stool that will make them look almost twice as tall.

PART A

The heights of objects in the set are proportional to the actual heights of objects. Complete the table.

The constant of proportionality is _____.

	Actual Height	Height on Set
Door	80 in.	44 in.
Table	28 in.	
Stool	18 in.	

PART B

How can the stage manager use the constant of proportionality to find the dimensions of any new props the director requires?

PART C

What should the height of a can of fruit juice used as a prop be if its actual height is 7 inches? Show your work.

3-ACT MATH ▶ ▶ ▶

Mixin' It Up

3-Act Mathematical Modeling:
Mixin' It Up

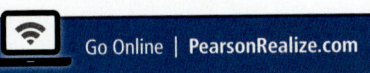

Go Online | PearsonRealize.com

ACT 1

1. After watching the video, what is the first question that comes to mind?

2. Write the Main Question you will answer.

3. **Construct Arguments** Predict an answer to this Main Question. Explain your prediction.

4. On the number line below, write a number that is too small to be the answer. Write a number that is too large.

   Too small ⟵——————————————⟶ Too large

5. Plot your prediction on the same number line.

Go Online | PearsonRealize.com   Topic 2 3-Act Mathematical Modeling   111

ACT 2

6. What information in this situation would be helpful to know? How would you use that information?

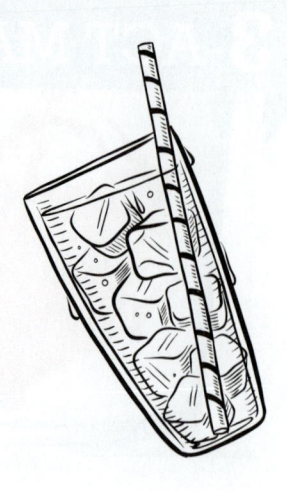

7. **Use Appropriate Tools** What tools can you use to get the information you need? Record the information as you find it.

8. **Model with Math** Represent the situation using the mathematical content, concepts, and skills from this topic. Use your representation to answer the Main Question.

9. What is your answer to the Main Question? Is it higher or lower than your prediction? Explain why.

ACT 3

10. Write the answer you saw in the video.

11. Reasoning Does your answer match the answer in the video? If not, what are some reasons that would explain the difference?

12. Make Sense and Persevere Would you change your model now that you know the answer? Explain.

Go Online | PearsonRealize.com

Topic 2 3-Act Mathematical Modeling

ACT 3 Extension

Reflect

13. Model with Math Explain how you used a mathematical model to represent the situation. How did the model help you answer the Main Question?

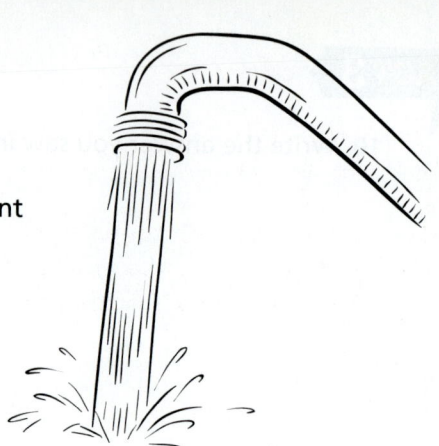

14. Critique Reasoning Choose a classmate's model. How would you adjust that model?

SEQUEL

15. Use Structure A classmate usually adds 6 drops to 16 ounces of water. Use your updated model to predict the number of drops she would use for the large container.

114 Topic 2 3-Act Mathematical Modeling

Lesson 2-5
Graph Proportional Relationships

Go Online | PearsonRealize.com

I can... use a graph to determine whether two quantities are proportional.

Explore It!

The graph shows the time it takes Jacey to print T-shirts for her school's math club.

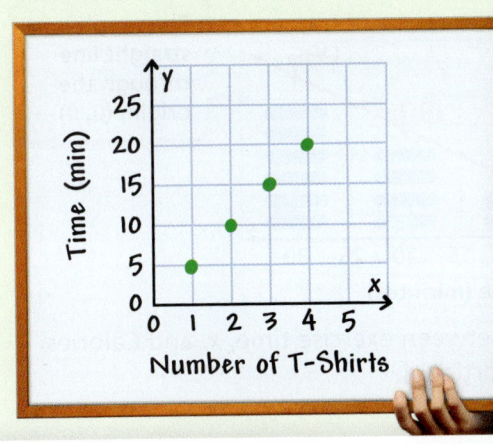

A. Use the points on the graph to complete the table. Are the quantities proportional? Explain.

Number of T-Shirts (x)				
Time in Minutes (y)				

B. Start at (1, 5). As you move from one point to the next on the graph, how does the x-coordinate change? How does the y-coordinate change?

C. Write the points for 0 T-shirts and for 5 T-shirts as ordered pairs. Graph the points and draw the line that passes through all six points.

Focus on math practices

Reasoning Suppose that after printing 4 T-shirts it takes Jacey 4 minutes to change the ink cartridge. Would this point for 5 T-shirts lie on the line you drew in Part C? Explain.

115

Essential Question What does the graph of a proportional relationship look like?

EXAMPLE 1 — Graph to Recognize a Proportional Relationship

Tanya exercised for 30 minutes. She noted the Calories burned at three times during her workout. How can Tanya use this information to find how many Calories she burned after 15 minutes of exercise?

- 10:00 TIME — 95 CALORIES
- 20:00 TIME — 190 CALORIES
- 30:00 TIME — 285 CALORIES

Model with Math You can represent the situation on the coordinate plane.

STEP 1 Use a graph to display the data.

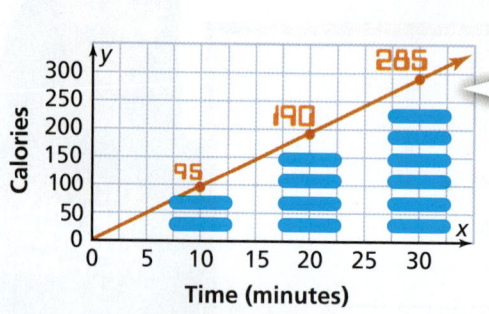

The graph is a straight line through the origin, (0, 0).

The relationship between exercise time, *x*, and Calories burned, *y*, is proportional.

STEP 2 Use the graph to find the constant of proportionality.

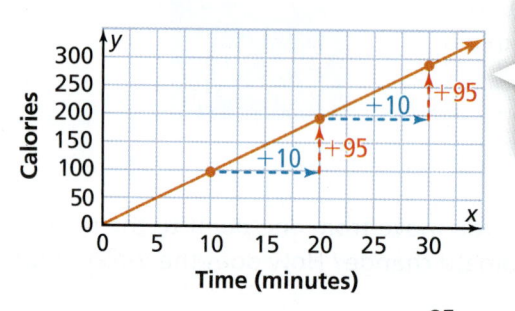

Find the differences between the coordinates of any two ordered pairs.

The constant of proportionality is $\frac{95}{10}$ or 9.5.

Tanya can use the graph and the constant of proportionality to determine that she burned 142.5 Calories in 15 minutes.

Try It!

Each $\frac{1}{4}$-cup serving of cereal has 3 grams of protein. How can you use the graph at the right to determine whether the quantities are proportional and to find how many grams of protein are in 1 cup of the cereal?

Convince Me! How can you find the constant of proportionality from the coordinates of one point on the graph?

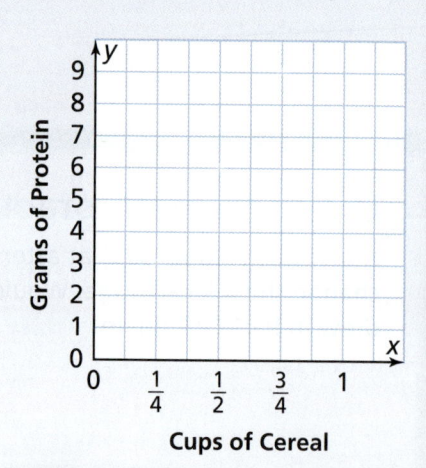

116   2-5 Graph Proportional Relationships

EXAMPLE 2 — Interpret the Graph of a Proportional Relationship

The graph shows a proportional relationship between the distance and the amount of time Mr. Brown drives.

a. What does each of these points represent in this situation: (0, 0), (1, 55), and (5, 275)?

(0, 0): Mr. Brown drives 0 miles in 0 hours.
(1, 55): Mr. Brown drives 55 miles in 1 hour.
(5, 275): Mr. Brown drives 275 miles in 5 hours.

b. What is the constant of proportionality?

Find the y-coordinate when x is 1.
The constant of proportionality is 55.

c. What equation relates the distance, y, and the time, x?

y = 55x

Mr. Brown's Road Trip

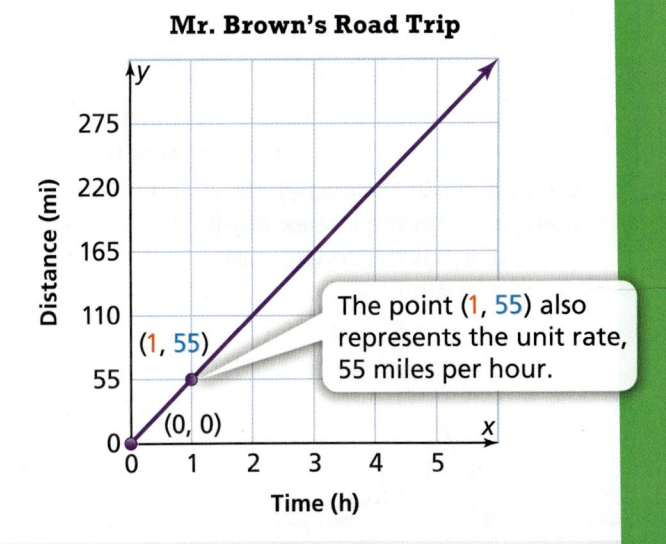

The point (1, 55) also represents the unit rate, 55 miles per hour.

✓ Try It!

Suppose the graph of Mr. Brown's Road Trip is extended. Find the ordered pair with an x-coordinate of 7. What does this point represent in the situation?

If the graph is extended, it will pass through the point (7, ☐). This means Mr. Brown drives ☐ miles in ☐ hours.

EXAMPLE 3 — Recognize Graphs of Proportional Relationships

Explain why each graph does or does not show a proportional relationship.

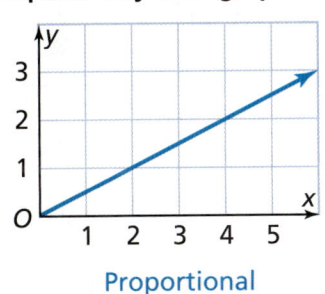

Proportional
The graph is a straight line that passes through the origin.

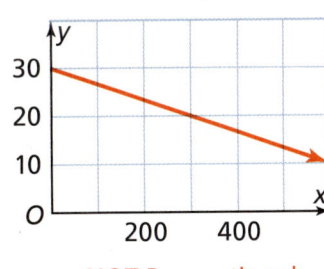

NOT Proportional
The graph is a straight line but does not pass through the origin.

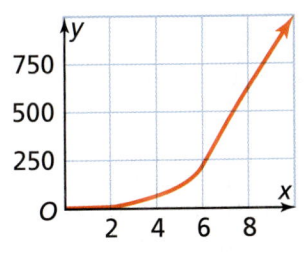

NOT Proportional
The graph passes through the origin but is not a straight line.

✓ Try It!

Draw two graphs that pass through the point (2, 3), one that represents a proportional relationship and one that does not. Label your graphs as *Proportional* or *NOT Proportional*.

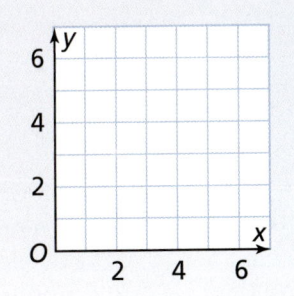

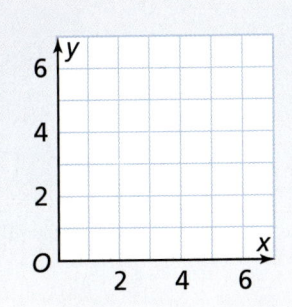

Go Online | PearsonRealize.com

2-5 Graph Proportional Relationships 117

KEY CONCEPT

The graph of a proportional relationship is a straight line through the origin.

This graph shows that the total cost of tickets at a county fair is proportional to the number of tickets purchased. For each point (x, y) on the line except (0, 0), $\frac{y}{x} = 5$, which is the constant of proportionality.

County Fair

Points on graph: (1, 5), (2, 10), (3, 15), (4, 20), (5, 25)

Each time x increases by 1, y increases by 5.

1 ticket costs $5. The constant of proportionality is 5.

0 tickets cost $0.

Do You Understand?

1. **Essential Question** What does the graph of a proportional relationship look like?

2. **Reasoning** Why will the graph of every proportional relationship include the point (0, 0)?

3. **Construct Arguments** Makayla plotted two points, (0, 0) and (3, 33), on a coordinate grid. Noah says that she is graphing a proportional relationship. Is Noah correct? Explain.

Do You Know How?

For 4–7, use the information below.

Martin and Isabelle go bowling. Each game costs $10, and they split that cost. Martin has his own bowling shoes, but Isabelle pays $3 to rent shoes.

4. Complete the graphs below.

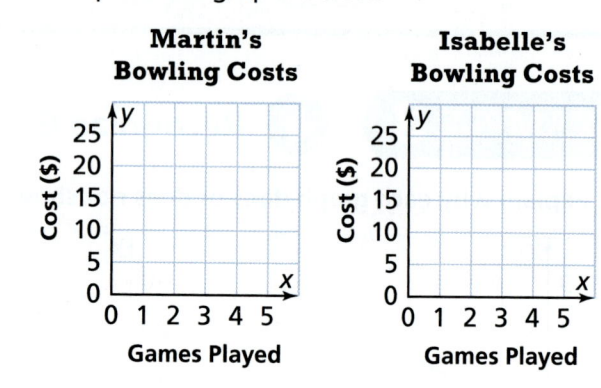

   Martin's Bowling Costs

   Isabelle's Bowling Costs

5. Which graph shows a proportional relationship? Explain why.

6. Choose one point on the graph of the proportional relationship and explain what this point means in terms of the situation.

7. What equation represents the proportional relationship?

118 2-5 Graph Proportional Relationships

Practice & Problem Solving

8. For each graph shown, tell whether it shows a proportional relationship. Explain your reasoning.

a.

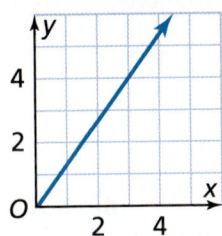

b.

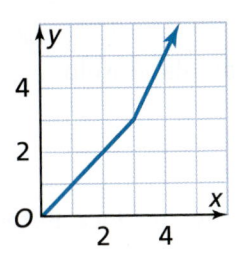

c.

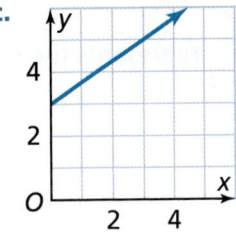

9. The graph shows the number of boxes a machine packages over time. Is the relationship proportional? How many boxes does the machine package in 4 minutes?

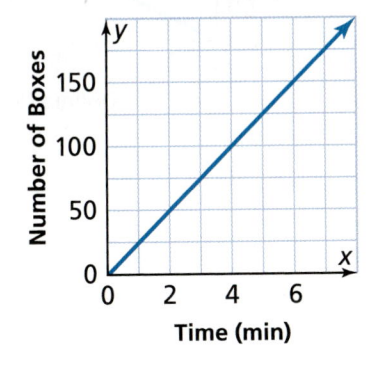

10. Does the graph show a proportional relationship? If so, use the graph to find the constant of proportionality.

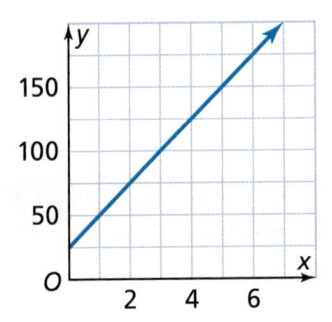

11. The graph shows a proportional relationship between the cups of flour a baker uses and the number of cookies made.

  a. **Use Structure** What does the point (0, 0) represent in the situation?

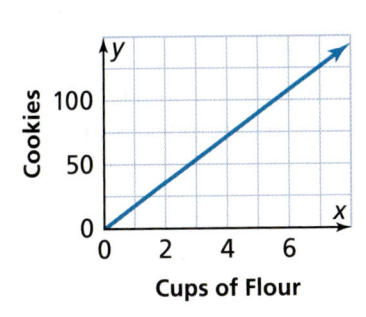

  b. What does the point (1, 18) represent?

2-5 Graph Proportional Relationships 119

12. The points $(0.5, \frac{1}{10})$ and $(7, 1\frac{2}{5})$ are on the graph of a proportional relationship.

   a. What is the constant of proportionality?

   b. Name one more point on the graph.

   c. Write an equation that represents the proportional relationship.

13. **Higher Order Thinking** Denmark uses the kroner as its currency. Before a trip to Denmark, Mia wants to exchange $1,700 for kroner.

   a. Does Bank A or Bank B have the better exchange rate? Explain.

   b. How many more kroner would Mia get if she exchanged her $1,700 at the bank with the better exchange rate?

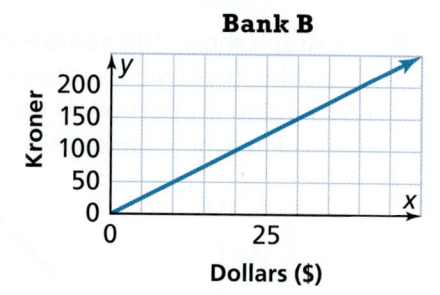

Bank A

Dollars ($)	Kroner
80	408
100	510
120	612

Bank B

Assessment Practice

14. Does the graph at the right show a proportional relationship between x and y? Explain.

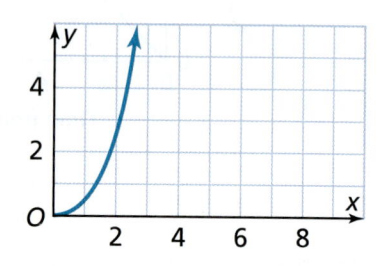

15. The graph at the right shows the relationship between rainfall during the growing season and the growth of a type of plant. Which of the following is true? Select all that apply.

    ☐ The point (1, 10) shows the constant of proportionality.

    ☐ The constant of proportionality is $\frac{5}{7}$.

    ☐ The graph does not show a proportional relationship.

    ☐ The point (0, 0) means without rain, there is no plant growth.

    ☐ The point (28, 20) means the type of plant grows 20 mm when it rains 28 cm.

Rainfall and Plant Growth

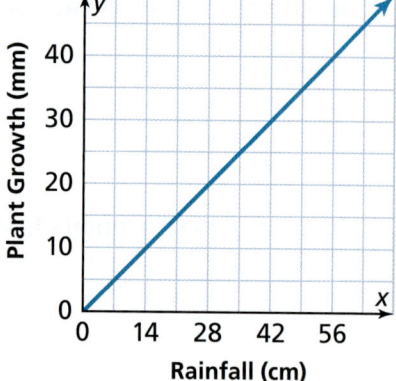

120   2-5 Graph Proportional Relationships

Lesson 2-6
Apply Proportional Reasoning to Solve Problems

Go Online | PearsonRealize.com

I can... determine whether a relationship is proportional and use representations to solve problems.

Solve & Discuss It!

Xander and Pedro are at an ice cream social. For every scoop of ice cream, Xander uses $\frac{1}{8}$ cup of fruit topping. Pedro uses one more tablespoon of fruit topping than the number of scoops. If Xander and Pedro each use the same amount of fruit topping, how many scoops of ice cream does each use?

Look for Relationships
There are 2 tablespoons in $\frac{1}{8}$ cup.

Focus on math practices

Reasoning For which person, Xander or Pedro, is the relationship between the quantities of ice cream and fruit topping proportional? Explain.

Essential Question How can proportional reasoning help solve a problem?

EXAMPLE 1 Use Proportional Reasoning to Solve a Problem

The ratio of collectible cards DeShawn owns to cards that Stephanie owns is 5:2. Stephanie has 36 cards. How will the ratio of DeShawn's cards to Stephanie's cards change if they both sell half their cards? Explain.

Make Sense and Persevere
How can you use proportional reasoning to compare the quantities of cards?

STEP 1 Draw a diagram that represents the ratio of DeShawn's cards to Stephanie's cards. You can use the diagram to find the number of cards DeShawn owns.

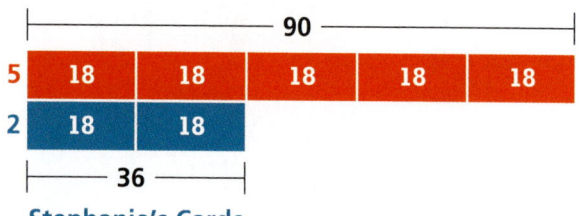

DeShawn's Cards
— 90 —
5 | 18 | 18 | 18 | 18 | 18
2 | 18 | 18
— 36 —
Stephanie's Cards

$$\frac{5}{2} = \frac{90}{36}$$
(× 18)

DeShawn owns 90 cards.

STEP 2 Find the ratio after they sell half their cards.

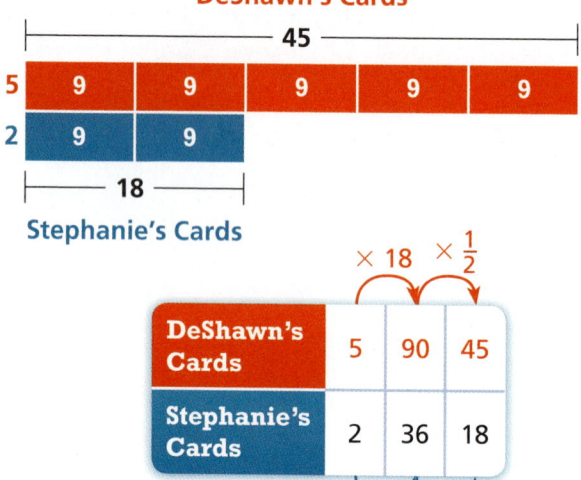

DeShawn's Cards
— 45 —
5 | 9 | 9 | 9 | 9 | 9
2 | 9 | 9
— 18 —
Stephanie's Cards

DeShawn's Cards	5	90	45
Stephanie's Cards	2	36	18

× 18   × ½

After they both sell half their cards, the ratio is $\frac{45}{18}$, or $\frac{5}{2}$. If the numbers of cards change by the same multiple, the ratio that relates them is equivalent, so it does not change.

✓ Try It!

After selling half their card collections, DeShawn and Stephanie each buy 9 new cards. What is the ratio of the number of cards DeShawn has to the number Stephanie has?

Convince Me! Why did the ratio stay the same in the Example but change in the Try It?

122   2-6 Apply Proportional Reasoning to Solve Problems

EXAMPLE 2 Recognize When to Use Proportional Reasoning

Martin is 6 years old when his sister Cassandra is 3 years old. How old will Martin be when Cassandra is 6 years old?

Make a table to find Martin's age.

Use Structure Look for a constant multiple to determine whether you can use proportional reasoning to solve this problem.

Martin's Age	Cassandra's Age
6	3
7	4
8	5
9	6

× 1.5   × 2

There is no constant multiple so you cannot use proportional reasoning. In 3 years when Cassandra is 6 years old, Martin will also be 3 years older, or 9 years old.

EXAMPLE 3 Apply Proportional Reasoning

A video streaming service charged Bryan $143.84 for a full year of access. Bryan thinks he was not charged the correct amount. What should Bryan say when he calls customer service?

STEP 1 Write an equation to represent the situation.

The rate is $8.99 per month. So an equation that represents the cost y after x months is $y = 8.99x$.

STEP 2 Substitute the given information into the equation and solve.

VIDEO STREAMING
Only $8.99 a month!

Option 1

$y = 8.99x$

$ = 8.99(12)$

$ = 107.88$

Bryan should have been charged $107.88. He should ask customer service for a credit of $143.84 − $107.88 = $35.96.

Option 2

$y = 8.99x$

$143.84 = 8.99x$

$\dfrac{143.84}{8.99} = \dfrac{8.99x}{8.99}$

$16 = x$

Bryan was charged for 16 months, so he should ask customer service to give him 4 months of free online service.

✓ Try It!

A florist makes bouquets that include 50 white flowers and 7 red flowers. If the florist orders 1,050 white flowers and 140 red flowers, there will be leftover flowers. How can the florist adjust the order so there are no leftover flowers?

2-6 Apply Proportional Reasoning to Solve Problems

KEY CONCEPT

Think about how two quantities are related before you decide to use proportional reasoning to solve a problem.

When Evie is 2 years old, Josh is 6 years old.

Josh is 4 years older than Evie.
Josh is 3 times as old as Evie.

In 2 years →

When Evie is 4 years old, Josh is 8 years old.

Josh is still 4 years older than Evie.
Josh is now 2 times as old as Evie.

You cannot use proportional reasoning to solve this problem because Josh's age is not a constant multiple of Evie's age.

Do You Understand?

1. **Essential Question** How can proportional reasoning help solve a problem?

2. **Use Appropriate Tools** How can knowing how to represent proportional relationships in different ways be useful in solving problems?

3. **Reasoning** How many ways are there to adjust two quantities so that they are in a given proportional relationship? Explain your reasoning.

Do You Know How?

4. A recipe calls for 15 oz of flour for every 8 oz of milk.

   a. Is the relationship between ounces of flour and ounces of milk proportional? Explain.

   b. If you use 15 oz of milk, how much flour should you use?

5. A food packing company makes a popular fruit cocktail. To ensure a good mixture of fruit, there are 3 cherry halves for every 8 white grapes in a jar. An inspector notices that one jar has 12 cherry halves and 20 white grapes. What can be done to fix the error?

124 2-6 Apply Proportional Reasoning to Solve Problems

Name: _____

Practice & Problem Solving

Scan for Multimedia

In 6 and 7, determine whether you can use proportional reasoning and then solve.

6. If Hector is 8 years old and Mary is 3 years old, how old will Mary be when Hector is 16?

7. Marco needs to buy some cat food. At the nearest store, 3 bags of cat food cost $15.75. How much would Marco spend on 5 bags of cat food?

8. An architect makes a model of a new house with a patio made with pavers. In the model, each paver in the patio is $\frac{1}{3}$ in. long and $\frac{1}{6}$ in. wide. The actual dimensions of the pavers are shown.

$\frac{1}{4}$ ft

$\frac{1}{8}$ ft

  a. What is the constant of proportionality that relates the length of a paver in the model and the length of an actual paver?

  b. What is the constant of proportionality that relates the area of a paver in the model and the area of an actual paver? Explain your reasoning.

9. Reasoning The table lists recommended amounts of food to order for 25 guests. Nathan is hosting a graduation party for 40 guests. There will also be guests stopping by for a short time. For ordering purposes, Nathan will count each of the 45 "drop-in" guests as half a guest. How much of each food item should Nathan order?

Party Food

Item	Amount
Fried Chicken	24 pieces
Deli Meats	$3\frac{2}{3}$ pounds
Lasagna	$10\frac{3}{4}$ pounds

10. Emily and Andy each go to a hardware store to buy wire. The table shows the relationship between the cost and the length of wire.

  a. Emily needs 24 feet of wire. How much will she spend on wire?

  b. Andy needs 13 yards of wire. How much will he spend on wire?

Cost of Wire

Length in Inches (x)	Cost in Dollars (y)
120	4.80
135	5.40
150	6.00
175	7.00

Go Online | PearsonRealize.com   2-6 Apply Proportional Reasoning to Solve Problems   125

11. **Make Sense and Persevere** The weights of Michael's and Brittney's new puppies are shown in the table and graph. Whose dog gains weight more quickly? Explain.

Weight of Michael's Puppy

Age (months)	1	2	3
Weight (pounds)	8.6	17.2	25.8

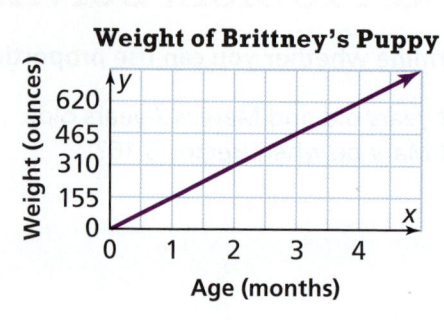

Weight of Brittney's Puppy

12. **Higher Order Thinking** Marielle's painting has the dimensions shown. The school asks her to paint a larger version that will hang in the cafeteria. The larger version will be twice the width and twice the height. Is the area of the original painting proportional to the area of the larger painting? If so, what is the constant of proportionality?

18 in.
24 in.

Assessment Practice

13. The ratio of orange juice concentrate to water that Zoe used to make orange juice yesterday was 3:7. She used 14 ounces of water in the juice yesterday. Today she wants to make twice as much orange juice.

    PART A
    How much orange juice concentrate does she need?

    Ⓐ 6 ounces

    Ⓑ 12 ounces

    Ⓒ 18 ounces

    Ⓓ 28 ounces

    PART B
    Explain your reasoning.

126 2-6 Apply Proportional Reasoning to Solve Problems

REVIEW — TOPIC 2

Topic Essential Question

How can you recognize and represent proportional relationships and use them to solve problems?

Vocabulary Review

Complete each definition and then provide an example of each vocabulary word.

Vocabulary: constant of proportionality, ratio, proportion, proportional relationship, rate, unit rate

Definition	Example
1. For two quantities x and y, if y is always a constant multiple of x, they have a(n) _____.	
2. The value of the ratio $\frac{y}{x}$ of two proportional quantities x and y is called the _____.	
3. An equation that shows that two ratios are equal is a(n) _____.	

Use Vocabulary in Writing

A sunflower grows 8 feet in 92 days. Assuming that it grows at a constant rate, explain how you could use this information to find the number of days it took for the sunflower to grow 6 feet. Use vocabulary words in your explanation.

Topic 2 Topic Review 127

Concepts and Skills Review

LESSONS 2-1 AND 2-2 | Connect Ratios, Rates, and Unit Rates | Determine Unit Rates with Ratios of Fractions

Quick Review

A **ratio** is a relationship in which for every *x* units of one quantity there are *y* units of another quantity. A **rate** is a ratio that relates two quantities with different units. A **unit rate** relates a quantity to 1 unit of another quantity. You can use what you know about equivalent fractions and calculating with fractions to write a ratio of fractions as a unit rate.

Example

In 3 days, a typical robin can eat up to 42.6 feet of earthworms. Write a rate to relate the number of feet of earthworms to the number of days. Then find the unit rate.

$$\frac{42.6 \text{ feet}}{3 \text{ days}} = \frac{14.2 \text{ feet}}{1 \text{ day}}$$

A robin eats 14.2 feet of earthworms per day.

Practice

1. Mealworms are a healthy food for wild songbirds. Adam buys a 3.5-oz container of mealworms for $8.75. Marco buys a 3.75-oz container of mealworms for $9.75. Which container is the better deal?

2. A painter mixes $2\frac{1}{2}$ pints of yellow paint with 4 pints of red paint to make a certain shade of orange paint. How many pints of yellow paint should be mixed with 10 pints of red paint to make this shade of orange?

LESSON 2-3 | Understand Proportional Relationships: Equivalent Ratios

Quick Review

Two quantities *x* and *y* have a proportional relationship if the ratios $\frac{y}{x}$ for every related pair of *x* and *y* are equivalent. You can write a proportion to show that two ratios have the same value.

Example

Does the table show a proportional relationship between *x* and *y*? Explain.

x	200	400	500
y	600	1,200	1,500

$\frac{600}{200} = \frac{3}{1}$ $\frac{1,200}{400} = \frac{3}{1}$ $\frac{1,500}{500} = \frac{3}{1}$

Because every ratio is equivalent, there is a proportional relationship between *x* and *y*.

Practice

In **1** and **2**, use the table below that shows information about squares.

Side Length (cm)	2	4	6
Perimeter (cm)	8	16	24

1. Are the perimeter and the side length of squares proportional? Explain.

2. Write and solve a proportion to find the perimeter of a square when its side length is 12.

LESSON 2-4 Describe Proportional Relationships: Constant of Proportionality

Quick Review

The equation $y = kx$ describes a proportional relationship between two quantities x and y, where k is the constant of proportionality. $k = \frac{y}{x}$ for any related pair of x and y except when $x = 0$.

Example

The table shows the wages Roger earned for the hours he worked. What equation relates the wages, w, and the number of hours, h?

Time (h)	Wages (w)
3	$27.00
5	$45.00
6	$54.00

Find the constant of proportionality, k.

$\frac{27}{3} = 9$ $\frac{45}{5} = 9$ $\frac{54}{6} = 9$

Write the equation in the form $y = kx$.

$w = 9h$

Practice

1. Sally is going on vacation with her family. In 2 hours they travel 90.5 miles. If they travel at the same speed, write an equation that represents how far they will travel, d, in h hours.

2. The table shows the weights of bunches of bananas and the price of each bunch. Identify the constant of proportionality. Write an equation to relate weight, w, to the price, p.

Weight (w)	Price (p)
3 pounds	$1.35
3.8 pounds	$1.71
5.2 pounds	$2.34

LESSON 2-5 Graph Proportional Relationships

Quick Review

The graph of a proportional relationship is a straight line through the origin. You can identify the constant of proportionality, k, from the point $(1, k)$ or by dividing $\frac{y}{x}$ for any point (x, y) except the origin.

Example

Is the number of sunny days proportional to the number of rainy days? If so, find the constant of proportionality, and explain its meaning in this situation.

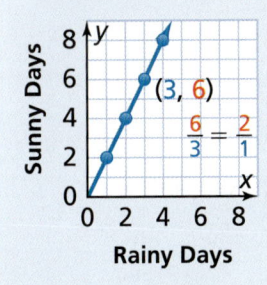

The graph is a straight line through the origin, so it shows a proportional relationship. The constant of proportionality is 2, which means for every 1 rainy day, there were 2 sunny days.

$\frac{6}{3} = \frac{2}{1}$

Practice

1. Does the graph show a proportional relationship? Explain.

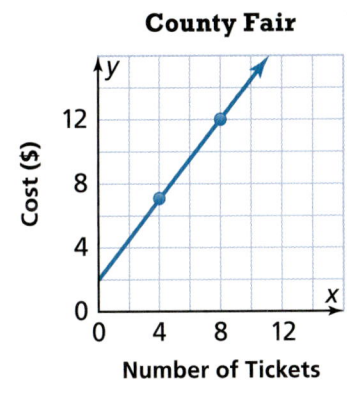

   County Fair

2. Sketch a graph that represents a proportional relationship.

LESSON 2-6: Apply Proportional Reasoning to Solve Problems

Quick Review
Think about how two quantities are related before you decide to use proportional reasoning to solve a problem.

Example
Ann-Marie makes gift baskets that each contain 3 pounds of gourmet cheese with every 2 boxes of crackers. She ordered 80 pounds of cheese and 50 boxes of crackers. How can she adjust her order to make 25 gift baskets, with no leftover items?

$$\frac{3 \times 25}{2 \times 25} = \frac{75}{50}$$

Ann-Marie can order 5 fewer pounds of cheese so that her order of 75 pounds of cheese and 50 boxes of crackers will make exactly 25 gift baskets.

Practice
Decide which problems can be solved by using proportional reasoning. Select all that apply.

☐ Yani buys 4 dozen flyers for $7.25. What is the cost of 12 dozen?

☐ First-class letters cost $0.49 for the first ounce and $0.22 for each additional ounce. What is the cost of a 5-oz letter?

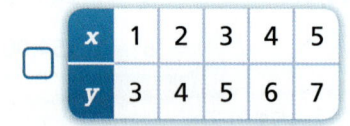

☐

x	1	2	3	4	5
y	3	4	5	6	7

What is the value of y when $x = 8$?

☐

x	1.5	3	5.2	6.5	8
y	4.5	9	15.6	19.5	24

What is the value of y when $x = 5$?

Fluency Practice

TOPIC 2

Pathfinder

Shade a path from START to FINISH. Follow the solutions from the least value to the greatest value. You can only move up, down, right, or left.

I can... add, subtract, multiply, and divide integers.

START

$3 - 24$	$3 \times (-13)$	-3×14	$44 - 49$	$-48 \div 16$
$-26 + 7$	$-7 - 27$	$13 \times (-4)$	$8 - 19$	$-18 \div (-6)$
$3 \times (-5)$	$28 \div (-2)$	$(-35) \div 2$	$4 + (-25)$	$-68 \div 17$
$23 - 46$	$-2 - 11$	$15 + (-26)$	$17 - 23$	$29 - 38$
$-12 \div (-3)$	$18 + (-32)$	$11 - 29$	$-60 \div 12$	$-3 \times (-2)$

FINISH

Topic 2 Topic Review 131

TOPIC 3: ANALYZE AND SOLVE PERCENT PROBLEMS

Topic Essential Question

How can percents show proportional relationships between quantities and be used to solve problems?

Topic Overview

- 3-1 Analyze Percents of Numbers
- 3-2 Connect Percent and Proportion
- 3-3 Represent and Use the Percent Equation
- 3-4 Solve Percent Change and Percent Error Problems
- 3-Act Mathematical Modeling: The Smart Shopper
- 3-5 Solve Markup and Markdown Problems
- 3-6 Solve Simple Interest Problems

Topic Vocabulary

- interest rate
- markdown
- markup
- percent change
- percent equation
- percent error
- percent markdown
- percent markup
- principal
- simple interest

Lesson Digital Resources

INTERACTIVE ANIMATION Interact with visual learning animations.

ACTIVITY Use with *Solve & Discuss It, Explore It*, and *Explain It* activities, and to explore Examples.

VIDEOS Watch clips to support *3-Act Mathematical Modeling Lessons* and *STEM Projects*.

PRACTICE Practice what you've learned.

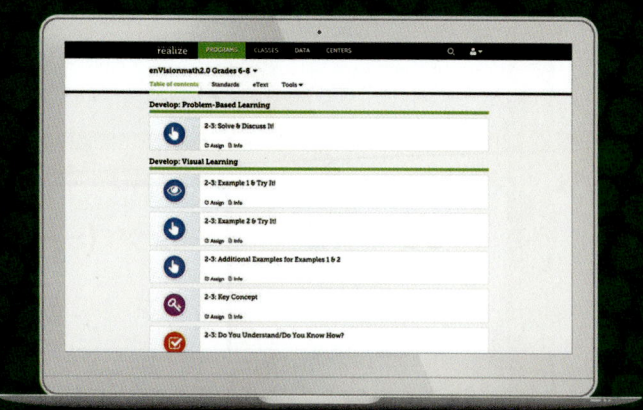

Go online | PearsonRealize.com

3-ACT MATH

The Smart Shopper

Why do stores and manufacturers print coupons? It seems like they lose money every time you use one. Well, some coupons are designed to steer you toward a specific brand and gain your loyalty. Stores also offer coupons to get you into the store, counting on you buying other items while you are there. If you're clever, you can use multiple coupons. Think about this during the 3-Act Mathematical Modeling lesson.

Additional Digital Resources

TUTORIALS Get help from *Virtual Nerd*, right when you need it.

KEY CONCEPT Review important lesson content.

GLOSSARY Read and listen to English/Spanish definitions.

ASSESSMENT Show what you've learned.

MATH TOOLS Explore math with digital tools.

GAMES Play Math Games to help you learn.

ETEXT Interact with your Student's Edition online.

Topic 3 Analyze and Solve Percent Problems

TOPIC 3 STEM Project

Did You Know?

One of the first popular activity trackers was a pedometer, which measures number of steps taken. Some sources trace the history of the pedometer back to Leonardo da Vinci.

A pedometer called *Manpo-kei* (10,000 steps meter) was introduced in Japan in the mid-1960s. Research led by Dr. Yoshiro Hatano indicated that **10,000 steps a day is the ideal energy output** to maintain health.

Today, most activity trackers are electronic devices that can **sync to a computer or a smartphone.**

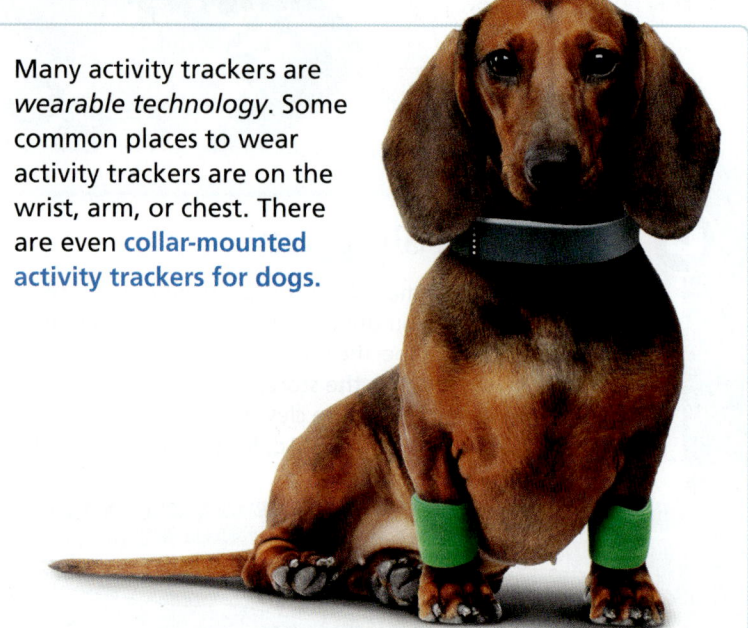

Many activity trackers are *wearable technology*. Some common places to wear activity trackers are on the wrist, arm, or chest. There are even **collar-mounted activity trackers for dogs.**

Your Task: Analyze Activity Tracker Data

Activity trackers, also called fitness trackers, have become quite popular in recent years. But is the data collected actually helpful to the user? You and your classmates will explore the types of data that an activity tracker collects, and how that data can help users reach their activity and fitness goals.

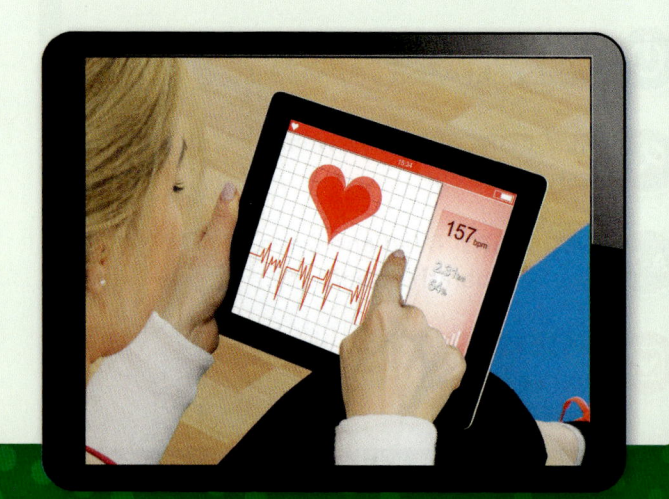

GET READY!

TOPIC 3

Review What You Know!

Vocabulary

Choose the best term from the box. Write it on the blank.

| percent |
| proportion |
| rate |
| ratio |

1. A _____ is a ratio in which the first term is compared to 100.

2. A ratio that relates two quantities with different units of measure is a _____.

3. A statement that two ratios are equal is called a _____.

4. The relationship "3 students out of 5 students" is an example of a _____.

Fractions, Decimals, and Percents

Write each number in two equivalent forms as a fraction, decimal, or percent.

5. 0.29

6. 35%

7. $\frac{2}{5}$

Proportions

Find the unknown number in each proportion.

8. $\frac{x \text{ days}}{4 \text{ years}} = \frac{365.25 \text{ days}}{1 \text{ year}}$

9. $\frac{33{,}264 \text{ feet}}{x \text{ miles}} = \frac{5{,}280 \text{ feet}}{1 \text{ mile}}$

10. A cooking magazine shows a photo of a main dish on the front cover of 5 out of the 12 issues it publishes each year. Write and solve a proportion to determine how many times a photo of a main dish will be on the front cover during the next 5 years.

Prepare for Reading Success

Before you begin Topic 3, complete the first and second columns of this table. While you work through the topic, return to complete the third column as you learn the answers to your questions from the second column.

What do I know about percents and how they are used?	What do I want to learn about how I will use percents in life?	What have I learned about how percents are used?

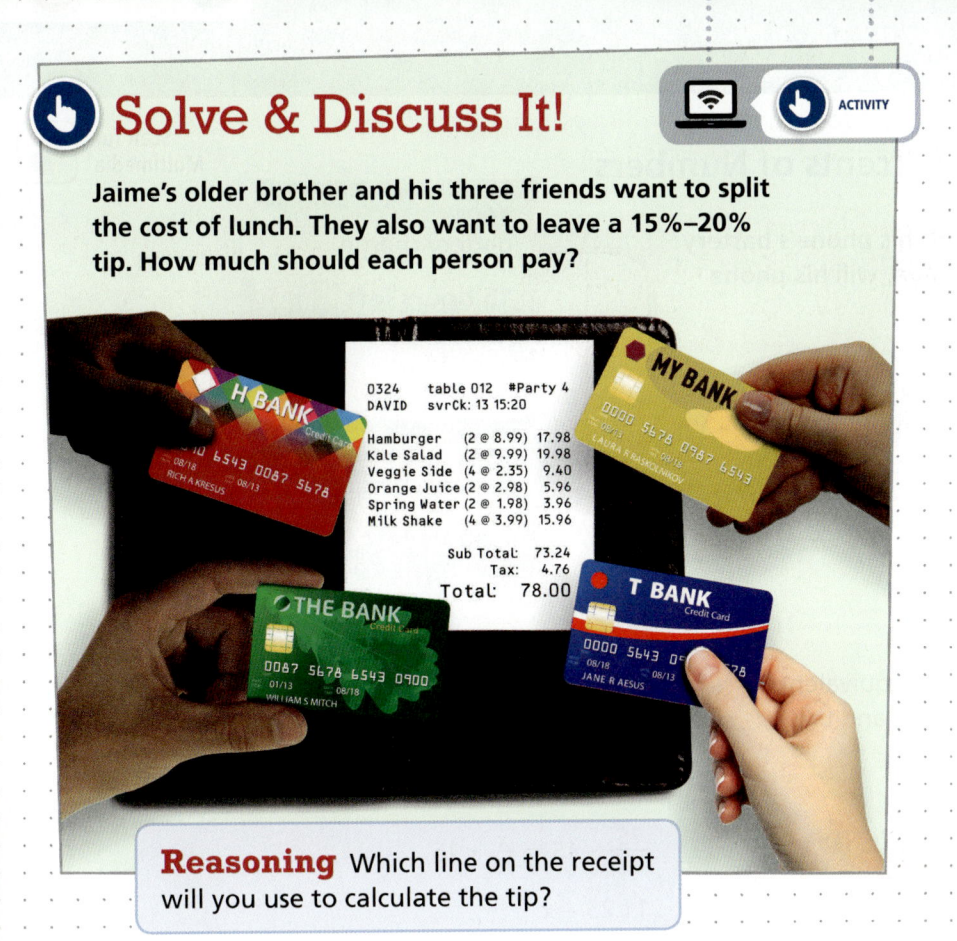

Lesson 3-1
Analyze Percents of Numbers

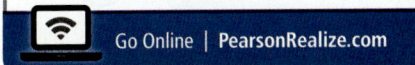

Go Online | PearsonRealize.com

I can... understand, find, and analyze percents of numbers.

Solve & Discuss It!

Jaime's older brother and his three friends want to split the cost of lunch. They also want to leave a 15%–20% tip. How much should each person pay?

```
0324      table 012   #Party 4
DAVID     svrCk: 13 15:20

Hamburger     (2 @ 8.99)   17.98
Kale Salad    (2 @ 9.99)   19.98
Veggie Side   (4 @ 2.35)    9.40
Orange Juice  (2 @ 2.98)    5.96
Spring Water  (2 @ 1.98)    3.96
Milk Shake    (4 @ 3.99)   15.96

            Sub Total:    73.24
                 Tax:      4.76
              Total:      78.00
```

Reasoning Which line on the receipt will you use to calculate the tip?

Focus on math practices

Reasoning How would the amount each person pays change if the tip is determined before or after the bill is split?

137

? **Essential Question** How do percents show the relationship between quantities?

EXAMPLE 1   Find Percents of Numbers

Diego starts a 12-hour road trip with his phone's battery charge at 75%. Given his normal usage, will his phone last the whole trip? Explain.

Look for Relationships How many hours will the phone last when the battery charge is at 75%?

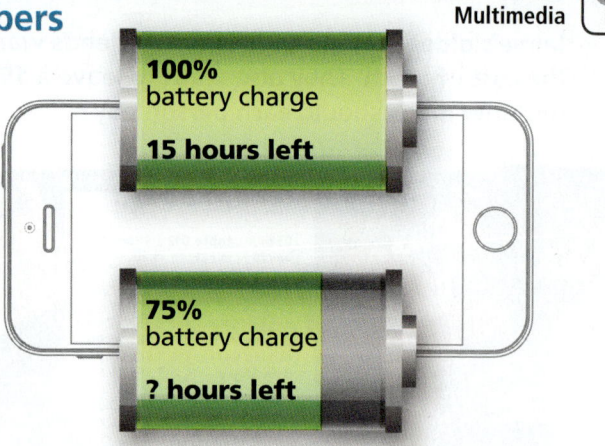

STEP 1 Draw a bar diagram and write equivalent ratios to represent the hours remaining and the battery charge.

15 hours of use
100%
75%
x hours of use

$$\frac{75}{100} = \frac{x}{15}$$

STEP 2 Use the equivalent ratios to find 75% of 15.

$$\frac{75}{100} = \frac{x}{15}$$ Solve for x.

$$\frac{75}{100} \cdot 15 = \frac{x}{15} \cdot 15$$

$$11.25 = x$$

75% of 15 is 11.25 hours.

The remaining battery life is 11.25 hours, so the phone will not last the whole 12-hour trip.

Try It!

Kita's phone had a fully charged battery. With normal usage, her phone will last 18 hours. How much time is left on Kita's phone battery with 12% charge remaining?

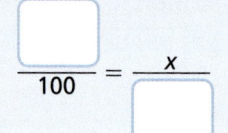

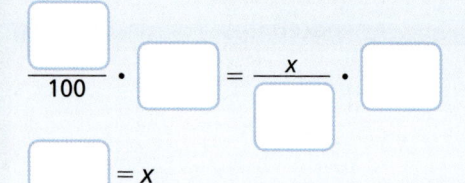

$$\frac{\Box}{100} = \frac{x}{\Box}$$

$$\frac{\Box}{100} \cdot \Box = \frac{x}{\Box} \cdot \Box$$

$$\Box = x$$

Kita's phone battery has ⬜ hours remaining.

Convince Me! Why is 51% of a number more than half of the number?

138   3-1 Analyze Percents of Numbers

EXAMPLE 2 Use Percents Greater than 100%

A full set of adult teeth includes 160% as many teeth as a full set of baby teeth. How many teeth are there in a full set of adult teeth?

Use the bar diagram to write equivalent ratios. Then solve for t to find the number of adult teeth.

t adult teeth

160%

100%

20 baby teeth

20 BABY TEETH

Types of Baby Teeth

4 central incisors (A and F)
4 lateral incisors (B and G)
4 cuspids (C and H)
4 first molars (D and I)
4 second molars (E and J)

Adults have 160% as many teeth as babies.

$$\frac{160}{100} = \frac{t}{20}$$

$$\frac{160}{100} \cdot 20 = \frac{t}{20} \cdot 20$$

$$32 = t$$

A full set of adult teeth includes 32 teeth.

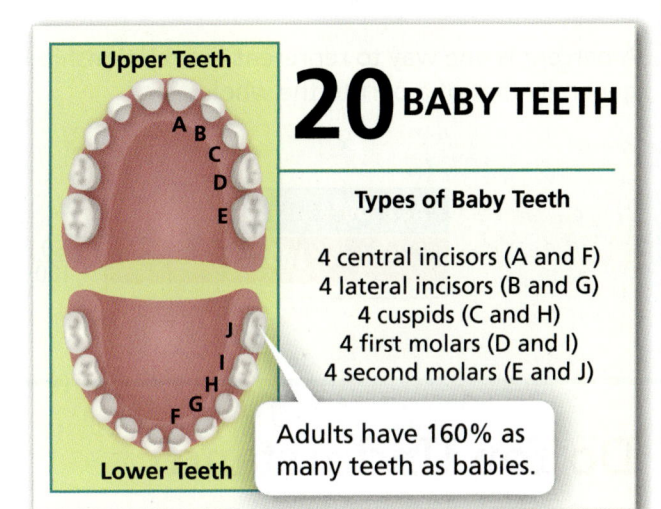

EXAMPLE 3 Use Percents Less than 1%

What is the approximate distance in miles from Earth to the Moon?

STEP 1 Draw a bar diagram and write equivalent ratios.

x miles

0.27%

100%

93 million miles

93,000,000 miles

0.27% of the distance between the Sun and Earth

$$\frac{x}{93{,}000{,}000} = \frac{0.27}{100}$$

STEP 2 Solve for x.

$$\frac{0.27}{100} \cdot 93{,}000{,}000 = \frac{x}{93{,}000{,}000} \cdot 93{,}000{,}000$$

$$251{,}100 = x$$

The distance from Earth to the Moon is about 251,100 miles.

Check Your Answer Use compatible numbers to estimate the solution. 93,000,000 is approximately 100,000,000. 1% of 100,000,000 miles is 1,000,000 miles.

0.27% is about $\frac{1}{4}$ of 1%, so the distance is about $\frac{1}{4}$ of 1,000,000, or 250,000 miles.

Reasoning The exact distance is close to the estimated distance, so the answer is reasonable.

✓ Try It!

a. Find 0.08% of 720.   b. Find 162.5% of 200.   c. Find 0.3% of 60.

Go Online | PearsonRealize.com   3-1 Analyze Percents of Numbers   139

KEY CONCEPT

A percent is one way to represent the relationship between two quantities, generally that of a part to the whole.

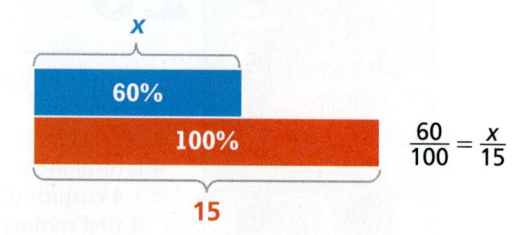

$$\frac{60}{100} = \frac{x}{15}$$

Do You Understand?

1. **Essential Question** How do percents show the relationship between quantities?

2. **Reasoning** How does a value that is greater than 100% of the original value or less than 1% of the original value compare to the original value?

3. **Construct Arguments** Gene stated that finding 25% of a number is the same as dividing the number by $\frac{1}{4}$. Is Gene correct? Explain.

Do You Know How?

4. An 8-ounce serving of apples contains 8% of your daily vitamin C. How many ounces of apples would you need to get 100% of your daily vitamin C?

5. Find the percent of each number.

   a. 59% of 640
   b. 0.20% of 3,542
   c. 195% of 568
   d. 74% of 920

6. Water is 2 parts hydrogen and 1 part oxygen (H_2O). For one molecule of water, each atom has the atomic mass unit, u, shown. What percent of the mass of a water molecule is hydrogen?

   O: 16.00 u
   H: 1.01 u
   H: 1.01 u

140 3-1 Analyze Percents of Numbers

Name: _____

Practice & Problem Solving

Scan for Multimedia

Leveled Practice In 7–8, fill in the boxes to solve.

7. A local Little League has a total of 60 players, 80% of whom are right-handed. How many right-handed players are there?

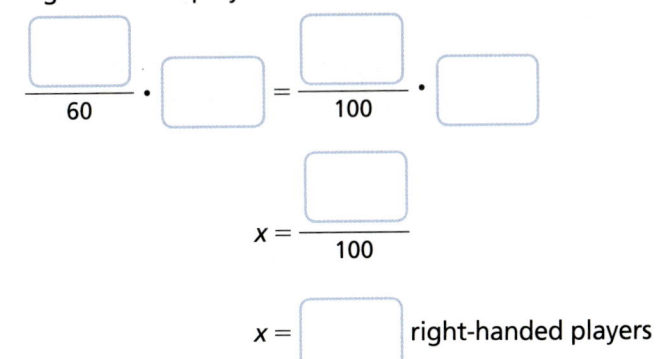

$$\frac{\square}{60} \cdot \square = \frac{\square}{100} \cdot \square$$

$$x = \frac{\square}{100}$$

$x = \square$ right-handed players

8. Sandra's volleyball team has a total of 20 uniforms. 20% are medium-sized uniforms. How many uniforms are medium-sized?

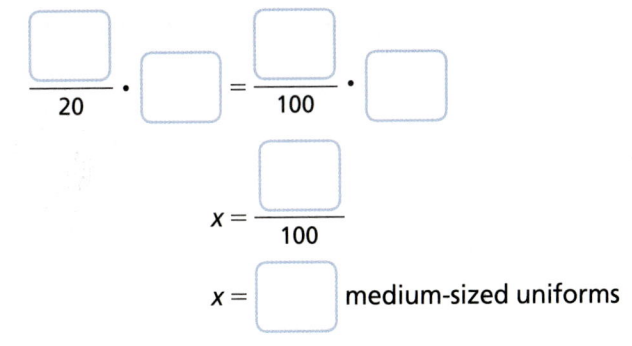

$$\frac{\square}{20} \cdot \square = \frac{\square}{100} \cdot \square$$

$$x = \frac{\square}{100}$$

$x = \square$ medium-sized uniforms

9. Meg is a veterinarian. In a given week, 50% of the 16 dogs she saw were Boxers. Steve is also a veterinarian. In the same week, 7 of the 35 dogs he saw this week were Boxers. Each wants to record the part, the whole, and the percent.

a. Does Meg need to find the part, the whole, or the percent?

b. Does Steve need to find the part, the whole, or the percent?

10. Olivia is a stockbroker. She makes 4% of her sales in commission. Last week, she sold $7,200 worth of stocks.

a. How much commission did she make last week?

b. If she were to average that same commission each week, how much would she make in commissions in a year, treating a year as having exactly 52 weeks?

11. The registration fee for a used car is 0.8% of the sale price of $5,700. How much is the fee?

12. The total cost of an item is the price plus the sales tax.

Find the sales tax to complete the table. Then find the total cost of the item.

Sales Tax

Selling Price	Rate of Sales Tax	Sales Tax
$40.00	4%	

13. Is 700% of 5 less than 10, greater than 10 but less than 100, or greater than 100? Explain your reasoning.

14. Is 250% of 44 less than 100, greater than 100 but less than 150, or greater than 150? Explain your reasoning.

Go Online | PearsonRealize.com

3-1 Analyze Percents of Numbers 141

15. The seed and skin of a typical avocado is about 30%–40% of the avocado's weight. For an 8-ounce avocado, how many ounces of edible fruit does it have?

16. A new health drink has 130% of the recommended daily allowance (RDA) for a certain vitamin. The RDA for this vitamin is 45 mg. How many milligrams of the vitamin are in the drink?

17. Make Sense and Persevere 153 is 0.9% of what number? Tell which equivalent ratios you used to find the solution.

18. Construct Arguments Brad says that if a second number is 125% of the first number, then the first number must be 75% of the second number. Is he correct? Justify your answer.

19. Higher-Order Thinking Mark and Joe work as jewelers. Mark has an hourly wage of $24 and gets overtime for every hour he works over 40 hours. The overtime pay rate is 150% of the normal rate. Joe makes 5% commission on all jewelry he sells. Who earns more money in a week if Mark works 60 hours and Joe sells $21,000 worth of jewelry? Explain.

Assessment Practice

20. A forest covers 43,000 acres. A survey finds that 0.2% of the forest is old-growth trees. How many acres of old-growth trees are there?

21. An Olympic-sized pool, which holds 660,000 gallons of water, is only 63% full. How many gallons of water are in the pool?

Ⓐ 244,200

Ⓒ 415,800

Ⓑ 396,000

Ⓓ 425,800

Lesson 3-2
Connect Percent and Proportion

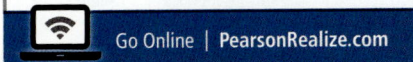

Go Online | PearsonRealize.com

I can... use proportions to solve percent problems.

Solve & Discuss It!

A florist is making flower arrangements for a party. He uses purple and white flowers in a ratio of 3 purple flowers to 1 white flower. How many flowers will he need in order to make 30 identical arrangements?

Look for Relationships
How are the number of purple flowers related to the number of white flowers?

Focus on math practices

Make Sense and Persevere If the florist can only buy white flowers in groups of flowers that have 3 white flowers and 2 red flowers, how many red flowers will the florist have to purchase? Explain your answer.

? Essential Question How does proportional reasoning relate to percent?

EXAMPLE 1 — Use a Proportion to Find the Percent

The basketball team statistician tracked the shots Emily made and the shots she missed during the last game. What percent of attempted shots did she make?

Legend
- Shots made
- Shots missed

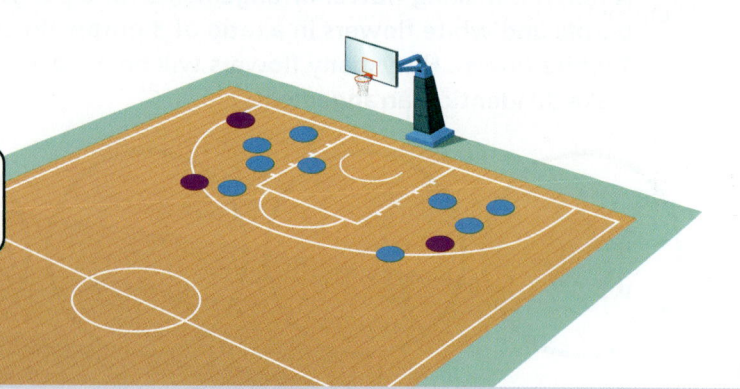

Draw a bar diagram and write a proportion to represent the number of shots made and the total number of shots.

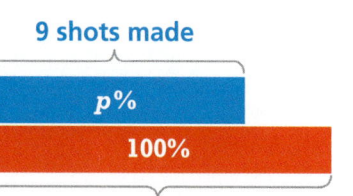

9 shots made

p%

100%

12 attempted shots

$$\frac{9}{12} = \frac{p}{100}$$

Solve the proportion to find the percent of shots made during the last game.

$$\frac{9}{12} = \frac{p}{100}$$

$$\frac{9}{12} \cdot 100 = \frac{p}{100} \cdot 100$$

$$75 = p$$

Reasoning The ratio of part to whole describes a proportional relationship.

Emily made 75% of her shots.

Try It!

Camila makes 2 of her 5 shots attempted. Is the percent of shots she made more than, less than, or the same as Emily's percent of shots?

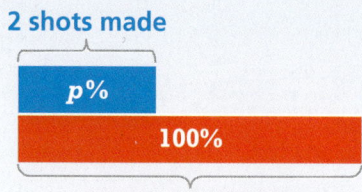

2 shots made

p%

100%

5 attempted shots

$$\frac{\Box}{\Box} = \frac{p}{\Box}$$

$$\frac{\Box}{\Box} = \frac{p}{\Box}$$

$$\Box = p$$

Camila made ☐ % of her shots.

Camila's percent of the shots made is ☐ Emily's.

Convince Me! A hockey goalie stops 37 out of 40 shots. What percent of attempted goals did she stop?

3-2 Connect Percent and Proportion

EXAMPLE 2 Use a Proportion to Find the Part

A plan to expand Megan's room will make the length of the room 175% of the current length. What will be the new length of her room?

Draw a bar diagram to represent the problem and then write a percent proportion to find the new length.

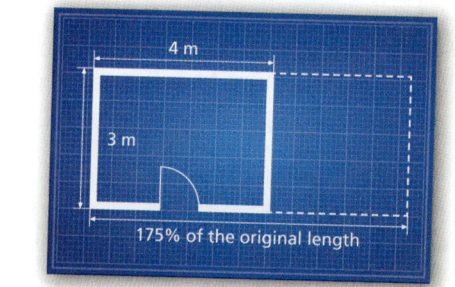

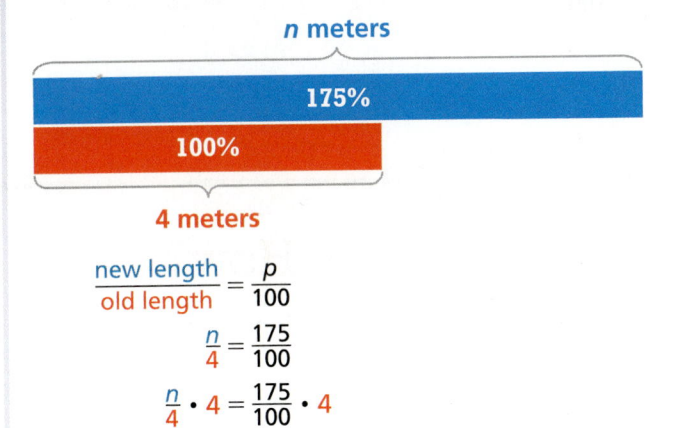

n meters
175%
100%
4 meters

$$\frac{\text{new length}}{\text{old length}} = \frac{p}{100}$$

$$\frac{n}{4} = \frac{175}{100}$$

$$\frac{n}{4} \cdot 4 = \frac{175}{100} \cdot 4$$

$$n = 7$$

The new length of the room will be 7 meters.

EXAMPLE 3 Use a Proportion to Find the Whole

The nutrition label shows the percents of the recommended daily intake for nutrients found in a serving of a soy milk. How many milligrams of calcium should you consume each day?

Write a percent proportion to find the amount of calcium.

$$\frac{\text{calcium per serving}}{\text{daily value}} = \frac{p}{100}$$

$$\frac{260}{w} = \frac{20}{100}$$

$$\frac{260}{w} \cdot w = \frac{20}{100} \cdot w \quad \text{Multiply both sides by the variable.}$$

$$260 = \frac{20w}{100}$$

$$260 \cdot \frac{100}{20} = \frac{20w}{100} \cdot \frac{100}{20} \quad \text{Multiply both sides by the reciprocal.}$$

$$1{,}300 = w$$

The daily value for calcium is 1,300 mg.

Try It!

a. Megan's room is expanded so the width is 150% of 3 meters. What is the new width?

b. Use the soy milk label in Example 3. What is the recommended amount of iron needed each day? Round your answer to the nearest mg.

3-2 Connect Percent and Proportion   145

KEY CONCEPT

Percent problems represent a kind of proportional relationship. You can use proportional reasoning to solve percent problems.

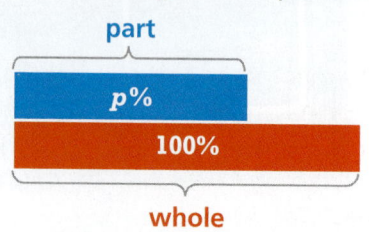

$$\frac{part}{whole} = \frac{p}{100}$$

Do You Understand?

1. **Essential Question** How does proportional reasoning relate to percent?

2. **Reasoning** Why does one of the ratios in a percent proportion always have a denominator of 100?

3. **Construct Arguments** The proportion $\frac{75}{w} = \frac{150}{100}$ can be used to find the whole, w. Use the language of percent to explain whether w is less than or greater than 75.

Do You Know How?

4. Write a percent proportion for the bar diagram shown.

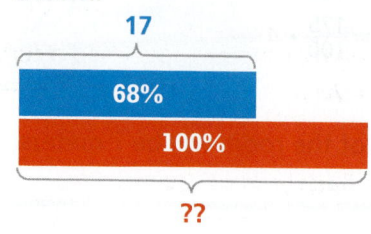

5. Use a proportion to find each value.
   a. 2% of 180
   $$\frac{n}{\square} = \frac{2}{\square}$$

   b. What percent is 17 out of 40?
   $$\frac{\square}{\square} = \frac{p}{\square}$$

6. **Construct Arguments** Gia researches online that her car is worth $3,000. She hopes to sell it for 85% of that value, but she wants to get at least 70%. She ends up selling it for $1,800. Did she get what she wanted? Justify your answer.

146 3-2 Connect Percent and Proportion

Practice & Problem Solving

Leveled Practice In 7–8, fill in the boxes to solve.

7. The rabbit population in a certain area is 200% of last year's population. There are 1,100 rabbits this year. How many were there last year?

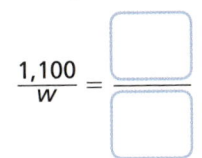

$\dfrac{1{,}100}{w} = \dfrac{\boxed{}}{\boxed{}}$

There were $\boxed{}$ rabbits last year.

8. A company that makes hair-care products had 3,000 people try a new shampoo. Of the 3,000 people, 9 had a mild allergic reaction. What percent of the people had a mild allergic reaction?

$\dfrac{9}{3{,}000} = \dfrac{p}{\boxed{}}$

Percent = $\boxed{}$ %

9. A survey was given to people who owned a certain type of car. What percent of the people surveyed were completely satisfied with the car?

Car Satisfaction Survey

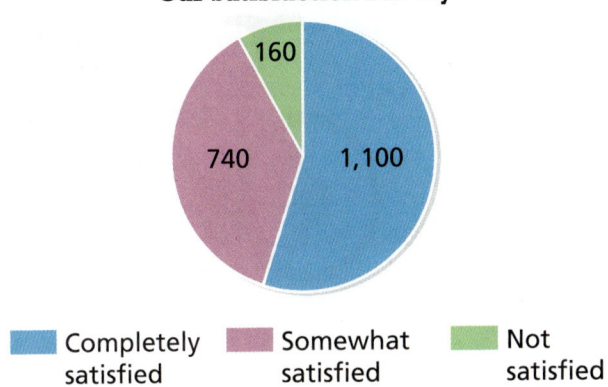

160
740
1,100

■ Completely satisfied   ■ Somewhat satisfied   ■ Not satisfied

10. The Washingtons buy a studio apartment for $240,000. They pay a down payment of $60,000.

a. Their down payment is what percent of the purchase price?

b. What percent of the purchase price would a $12,000 down payment be?

11. A restaurant customer left $3.50 as a tip. The tax on the meal was 7% and the tip was 20% of the cost including tax.

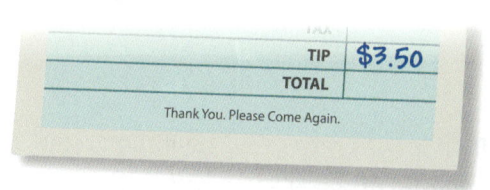

TIP $3.50
TOTAL
Thank You. Please Come Again.

a. What piece of information is not needed to compute the bill after tax and tip?

b. Make Sense and Persevere What was the total bill?

12. Reasoning What is a good estimate for 380% of 60? Explain.

Go Online | PearsonRealize.com

3-2 Connect Percent and Proportion   147

13. **Critique Reasoning** Marna thinks that about 35% of her mail is junk mail. She gets about twice as much regular mail as junk mail. Is she correct? Explain.

14. Hypatia has read 13 chapters of a 22-chapter book.

    a. What percent of the chapters has she read?

15. A school year has 4 quarters. What percent of a school year is 7 quarters?

16. **Construct Arguments** A survey found that 27% of high school students and 94% of teachers and school employees drive to school. The ratio of students to employees is about 10 to 1. Roger states that the number of students who drive to school is greater than the number of teachers and employees who drive to school. Explain how Roger's statement could be correct.

17. **Higher Order Thinking** Stefan sells Jin a bicycle for $114 and a helmet for $18. The total cost for Jin is 120% of what Stefan spent originally to buy the bike and helmet. How much did Stefan spend originally? How much money did he make by selling the bicycle and helmet to Jin?

Assessment Practice

18. Last month you spent $30. This month you spent 140% of what you spent last month. Set up a proportion to model this situation. How much did you spend this month?

19. The owner of a small store buys coats for $50.00 each.

    PART A
    She sells the coats for $90.00 each. What percent of the purchase price is the selling price?

    PART B
    The owner increases the sale price the same percent that you found in Part A when she buys jackets for $35 and sells them. How many jackets must the owner buy for the total jacket sales to be at least $250? Explain your answer.

148 3-2 Connect Percent and Proportion

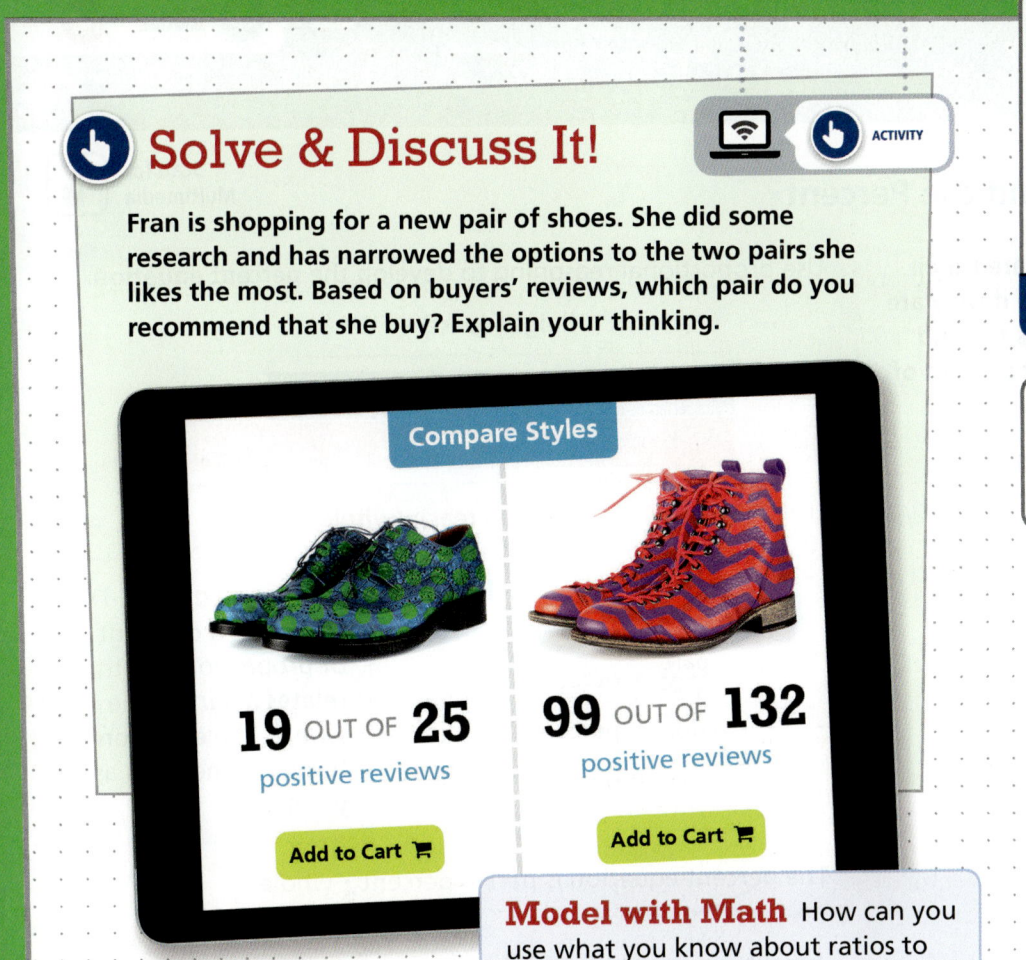

Lesson 3-3
Represent and Use the Percent Equation

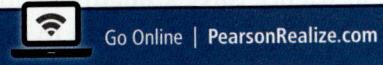

Go Online | PearsonRealize.com

I can... represent and solve percent problems using equations.

Solve & Discuss It!

Fran is shopping for a new pair of shoes. She did some research and has narrowed the options to the two pairs she likes the most. Based on buyers' reviews, which pair do you recommend that she buy? Explain your thinking.

Compare Styles

19 OUT OF 25 positive reviews

Add to Cart

99 OUT OF 132 positive reviews

Add to Cart

Model with Math How can you use what you know about ratios to compare the reviews?

Focus on math practices

Model with Math Describe another situation in which you could use ratios to make a decision.

Essential Question How are percent problems related to proportional reasoning?

EXAMPLE 1 Find the Percent

In science class, students compared their vertical reach and height to see if they are proportional. Maria is 60 inches tall and can reach 75 inches high. What percent of her total vertical reach is her height?

Vertical Reach 75 in.

Height 60 in.

Use proportional reasoning to develop the **percent equation**.

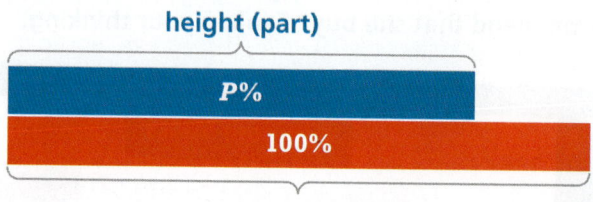

height (part)

$P\%$

100%

vertical reach (whole)

$$\frac{\text{part}}{\text{whole}} = \frac{p}{100}$$

$$\frac{\text{part}}{\text{whole}} = \text{percent}$$

$$\frac{\text{part}}{\text{whole}} \cdot \text{whole} = \text{percent} \cdot \text{whole}$$

$$\text{part} = \text{percent} \cdot \text{whole}$$

Use Structure The percent is a constant of proportionality that relates a *part* to the *whole*. The equation has the same form as $y = mx$.

The percent equation is part = percent • whole.

height = percent • vertical reach

60 = P • 75

$$\frac{60}{75} = \frac{P \cdot 75}{75}$$

0.80 = P

To represent a decimal as a percent, multiply by 100 and add the percent symbol.

Maria's height is 80% of her total vertical reach.

Try It!

An elephant weighs 15,000 pounds on Earth and 2,500 pounds on the Moon. Assuming the weights are proportional, what percent of its weight on Earth is its weight on the Moon?

Convince Me! How does the percent describe how the weights are related?

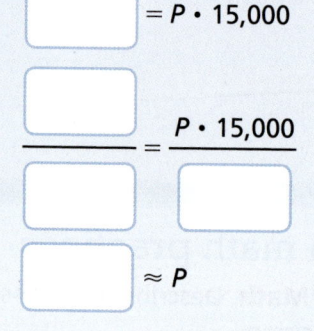

☐ = P • 15,000

$$\frac{\boxed{}}{\boxed{}} = \frac{P \cdot 15,000}{\boxed{}}$$

☐ ≈ P

The elephant's weight on the Moon is about ☐ % of its weight on Earth.

150 3-3 Represent and Use the Percent Equation

EXAMPLE 2 — Find the Part

Many states have a meal tax that is proportional to the total spent on food and beverages. In one state, the meal tax is 8.44%. How much tax will a customer pay if the food and beverages total $54?

Tax ($)

8.44%	
	100%

Total food and beverage ($)

part = percent · whole
tax = percent · bill

$t = 8.44\% \cdot b$

Use t for the tax and b for the food and beverages bill.

$t = 0.0844 \cdot 54$

Express the percent as a decimal.

$t = 4.5576$

Reasoning What does 4.5576 mean in this situation?

The customer will pay $4.56 in tax.

EXAMPLE 3 — Find the Whole

Jane earns a 5.5% commission on the selling price of each home she sells. She earned $9,020 in commission on the sale of a home. What was the selling price of the home?

Be Precise Instead of a salary, some workers earn a percent of the value of a transaction, called a *commission*.

Commission ($)

5.5%	
	100%

Selling price ($)

part = percent · whole

$c = 5.5\% \cdot h$

Use c for the commission and h for the selling price of the home.

$9{,}020 = 0.055h$

$$\frac{9{,}020}{0.055} = \frac{0.055h}{0.055}$$

$164{,}000 = h$

Jane sold the home for $164,000.

✓ Try It!

To make a profit, a clothing store sells jeans at 115% of the amount they paid for them. How much did the store pay for the jeans shown?

$28

Go Online | PearsonRealize.com   3-3 Represent and Use the Percent Equation

KEY CONCEPT

The percent equation shows how a percent relates proportional quantities. The percent is a constant of proportionality and the equation has the same form as $y = mx$.

$$\frac{\text{part}}{\text{whole}} = \text{percent}$$

$$\text{part} = \text{percent} \cdot \text{whole}$$

Do You Understand?

1. **Essential Question** How are percent problems related to proportional reasoning?

2. **Reasoning** A waiter at a restaurant receives $11 as a tip on a $47.20 bill. He usually receives tips that are 20% of the total bill. Is the tip amount what the waiter typically receives? Explain.

3. **Construct Arguments** Sara used an equation to solve the problem below. Justify each step of her work.

   About 11% of people are left-handed. How many people would you expect to be left-handed in a class of 30 students?

   $\ell = 0.11 \cdot 30$
   $\ell = 3.3$
   about 3 students

Do You Know How?

4. An auto insurance company pays 12% commission to its agents for each new insurance policy they sell. How much commission does an agent make on a $1,000 policy?

5. Curt and Melanie are mixing blue and yellow paint to make seafoam green paint. Use the percent equation to find how much yellow paint they should use.

   70%   30%
   1.5 QUARTS
   Seafoam green

6. Bill paid $35.99 in tax on a laptop that cost $449.99. About what percent sales tax did Bill pay?

Practice & Problem Solving

Leveled Practice In **7** and **8**, solve each percent problem.

7. In a survey of 500 voters, 430 said they would vote for the same candidate again. What percent of the voters would vote the same way again?

part = percent · whole

☐ = P% · ☐

☐ = P%

8. The local newspaper has letters to the editor from 40 people. If this number represents 5% of all of the newspaper's readers, how many readers, *r*, does the newspaper have?

part = percent · whole

☐ = ☐ · r

☐ = r

9. Make Sense and Persevere What percent of the 16-gigabyte hard drive shown is used for photos?

3.32 GB

| Music | Photos | Apps | Other | Free Space |

⟵ 16 GB ⟶

10. A shirt that normally costs $30 is on sale for $21.75. What percent of the regular price is the sale price?

11. Complete the table.

Earning Commission

Sales	Commission Rate	Commission
$768	4%	☐

12. Complete the table.

Sales Tax

Selling Price	Tax Rate	Sales Tax
$39.98	4.5%	☐

13. A restaurant automatically charges a 20% gratuity if a party has 6 or more people. How much gratuity is added to a party of 6 on a $141 bill?

3-3 Represent and Use the Percent Equation

14. Make Sense and Persevere A large university accepts 70% of the students who apply. Of the students the university accepts, 25% actually enroll. If 20,000 students apply, how many enroll?

15. Model with Math There are 4,000 books in the town's library. Of these, 2,600 are fiction. Write a percent equation that you can use to find the percent of the books that are fiction. Then solve your equation.

16. A salesperson earns 4% commission on furnace sales.

   a. What is the commission that the salesperson earns on the sale of $33,000 worth of furnaces?

   b. Suppose the salesperson doubles his sales of furnaces. What would be true about the commission? Explain without using any calculations.

17. Heidi earns 3% commission on the jewelry she sells each week. Last week, she sold the pieces of jewelry shown.

   a. How much did she make in commission?

   b. Reasoning How much did the jewelry store take in from her sales? How do you know?

$110
$275
$200
$145

18. Higher Order Thinking In a company, 60% of the workers are men. If 1,380 women work for the company, how many workers are there in all? Show two different ways that you can solve this problem.

Assessment Practice

19. A salesperson works 40 hours per week at a job where he has two options for being paid. Option A is an hourly wage of $19. Option B is a commission rate of 8% on weekly sales. How much does he need to sell in a given week to earn the same amount with each option?

20. At a real estate agency, an agent sold a house for $382,000. The commission rate is 5.5% for the real estate agency. The commission for the agent is 30% of the amount the real estate agency gets.

PART A
How much did the agency make on the house? Show your work.

PART B
How much did the agent earn in commission? Explain.

Name: _____

MID-TOPIC CHECKPOINT
TOPIC 3

1. **Vocabulary** How does the percent equation relate proportional quantities? *Lesson 3-3*

2. Colleen buys a movie for $20 and pays 7% sales tax. Her cousin, Brad, lives in another state. Brad buys the same movie for $22 and pays 6% sales tax. Who pays more sales tax? How much more? *Lessons 3-1 and 3-3*

3. Kamesh and Paolo each read 40 books in one year. Kamesh read 12 nonfiction books. Thirty-five percent of the books Paolo read were nonfiction. Who read more nonfiction books? How many more? *Lesson 3-2*

4. Val buys a computer for $920. If this is 115% of what the store paid for the same computer, how much did the store earn on the sale? *Lesson 3-3*

5. Draw lines to match each situation on the left with a percent on the right. *Lessons 3-1, 3-2, and 3-3*

Situation	Percent
At an auto repair shop, 14 of the 56 cars received oil changes. What percent of the cars received oil changes?	5%
Harry pays $3.50 sales tax on a $70 item. What is the sales tax rate?	15%
In a box of 250 paperclips, 50 are red. What percent of the paperclips is red?	20%
Rylee saved $9 on a $60 pair of shoes. What percent did she save?	25%

6. Explain how you can use proportional reasoning to determine the whole if you know that 21 is 60% of the whole. *Lesson 3-2*

How well did you do on the mid-topic checkpoint? Fill in the stars.

TOPIC 3: MID-TOPIC PERFORMANCE TASK

The coach of a women's basketball team wants each of her starting players to make at least 75% of the free throws attempted during regular season games. The table shows the statistics for the starting players after the first 15 games.

Player	Free Throws Attempted	Free Throws Made	Percent
Wilson	36	24	
Bartholdi	42	37	
Johnson	22	15	
Garcia	29	16	
O'Malley	14	12	

PART A

Complete the table. Find the percentage of free throws made by each player. Round to the nearest whole percent.

PART B

Choose one of the players with a percentage that is less than 75%. Determine a number of free throws she could attempt and make during the next 10 games to increase her free throw percentage to at least 75%.

PART C

Choose one of the players with a percentage that is greater than 75%. Determine the number of free throws that she could miss during the next 10 games and still maintain an overall percentage of at least 75%.

Lesson 3-4
Solve Percent Change and Percent Error Problems

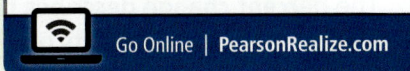

Go Online | PearsonRealize.com

I can... solve problems involving percent change and percent error.

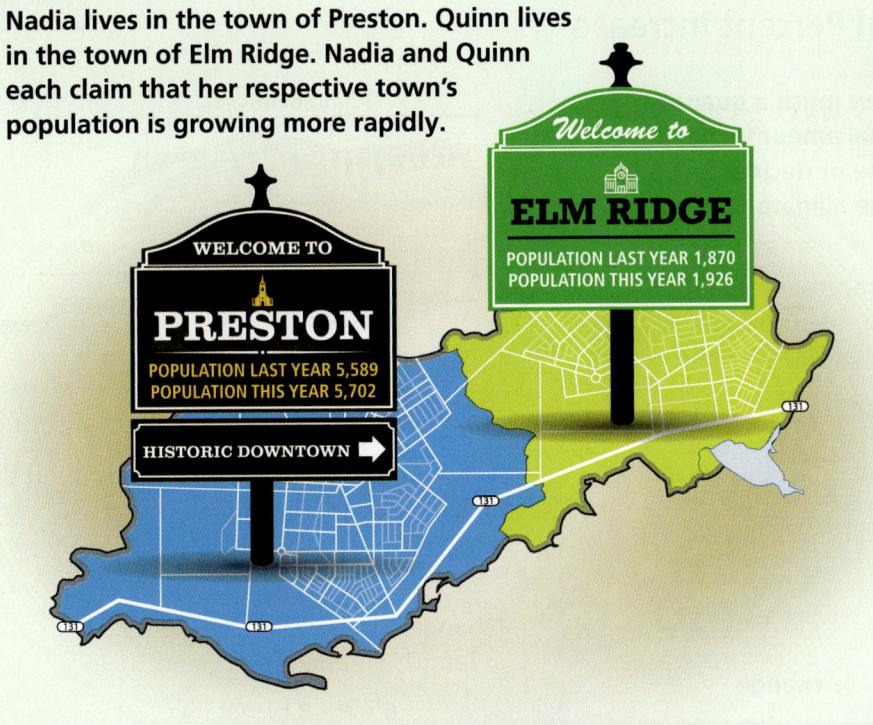

Explain It!

Nadia lives in the town of Preston. Quinn lives in the town of Elm Ridge. Nadia and Quinn each claim that her respective town's population is growing more rapidly.

Welcome to ELM RIDGE
POPULATION LAST YEAR 1,870
POPULATION THIS YEAR 1,926

WELCOME TO PRESTON
POPULATION LAST YEAR 5,589
POPULATION THIS YEAR 5,702
HISTORIC DOWNTOWN

A. Write an argument to support Nadia. Why might she argue that Preston's population is growing more rapidly?

B. Write an argument to support Quinn. Why might she argue that Elm Ridge's population is growing more rapidly?

C. Whose reasoning is more logical? Explain why.

Focus on math practices

Critique Reasoning Suppose Preston's population is expected to grow 3% next year. Nadia says that means the population will increase by 300 people. Is Nadia's reasoning correct? Explain.

? **Essential Question** How is finding percent error similar to finding percent change?

EXAMPLE 1 Find Percent Increase

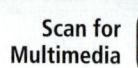

The **percent change** describes how much a quantity has changed relative to its original amount. The percent change can be an increase or decrease. What is the percent change of the alligator's length?

Model with Math What representation can show the change in the alligator's length?

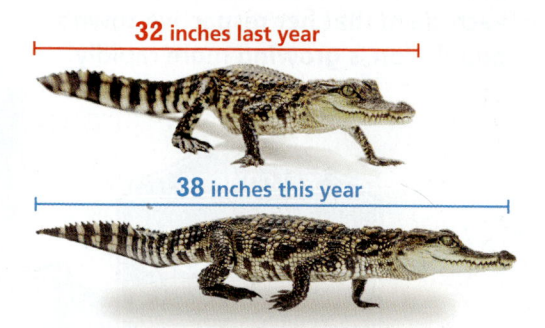

32 inches last year

38 inches this year

STEP 1 Draw a bar diagram to represent the percent change from last year to this year.

The percent change is a *percent increase* because the alligator's length increased.

% change

32 inches | 6 in.
32 inches
100%

The change in length is 6 inches.

STEP 2 Use the percent equation to find the percent change.

part = percent • whole

change in length = percent change • original length

$6 = P \cdot 32$

$\frac{6}{32} = P$

$0.1875 = P$

Express the decimal as a percent by multiplying by 100.

The alligator's length increased by 18.75% this year.

✓ Try It!

What will be the length of the alligator next year if its length changes by the same percent as it changed this year?

18.75%

38 inches | ? in.
38 inches
100%

percent change • length this year = change in length

0.1875 • ☐ = ☐

☐ + ☐ = ☐

Next year, the length of the alligator will be ☐ inches long.

Convince Me! Why is the increase in the alligator's length different from year to year, even though the percent change stayed the same?

158 3-4 Solve Percent Change and Percent Error Problems

EXAMPLE 2 Find Percent Decrease

Last year, a website had 40,000 visitors and this year, it had 37,000 visitors. What is the percent change in the number of visitors to the website from last year to this year?

Find the decrease in the number of visitors. Then use the percent equation to find the percent change.

The percent change is a *percent decrease* because the number of visitors decreased.

% change

37,000 visitors
40,000 visitors
100%

The change in attendance is 3,000.

change in number of visitors = percent change • number of visitors last year

$$3{,}000 = P \cdot 40{,}000$$

$$\frac{3{,}000}{40{,}000} = P$$

$$0.075 = P$$

The number of visitors decreased by 7.5% this year.

EXAMPLE 3 Find Percent Error

Shaun estimated that the attendance at a college lacrosse game was 3,000. The actual attendance was 3,296. What is the percent error of Shaun's estimate? Round to the nearest whole percent.

Percent error describes the accuracy of a measured or estimated value compared to an actual value. It is always a positive percent.

Use absolute value to find the positive difference between the estimated and actual attendance. Then use the percent equation to find the percent error.

$$|3{,}000 - 3{,}296| = 296$$

difference in attendance = percent error • actual attendance

$$296 = P \cdot 3{,}296$$

$$\frac{296}{3{,}296} = P$$

$$0.0898 \approx P$$

Remember to express the decimal value as a percent.

Shaun's attendance estimate has a percent error of about 9%.

✓ Try It!

The specification for the length of a bolt is 4.75 inches. A machinist makes a bolt that is 4.769 inches long. What is the percent error of the bolt's length?

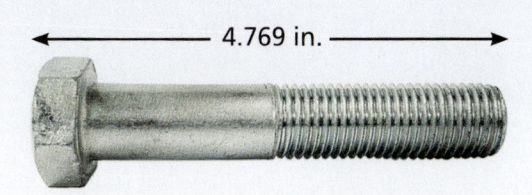

← 4.769 in. →

Go Online | PearsonRealize.com

3-4 Solve Percent Change and Percent Error Problems   159

KEY CONCEPT

Percent change and percent error problems are kinds of percent problems. You can use the percent equation to solve them.

$$\frac{\text{amount of change}}{} = \text{percent change} \cdot \text{original amount}$$

The amount of change is the difference between original and new values.

% change (increase): New value > Original value (100%)

% change (decrease): New value < Original value (100%)

Do You Understand?

1. **Essential Question** How is finding percent error similar to finding percent change?

2. **Reasoning** Give an example of a problem in which the percent error is greater than 20%, but less than 50%. Explain how you determined the percent error.

3. **Construct Arguments** A store manager marked up a $10 flash drive by 20%. She then marked it down by 20%. Explain why the new price of the flash drive is not $10.

Do You Know How?

4. Lita's softball team won 8 games last month and 10 this month. What was the percent change in games the team won? Was it an increase or decrease?

5. What is the percent change in the price of a gallon of gas, to the nearest whole percent? Is it an increase or a decrease?

   $ 3.499 Price Per Gallon
   → $ 3.079 Price Per Gallon

6. Several students measured a 25-mm-long nail and wrote the measurements shown in the table below. Whose measurement had the greatest percent error? Round to the nearest percent.

Student	Measurement (mm)	Percent Error
Layne	26	%
Tenicia	23	%
Juan	25	%

160   3-4 Solve Percent Change and Percent Error Problems

Practice & Problem Solving

Leveled Practice In 7–8, use the bar diagram and fill in the boxes to solve.

7. The original quantity is 10 and the new quantity is 13. What is the percent change? Is it an increase or decrease?

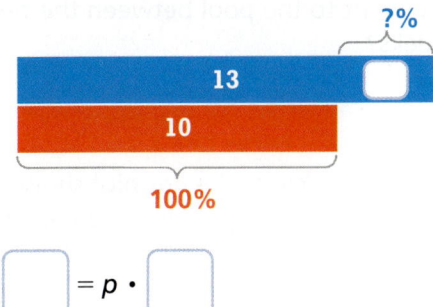

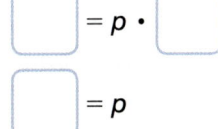

☐ = p · ☐

☐ = p

The percent increase is ☐ %.

8. The original quantity is 5 and the new quantity is 3. What is the percent change? Is it an increase or decrease?

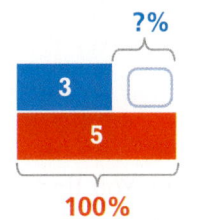

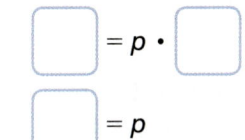

☐ = p · ☐

☐ = p

The percent decrease is ☐ %.

9. At noon, a tank contained 10 cm of water. After several hours, it contained 7 cm of water. What is the percent decrease of water in the tank?

10. Craig likes to collect vinyl records. Last year he had 10 records in his collection. Now he has 12 records. What is the percent increase of his collection?

11. Carl bought an airline ticket. Two weeks ago, the cost of this flight was $300.

What is the percent increase?

12. On Monday, a museum had 150 visitors. On Tuesday, it had 260 visitors.

   a. Estimate the percent change in the number of visitors to the museum.

   b. About how many people would have to visit the museum on Wednesday to have the same percent change from Tuesday to Wednesday as from Monday to Tuesday? Explain your answer.

13. Rihanna has a container with a volume of 1.5 liters. She estimates the volume to be 2.1 liters. What is the percent error?

14. The label on a package of bolts says each bolt has a diameter of 0.35 inch. To be in the package, the percent error of the diameter must be less than 5%. One bolt has a diameter of 0.33 inch. Should it go in the package? Why or why not?

3-4 Solve Percent Change and Percent Error Problems

15. A band expects to have 16 songs on their next album. The band writes and records 62.5% more songs than they expect to have in the album. During the editing process, 50% of the songs are removed. How many songs will there be in the final album?

16. **Make Sense and Persevere** In the first week of July, a record 1,060 people went to the local swimming pool. In the second week, 105 fewer people went to the pool. In the third week, 135 more people went to the pool than in the second week. In the fourth week, 136 fewer people went to the pool than in the third week.

    What is the percent change in the number of people who went to the pool between the first and last weeks?

17. **Be Precise** You have 20 quarters. You find 40% more quarters in your room. Then you go shopping and spend 50% of the total number of quarters.

    a. Write an expression that represents the total number of quarters you take with you when you go shopping.

    b. How much money do you have left?

18. **Higher Order Thinking** The dot plot shows predictions for the winning time in a 200-meter sprint. The winner finished the race in 22.3 seconds. Find the greatest percent error for a prediction to the nearest tenth of a percent. Justify your answer.

    Race Times

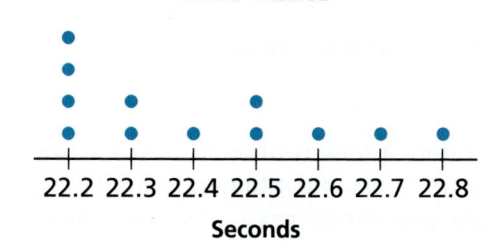

    22.2 22.3 22.4 22.5 22.6 22.7 22.8
    Seconds

Assessment Practice

19. The amount of money in a savings account increases from $250 to $270. What is the percent increase of the money in the savings account?

20. A meteorologist predicted that there would be 10 inches of snowfall from a snowstorm. Instead, there were 22 inches of snowfall. Which of the following statements is true? Select all that apply.

    ☐ The prediction was off by 35%.

    ☐ If the percent error should be less than 60%, the prediction was acceptable.

    ☐ The percent error of the prediction was about 55%.

    ☐ If the percent error should be less than 20%, the prediction was acceptable.

    ☐ The difference between the predicted and actual snowfall was 12 inches.

3-ACT MATH ▶ ▶ ▶

3-Act Mathematical Modeling:
The Smart Shopper

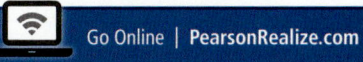

Go Online | PearsonRealize.com

ACT 1

1. After watching the video, what is the first question that comes to mind?

2. Write the Main Question you will answer.

3. **Construct Arguments** Make a prediction to answer this Main Question. Explain how you arrived at your prediction.

4. On the number line below, write a number that is too small to be the answer. Write a number that is too large.

Too small ←—————————————————→ Too large

5. Plot your prediction on the same number line.

Topic 3 3-Act Mathematical Modeling 163

ACT 2

6. What information in this situation would be helpful to know? How would you use that information?

7. **Use Appropriate Tools** What tools can you use to get the information you need? Record the information as you find it.

8. **Model with Math** Represent the situation using the mathematical content, concepts, and skills from this topic. Use your representation to answer the Main Question.

9. What is your answer to the Main Question? Is it higher or lower than your prediction? Explain why.

ACT 3

10. Write the answer you saw in the video.

11. Reasoning Does your answer match the answer in the video? If not, what are some reasons that would explain the difference?

12. Make Sense and Persevere Would you change your model now that you know the answer? Explain.

ACT 3 Extension

Reflect

13. Model with Math Explain how you used a mathematical model to represent the situation. How did the model help you answer the Main Question?

14. Be Precise Describe how you would tell the friends to use their coupons.

SEQUEL

15. Make Sense and Persevere Suppose the $20 coupon requires a purchase of $100 or more. How would that affect your solution?

Lesson 3-5
Solve Markup and Markdown Problems

Go Online | PearsonRealize.com

I can...
solve problems involving percent markup and markdown.

Solve & Discuss It!

Clare subscribes to an online music streaming service for a yearly fee of $96. Starting next month, there will be a 12% increase in the fee.

The ad for another music streaming service is shown below. Should Clare switch? Explain.

Welcome to our *Music* site

DIGITAL STREAMING OF MUSIC

$8.75 per month

Home | About Us | Services | FAQ | Contact Us

Model with Math
You can use the percent equation to determine the percent increase.

Focus on math practices

Make Sense and Persevere What is another problem-solving method you could use to check that your solution makes sense?

167

Essential Question How are the concepts of percent markup and percent markdown related to the percent equation?

EXAMPLE 1 Find the Percent Markup

Marty buys plain cell phone cases and then decorates them to resell online at a higher price. What is the percent markup on each phone case?

$7.20 → Selling price: $11.25 each

Markup is the amount of increase from the cost of an item to its selling price. The markup as a percent increase from the original cost is the **percent markup**.

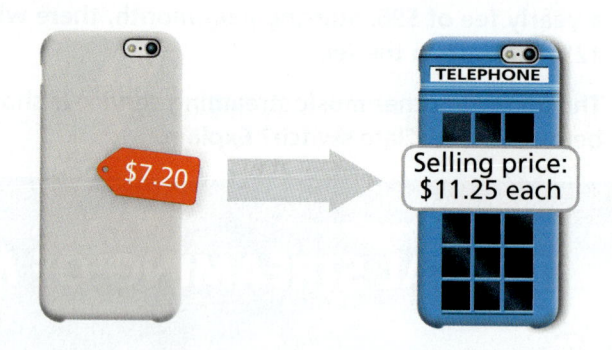

STEP 1 Draw a bar diagram to represent the problem and to find the markup.

% markup
$11.25
$7.20
100%
The markup is $4.05.

STEP 2 Use the percent equation to find the percent markup.

markup = percent markup • cost

$4.05 = P \cdot 7.20$

$\dfrac{4.05}{7.20} = P$

$0.5625 = P$

Remember to express the decimal value as a percent.

The percent markup on each cell phone case is about 56%.

Try It!

What is the percent markup on a $300 phone sold for $465?

markup = percent markup • cost

☐ = P • 300

☐ = P

$465
$300
100%
The markup is ☐.

The percent markup on the phone is ☐ %.

Convince Me! How does the percent equation help solve markup problems?

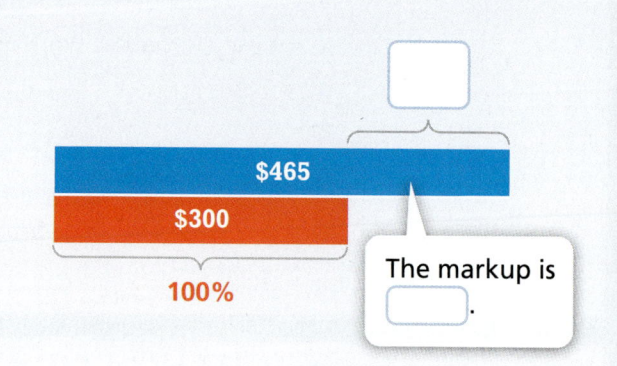

168   3-5 Solve Markup and Markdown Problems

EXAMPLE 2   Find the Selling Price

The local furniture store pays $110 for a chest of drawers and sells it with a 40% markup. What is the selling price of the chest of drawers?

STEP 1 Draw a bar diagram to represent the problem.

40% markup

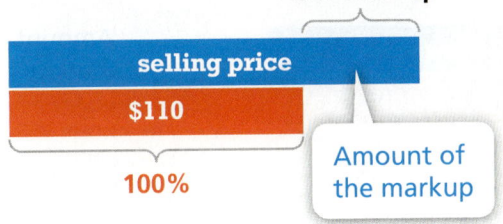

selling price
$110
100%
Amount of the markup

STEP 2 Use the percent equation to find the markup and the selling price.

markup = percent markup · cost
$a = 0.40 \cdot 110$
$a = 44$

The markup is $44.

$110 + 44 = 154$

The selling price of the chest of drawers is $100 + $44 or $154.

Try It!

What is the selling price for a $45 pair of shoes with a 15% markup?

EXAMPLE 3   Find Markdown and Sales Tax

Edward wants to buy a snowboard that is on sale. If the sales tax in Edward's state is 7.5%, how much will he pay for the snowboard?

Markdown is the decrease from the original price of an item to its sale price. The markdown as a percent decrease of the original price is the **percent markdown**.

$180
30% OFF

STEP 1 Use the percent equation to find the marked down price of the snowboard.

markdown = percent markdown · original price
$m = 0.30 \cdot 180$
$m = 54$

The sale price is $180 − $54, or $126.

STEP 2 Use the percent equation to find the sales tax board.

sales tax = percent · sale price
$s = 0.075 \cdot 126$
$s = 9.45$

Edward will pay 126 + 9.45, or $135.45, for the snowboard.

Try It!

Find the percent markdown for an $80 jacket that is on sale for $48.

Go Online | PearsonRealize.com   3-5 Solve Markup and Markdown Problems   169

KEY CONCEPT

You can solve markup and markdown problems using the percent equation.

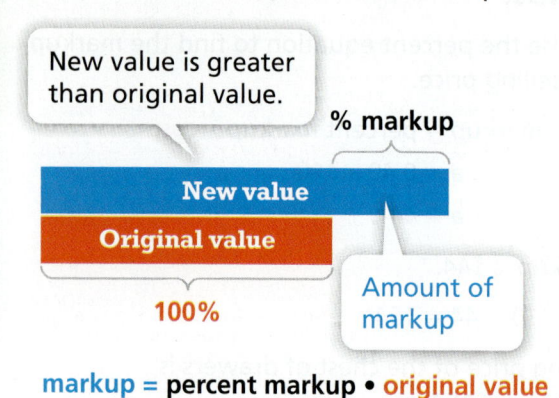

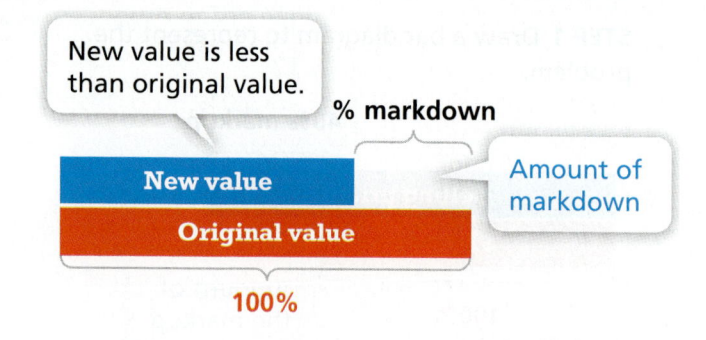

New value is greater than original value.

% markup

New value
Original value
100%
Amount of markup

markup = percent markup • original value

New value is less than original value.

% markdown

New value
Original value
100%
Amount of markdown

markdown = percent markdown • original value

Do You Understand?

1. **Essential Question** How are the concepts of markup and markdown related to the percent equation?

2. **Reasoning** What does the amount of the markup or markdown represent in the percent equation?

3. **Generalize** When an item is marked up by a certain percent and then marked down by the same percent, is the sale price equal to the price before the markup and markdown?

Do You Know How?

4. An item costs $4 before tax and $4.32 after sales tax. What is the sales tax rate?

5. Sheila buys two concert tickets from her friend. She pays $90 for the two tickets. She looks at the tickets and sees that each ticket has a face value of $52.50.

   a. How much of a markdown did her friend give Sheila? Explain how you know.

   b. What was the percent markdown, rounded to the nearest whole percent?

6. Find the sale prices.

   a. $4,200 with a 35% markdown

   b. $5,000 with a 44% markdown

Name: _____

Practice & Problem Solving

Leveled Practice In 7–8, fill in the boxes to solve.

7. A $300 suit is marked down by 20%. Find the sale price rounded to the nearest dollar.

markdown = percent markdown • original price

markdown = ☐ % • $☐

markdown = $☐

original price − markdown = sale price

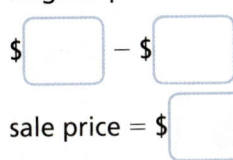

$☐ − $☐

sale price = $☐

8. The selling price of an item is $650 marked up from the wholesale cost of $450. Find the percent markup from wholesale cost to selling price.

selling price − markup = wholesale cost

$☐ − $☐ = $☐

markup = percent markup × wholesale cost

☐ = ☐ × ☐

The percent markup is about ☐.

9. Karen purchased the DVD player shown in the sign on the right. Find the percent markdown rounded to the nearest percent.

SALE!
WAS $175.90
NOW $153.77

10. A store manager instructs his employees to mark up all items by 30%. A store clerk puts a price tag of $30 on an item that the store bought for $27. As an employee, you notice that this selling price is incorrect.

  a. Find the correct selling price. Round to the nearest dollar.

  b. What was the clerk's likely error?

11. Nate has $50 to spend at the grocery store. He fills his shopping cart with items totaling $46. At checkout he will have to pay 6% sales tax on all items in the cart. Does he have enough money to buy everything in his cart? Explain.

12. A department store buys 300 shirts at a cost of $1,800 and sells them for $10 each. Find the percent markup rounded to the nearest percent.

3-5 Solve Markup and Markdown Problems

13. **Make Sense and Persevere** A computer store buys a computer system at a cost of $465.60. The selling price was first at $776, but then the store advertised a 30% markdown on the system.

    a. Find the current sale price. Round to the nearest cent if necessary.

    b. Members of the store's loyalty club get an additional 10% off their computer purchases. How much do club members pay for the computer with their discount?

14. **Higher Order Thinking** A sporting goods store manager was selling a ski set for a certain price. The manager offered the markdowns shown on the right, making the one-day sale price of the ski set $328. Find the original selling price of the ski set.

    SKI SET
    10% OFF
    Today only!
    EXTRA 30% OFF

Assessment Practice

15. Eliza cannot decide which of two bicycles to buy. The original price of each is $380. The first is marked down by 50%. The second is marked down by 30% with an additional 20% off.

    PART A

    Find the sale price of each bicycle. Show your work.

    PART B

    Which bicycle should Eliza buy if the bicycles are the same except for the selling price?

16. A shoe store uses a 50% markup for all of the shoes it sells. What would be the selling price of a pair of shoes that has a wholesale cost of $57?

172 3-5 Solve Markup and Markdown Problems

Explore It!

Lesson 3-6
Solve Simple Interest Problems

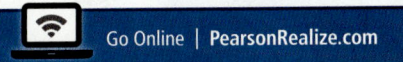

Go Online | PearsonRealize.com

Gerard compares the offers at two different banks to decide where he should open a savings account.

I can...
apply percent reasoning to solve simple interest problems.

Billboard 1 (MY BANK): Open a savings account - we'll add $100 to your first deposit!

Billboard 2 (New Bank): When you open a savings account with us, we'll add 5% of your first deposit to the account!

A. Draw a representation to show how much would be in the first savings account if Gerard's initial deposit were d dollars.

B. Draw a representation to show how much would be in the second savings account if Gerard's initial deposit were d dollars.

C. Use the two representations you drew to explain how the offers at the two banks are similar and how they are different.

Focus on math practices

Construct Arguments Gerard's first deposit is $500. Which bank should he choose? Explain.

? **Essential Question** How does simple interest show proportional reasoning and relate to the percent equation?

EXAMPLE 1 — Find Simple Interest

Victoria opens a savings account with a deposit of $300. She will earn 1.6% simple interest each year on her money. How much interest will she earn over 5 years (assuming she does not add or take out any money)?

Interest that is applied to the initial amount only is called **simple interest**.

The initial amount is called the **principal**.

0 years 1 year 2 years 3 years 4 years 5 years

STEP 1 Use the percent equation to find the amount of interest earned in one year, s.

An **interest rate** is a percent used to calculate interest on the principal.

interest amount = interest rate • principal
$$s = 0.016 \cdot 300$$
$$s = 4.80$$

The simple interest earned on the principal in one year is $4.80.

STEP 2 Multiply the interest earned in one year by 5 to calculate the total interest Victoria will earn over 5 years.

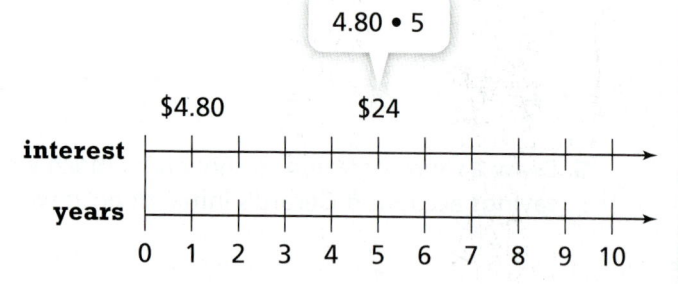

4.80 • 5

$4.80 $24

interest
years
0 1 2 3 4 5 6 7 8 9 10

Victoria will earn $24 in interest over 5 years.

✓ Try It!

Victoria has another account at the bank that pays $2\frac{1}{2}$% simple interest. How much interest will she earn in 8 years on an initial deposit of $250 assuming she neither adds to nor withdraws from the account?

$2\frac{1}{2}$% interest expressed as a decimal is ☐.

Interest after 1 year: s = ☐ • $☐

= $☐

Interest after 8 years: $☐ • ☐

= $☐

Victoria will earn $☐ in interest over 8 years.

Convince Me! Would the interest for the second year be the same if it were calculated on the total after the first year? Why or why not?

3-6 Solve Simple Interest Problems

EXAMPLE 2   Find the Percent of Interest

Maya's older sister got a loan to buy a used car for $3,400. What is the interest rate on the loan?

STEP 1 Multiply the interest amount by 12 to find the interest for 1 year.

$$8.50 \cdot 12 = 102$$

STEP 2 Use the percent equation to find the interest rate.

interest amount = interest rate · loan amount

$$102 = P \cdot 3{,}400$$
$$\frac{102}{3{,}400} = P \cdot \frac{3{,}400}{3{,}400}$$
$$0.03 = P$$

The simple interest rate is 3% for 1 year.

WE LEND IT!
Borrow $3,400 for this car today.. and pay only $8.50 interest
...every month!!!

JIM'S USED CARS   1-555-JIM-CARS
WE HAVE THE PERFECT CAR FOR YOU
Route 7 off Interstate 11, Mathville, U.S.A.

✓ Try It!

Another company will lend Maya's older sister $4,000. Every month, she will pay $11.88 in interest. What is the interest rate, rounded to the nearest tenth of a percent, for 1 year?

EXAMPLE 3   Find the Principal

Jake opened a savings account that earns 1.5% interest. Jake estimates that, assuming he neither adds to nor withdraws from his account, he will earn $240 in interest after 10 years. How much did Jake deposit when he opened the account?

First, find the amount of interest for 1 year.

$$240 \div 10 = 24$$

Then, use the percent equation to find the initial deposit or principal, d.

interest amount = interest rate · initial deposit

$$24 = 0.015 \cdot d$$
$$\frac{24}{0.015} = d \cdot \frac{0.015}{0.015}$$
$$1{,}600 = d$$

Calculating simple interest is a good way to estimate how much interest Jake will have in the bank after 10 years.

Jake deposited $1,600.

Make Sense and Persevere
How can using an equation help make sense of the problem situation?

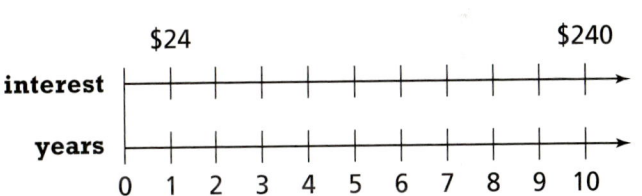

✓ Try It!

Katelyn's older brother borrowed money for school. He took out a loan that charges 6% simple interest. He will end up paying $720 in interest after 6 years. How much did Katelyn's brother borrow for school?

3-6 Solve Simple Interest Problems   175

KEY CONCEPT

Simple interest represents a proportional relationship between the yearly interest and the principal, or initial amount. The ratio of yearly interest to principal is the interest rate.

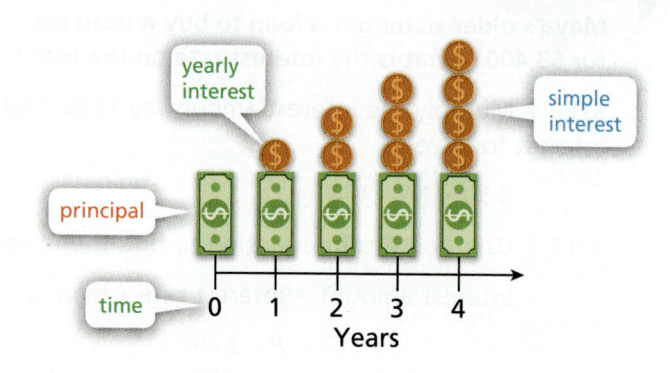

Do You Understand?

1. **Essential Question** How does simple interest show proportional reasoning and relate to the percent equation?

2. **Reasoning** If the interest earned on an account after 2 years is $15, how much would it be after 10 years? Why?

3. **Be Precise** Angelina is deciding which bank would give her the best simple interest rate on a $300 deposit. One bank says that she will have $320 in her account if she leaves the principal for 2 years. Is this enough information for Angelina to find the interest rate? Explain.

Do You Know How?

4. Find the missing value in each row. Use the percent equation.

Principal (P)	Interest Rate (r)	Time in years (t)	Interest Earned (I)
$100	5%	3	
$500	4%		$20
	10%	7	$35
$200		2	$6

5. Annika's older cousin borrowed $800 to repair her car. She will pay off the loan after 2 years by paying back the principal plus 4.5% simple interest for each year.

   a. How much will she pay in interest? Show your work.

   b. How much will she pay back altogether?

6. J.D. opened a savings account with $425. After 2 years, the total interest he earned was $10.20. What was the annual interest rate?

176 3-6 Solve Simple Interest Problems

Name: _____

Practice & Problem Solving

Leveled Practice In 7–8, fill in the boxes to solve.

7. Edward deposited $6,000 into a savings account 4 years ago. The simple interest rate is 3%.

   How much money did Edward earn in interest?

   Interest = $ ☐ · ☐ · ☐ years

   Edward earned $ ☐ in interest.

8. The interest on $2,000 for 2 years is $320. What is the simple interest rate?

   $ ☐ = $2,000 · r · ☐

   $ ☐ = $ ☐ · r

   ☐ = r

   ☐ % = r

9. Suppose you deposited $100 in a savings account 4 years ago with a simple interest rate of 2.2%. The interest that you earned in those 4 years is $8.80. Which of the following is true? Select all that apply.

   ☐ The interest rate is 0.022.

   ☐ The principal was $100.

   ☐ The interest earned is $4.

   ☐ The account was opened 8 years and 8 months ago.

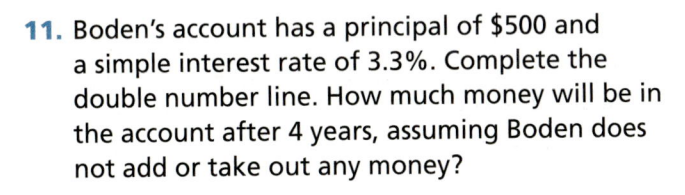

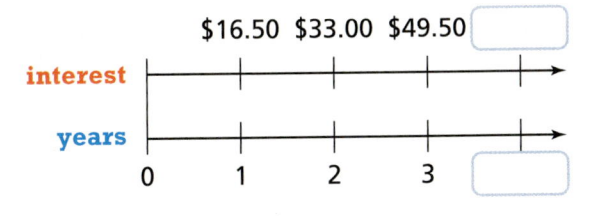

10. A new bank customer with $3,000 wants to open a money market account. The bank is offering a simple interest rate of 1.1%.

    a. How much interest will the customer earn in 20 years?

    b. What will be the account balance after 20 years?

11. Boden's account has a principal of $500 and a simple interest rate of 3.3%. Complete the double number line. How much money will be in the account after 4 years, assuming Boden does not add or take out any money?

    interest: $16.50 $33.00 $49.50 ☐
    years: 0 1 2 3 ☐

12. **Critique Reasoning** Monica deposits $100 into a savings account that pays a simple interest rate of 3.4%. Paul deposits $200 into a savings account that pays a simple interest rate of 2.2%. Monica says that she will earn more interest in one year because her interest rate is higher. Do you agree? Justify your response.

13. **Construct Argument** Tommy earned $76.00 in interest after 5 years on a principal of $400. Jane earned $82.00 in interest after 2 years on a principal of $1,000.

    Which bank would you rather use, Tommy's or Jane's? Why?

3-6 Solve Simple Interest Problems   177

14. **Reasoning** A bank manager wants to encourage new customers to open accounts with initial deposits of at least $3,000. He has posters made for the promotion.

   a. Under the new promotion, what is the minimum amount of interest a new account would make in one year if there were no withdrawls from the account?

   b. The manager wants to add the sentence, "Open an account with $3,000 and earn at least $120 interest each year!" to the poster. Do you agree? Explain.

EAST BANK

Earn **4.8%** (simple interest rate) **on** new deposits of **$3,000** or more.

15. Suppose you deposit $100 in Account A with a simple interest rate of 3.4%, and $300 in Account B with a simple interest rate of 1.8%. One year later, you get a bank statement that shows the interest for Account A is $3.40 and the interest for Account B is $540.00.

   a. Which account statement is incorrect?

   b. What may have been the bank's error?

16. **Higher Order Thinking** You have two different savings accounts. For Account A, the interest earned after 18 months is $12.00. For Account B, the interest earned after 27 months is $27.00.

   a. If the interest rate is 3.2% for Account A, how much is the principal?

   b. If the interest rate is 2.4% for Account B, how much is the principal?

   c. Which account earned you the most interest in the first year? Explain.

Assessment Practice

17. Which of these would earn the same interest as a $150 principal at 4% annual interest for 2 years? Select all that apply.

    ☐ $300 at 2% for 2 years

    ☐ $150 at 6% for 18 months

    ☐ $400 at 3% for 1 year

    ☐ $100 at 1% for 8 years

    ☐ $50 at 48% for 6 months

18. Dakota earned $15.75 in interest in Account A and $28.00 in interest in Account B after 21 months. If the simple interest rate is for 3.0% for Account A and 4.0% for Account B, which account had the greater principal? Explain.

REVIEW — TOPIC 3

? Topic Essential Question

How can percents show proportional relationships between quantities and be used to solve problems?

Vocabulary Review

Complete each definition and then provide an example of each word.

Vocabulary: markdown, markup, percent change, principal, simple interest

Definition	Example
1. The _____ is the decrease from the original price of an item to its sale price.	
2. The accuracy of a measured or estimated value compared to its actual value is described as the _____.	
3. An initial amount of money that is deposited in an account is called the _____.	
4. The _____ describes how much a quantity has changed relative to its original amount.	

Use Vocabulary in Writing

Birute deposits $500 in a savings account with a simple interest rate of 1.3%. How could you use this information to find the interest she would earn in 4 years and determine the percent change in her savings account?

Concepts and Skills Review

LESSON 3-1 | Analyze Percents of Numbers

Quick Review
You can use equivalent ratios to find the percent of a number. Remember that a percent is a ratio that relates a number to 100.

Example
Find 57% of 690.

$$\frac{57}{100} = \frac{x}{690}$$

$$\frac{57}{100} \cdot 690 = \frac{x}{690} \cdot 690$$

$$393.3 = x$$

Practice
1. Find 0.8% of 1,046.

2. Find 160% of 98.

3. A company charges a shipping fee that is 4.5% of the purchase price for all items it ships. What is the fee to ship an item that costs $56?

LESSON 3-2 | Connect Percent and Proportion

Quick Review
You can use proportions to solve different types of percent problems. There are three values in a percent problem—the percent, the part, and the whole. If you know two of these values, you can set up a proportion to find the third value.

Example
What percent of 19 is 4.75?

The whole is 19 and the part is 4.75. Write a proportion, and solve for the percent, p.

$$\frac{\text{part}}{\text{whole}} = \frac{p}{100}$$

$$\frac{4.75}{19} = \frac{p}{100}$$

$$\frac{4.75}{19} \cdot 100 = \frac{p}{100} \cdot 100$$

$$25 = p$$

So, 4.75 is 25% of 19.

Practice
1. 24.94 is 29% of what number?

2. On Thursday, a restaurant serves iced tea to 35 of its 140 customers. What percent of the customers order iced tea?

3. Liam puts $40 in savings in March and 175% of this amount in savings in April. How much does Liam put in savings in April?

LESSON 3-3: Represent and Use the Percent Equation

Quick Review
You can use the percent equation to solve percent problems.

part = percent • whole

Substitute two of the three values to solve for the unknown value.

Example
Michael earns a 6% commission on each house he sells. If he sells a house for $180,000, how much does he earn in commission, c?

$c = 0.06 \cdot 180{,}000$

$c = 10{,}800$

Michael earns $10,800 in commission.

Practice
1. Sharon paid $78 sales tax on a new camera. If the sales tax rate is 6.5%, what was the cost of the camera?

2. There are 45 students who play a woodwind instrument in the school band. Of these, 18 play the saxophone. What percent of these students play the saxophone?

LESSON 3-4: Solve Percent Change and Percent Error Problems

Quick Review
A percent change can be an increase or a decrease. You can use an equation to find a percent change.

change = percent change • original amount

A percent error is always a nonnegative value. You can use an equation to find a percent error.

difference = percent error • actual

Example
Juan's puppy weighed 16 pounds at the age of 2 months. The puppy weighed 60 pounds at the age of 8 months. What is the percent change in the puppy's weight?

change in pounds = 60 − 16 = 44

$44 = P \cdot 16$

$\frac{44}{16} = P$

$2.75 = P$

The puppy's weight increased by 275%.

Practice
1. In 2014, the attendance at Jefferson School's Fall Festival was 650. In 2015, the attendance was 575. What was the percent change in attendance from 2014 to 2015?

   Round to the nearest whole percent.

2. Melissa estimated that she would read 250 pages last week. She read 290 pages. What is the percent error of Melissa's estimate? Round to the nearest whole percent.

LESSON 3-5 Solve Markup and Markdown Problems

Quick Review
You can use the percent equation to solve markup and markdown problems.

markup = percent markup • cost
markdown = percent markdown • selling price

Example
Bree buys a purse for $90. She sells it at her store for $135. What is the percent markup on the purse?

markup = $135 − $90 = $45

$45 = P \cdot 90$

$\frac{45}{90} = P$

$0.5 = P$ — The decimal 0.5 is equivalent to 50%.

The percent markup on the purse is 50%.

Practice
1. Hank buys a used car for $7,200 and plans to sell it on his used car lot. What is the price of the car after a markup of 15%?

2. Nya wants to buy a sweater that had an original price of $55. The sweater is now discounted 20% and the sales tax rate is 5.5%. How much will Nya pay for the sweater?

LESSON 3-6 Solve Simple Interest Problems

Quick Review
You consider four quantities when solving problems involving simple interest.

- initial amount, or principal, p
- interest rate, r
- time, t
- amount of simple interest, I

Example
Yuni loaned $400 to her brother. He will repay the loan by paying 2.5% simple interest for 3 years. How much will he pay in interest?

$I = 400 \cdot 0.025 \cdot 3 = \$30$

He will pay $30 in interest.

Practice
1. Ethan put $700 into a Certificate of Deposit (CD) account that earns 1.8% interest each year. What will the interest of the CD account be after 6 years?

2. Kelly opened a bank account that earns 1.2% simple interest each year. After 7 years, Kelly will earn $126 in interest. How much did Kelly deposit when she opened the account?

Fluency Practice — Topic 3

Riddle Rearranging

Find the value of x in each unit rate. Then arrange the answers in order from least to greatest. The letters will spell out the answer to the riddle below.

I can... find unit rates with ratios of fractions.

K) $\dfrac{\frac{3}{4}\,c}{\frac{1}{3}\,h} = \dfrac{x\,c}{1\,h}$

N) $\dfrac{\frac{3}{5}\,mL}{\frac{2}{5}\,min} = \dfrac{x\,mL}{1\,min}$

A) $\dfrac{\frac{1}{4}\,mi}{\frac{5}{8}\,h} = \dfrac{x\,mi}{1\,h}$

I) $\dfrac{\frac{1}{4}\,ft}{\frac{3}{4}\,h} = \dfrac{x\,ft}{1\,h}$

E) $\dfrac{\frac{6}{5}\,m}{\frac{1}{2}\,s} = \dfrac{x\,m}{1\,s}$

Y) $\dfrac{\frac{5}{6}\,pt}{\frac{1}{3}\,min} = \dfrac{x\,pt}{1\,min}$

S) $\dfrac{\frac{1}{4}\,in.}{\frac{1}{12}\,min} = \dfrac{x\,in.}{1\,min}$

O) $\dfrac{\frac{5}{3}\,pt}{\frac{5}{6}\,h} = \dfrac{x\,pt}{1\,h}$

P) $\dfrac{\frac{3}{10}\,mm}{\frac{6}{5}\,s} = \dfrac{x\,mm}{1\,s}$

What keys cannot be put in a lock?

◯ ◯ ◯ ◯ ◯   ◯ ◯ ◯ ◯

TOPIC 4
GENERATE EQUIVALENT EXPRESSIONS

? Topic Essential Question

How can properties of operations help to generate equivalent expressions that can be used in solving problems?

Topic Overview

- 4-1 Write and Evaluate Algebraic Expressions
- 4-2 Generate Equivalent Expressions
- 4-3 Simplify Expressions
- 4-4 Expand Expressions
- 4-5 Factor Expressions
- 3-Act Mathematical Modeling: I've Got You Covered
- 4-6 Add Expressions
- 4-7 Subtract Expressions
- 4-8 Analyze Equivalent Expressions

Lesson Digital Resources

INTERACTIVE ANIMATION
Interact with visual learning animations.

ACTIVITY Use with *Solve & Discuss It, Explore It,* and *Explain It* activities, and to explore Examples.

VIDEOS Watch clips to support *3-Act Mathematical Modeling Lessons* and *STEM Projects*.

PRACTICE Practice what you've learned.

Go online | **PearsonRealize.com**

184 Topic 4 Generate Equivalent Expressions

3-ACT MATH

I've Got You Covered

I've Got You Covered

Did you know that DIY stands for Do It Yourself? Do-it-yourself projects are a fun way to save money, learn new skills, and make your home unique.

From painting furniture to turning an old T-shirt into a pillow, there are plenty of projects for everyone.

TUTORIALS Get help from *Virtual Nerd*, right when you need it.

KEY CONCEPT Review important lesson content.

GLOSSARY Read and listen to English/Spanish definitions.

ASSESSMENT Show what you've learned.

Additional Digital Resources

MATH TOOLS Explore math with digital tools.

GAMES Play Math Games to help you learn.

ETEXT Interact with your Student's Edition online.

Topic 4 Generate Equivalent Expressions 185

TOPIC 4 STEM Project

Did You Know?

In 2013, just over 30% of American consumers knew about activity trackers. By 2015, about **82%** recognized them.

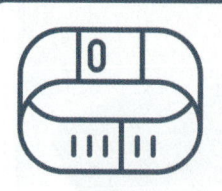

About **3.3 million** fitness bands and activity trackers were sold in the U.S. between April 2013 and March 2014.

The fitness tracker industry is expected to almost **triple in value** between 2014 and 2019.

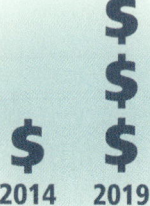

% of people aware of activity trackers

2013 30%

2015 82%

Continued research and development leads to technological advances and breakthroughs, such as the use of biosensing apparel to track activity.

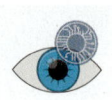

Your Task: Analyze Activity Tracker Data

The ways that data are communicated and presented to the user are just as important as the types of data collected. You and your classmates will continue your exploration of activity trackers and use data to develop models based on individual fitness goals.

Analyzing Activity Tracker Data

Review What You Know!

GET READY!

TOPIC 4

Vocabulary

Choose the best term from the box to complete each definition.

evaluate
expression
factor
order of operations
substitute
term

1. When you _____ an expression, you replace each variable with a given value.

2. To evaluate $a + 3$ when $a = 7$, you can _____ 7 for a in the expression.

3. The set of rules used to determine the order in which operations are performed is called the _____.

4. Each part of an expression that is separated by a plus or minus sign is a(n) _____.

5. A(n) _____ is a mathematical phrase that can contain numbers, variables, and operation symbols.

6. When two numbers are multiplied to get a product, each number is called a(n) _____.

Order of Operations

Evaluate each expression using the order of operations.

7. $3(18 - 7) + 2$

8. $(13 + 2) \div (9 - 4)$

9. $24 \div 4 \cdot 2 - 2$

Equivalent Expressions

Evaluate each expression when $a = -4$ and $b = 3$.

10. ab

11. $2a + 3b$

12. $2(a - b)$

13. Explain the difference between evaluating $3 \cdot 7 - 4 \div 2$ and evaluating $3(7 - 4) \div 2$.

Go Online | PearsonRealize.com   Topic 4 Generate Equivalent Expressions

Prepare for Reading Success

Use the graphic organizer to record details you learn about equivalent expressions during Topic 4.

☐

Write one word that describes one major idea of Topic 4.

☐ ☐

Write two words that describe things you can do with an expression.

☐ ☐ ☐

Write three words that describe how the Distributive Property is used.

☐ ☐ ☐ ☐

Write four words that describe the operations that can be used with expressions.

☐ ☐ ☐ ☐ ☐

Write five words that describe the Order of Operations.

☐ ☐ ☐ ☐ ☐ ☐

Write six important vocabulary words.

☐ ☐ ☐ ☐ ☐ ☐ ☐

Name seven types of problems that you solved in Topic 4.

188 Topic 4 Generate Equivalent Expressions

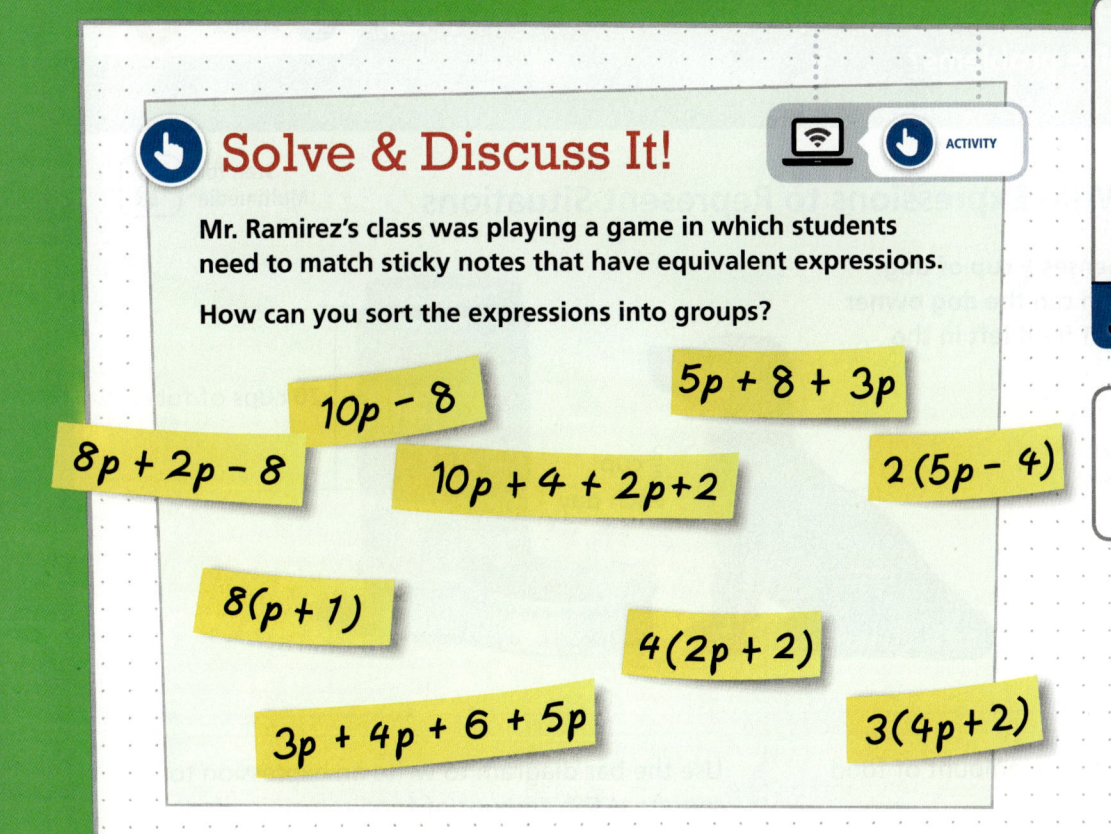

Lesson 4-1
Write and Evaluate Algebraic Expressions

Go Online | PearsonRealize.com

I can... write and evaluate algebraic expressions.

Solve & Discuss It!

Mr. Ramirez's class was playing a game in which students need to match sticky notes that have equivalent expressions.

How can you sort the expressions into groups?

- $10p - 8$
- $5p + 8 + 3p$
- $8p + 2p - 8$
- $10p + 4 + 2p + 2$
- $2(5p - 4)$
- $8(p + 1)$
- $4(2p + 2)$
- $3p + 4p + 6 + 5p$
- $3(4p + 2)$

Focus on math practices

Reasoning Is there more than one way to group the expressions? Give an example.

? **Essential Question** How can algebraic expressions be used to represent and solve problems?

EXAMPLE 1 Write Expressions to Represent Situations

An automatic dog feeder dispenses $\frac{2}{5}$ cup of dog food each day. What expression can the dog owner use to determine the amount of food left in the feeder after d days?

Model with Math How can a bar diagram represent the situation?

20 cups of food

$\frac{2}{5}$ cup each day

Draw a bar diagram to represent the amount of food remaining in the feeder after d days.

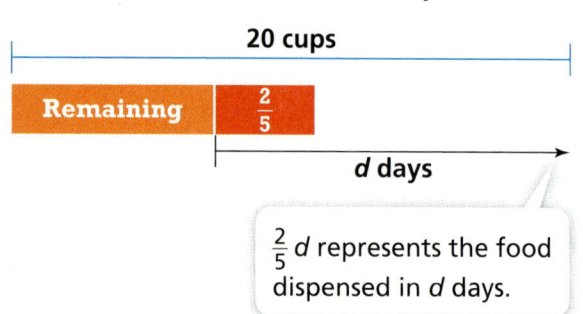

20 cups
Remaining	$\frac{2}{5}$

d days

$\frac{2}{5}d$ represents the food dispensed in d days.

Use the bar diagram to write an expression to represent the amount of food remaining in the feeder after d days.

$$20 - \frac{2}{5}d$$

the number of cups of food the feeder holds

the number of cups of food dispensed in d days

The dog owner can use the expression $20 - \frac{2}{5}d$ to determine the amount of food left in the feeder after d days.

✓ Try It!

Misumi started with $217 in her bank account. She deposits $25.50 each week and never withdraws any money. What expression can Misumi use to determine her account balance after w weeks?

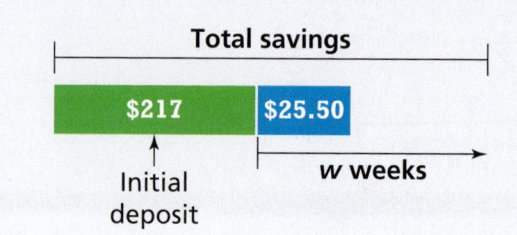

☐ + ☐ w

Total savings

$217 | $25.50

Initial deposit | w weeks

Convince Me! How did you determine which value to use for the constant and which value to use for the coefficient?

190 4-1 Write and Evaluate Algebraic Expressions

EXAMPLE 2 Evaluate Expressions

The expression 9.99d + 12.99c can be used to find the total cost of d pounds of almonds and c pounds of cashews. How much does it cost to buy $1\frac{1}{2}$ pounds of almonds and $2\frac{1}{2}$ pounds of cashews?

Almonds $9.99/lb

Cashews $12.99/lb

Evaluate the expression for the given values.

Total cost of almonds

Total cost of cashews

9.99d + 12.99c

$= 9.99\left(1\frac{1}{2}\right) + 12.99\left(2\frac{1}{2}\right)$

$= 14.985 + 32.475$

$= 47.46$

It costs $47.46 to buy $1\frac{1}{2}$ pounds of almonds and $2\frac{1}{2}$ pounds of cashews.

Try It!

The cost to rent a scooter is $15.50 per hour and the cost to rent a watercraft is $22.80 per hour. Use the expression 15.5s + 22.8w to determine how much it would cost to rent a scooter for $3\frac{1}{2}$ hours and a watercraft for $1\frac{3}{4}$ hours.

EXAMPLE 3 Write and Evaluate Expressions

Malik and two friends earn m dollars in one week doing odd jobs. They split the earnings so that each friend gets $\frac{1}{3}$ of the total earnings. Malik uses $32.50 of his earnings on lunch each week. Last week, the three friends earned $963. How much money did Malik have left after paying for lunch?

Write an expression to represent how much Malik has left. Then evaluate the expression for the given value.

$\frac{1}{3}m - 32.5$

$= \frac{1}{3}(963) - 32.5$

$= 288.5$

Malik had $288.50 left after paying for lunch.

Try It!

Emelia earns $8.74 per hour plus a gas allowance of $3.50 per day at her job. How much does Emelia's job pay in a day when she works $5\frac{1}{2}$ hours? Write an expression and evaluate for $5\frac{1}{2}$ hours.

KEY CONCEPT

Algebraic expressions can be used to represent problems with unknown or variable values.

Values can be substituted for variables to evaluate the expression.

Do You Understand?

1. **Essential Question** How are algebraic expressions used to represent and solve problems?

2. **Use Structure** How is a constant term different than a variable term for an expression that represents a real-world situation?

3. **Look for Relationships** Explain why you can have different values when evaluating an algebraic expression.

Do You Know How?

4. A tank containing 35 gallons of water is leaking at a rate of $\frac{1}{4}$ gallon per minute. Write an expression to determine the number of gallons left in the tank after m minutes.

5. Write an algebraic expression that Marshall can use to determine the total cost of buying a watermelon that weighs w pounds and some tomatoes that weigh t pounds. How much will it cost to buy a watermelon that weighs $18\frac{1}{2}$ pounds and 5 pounds of tomatoes?

    Watermelons $0.68 per lb
    Tomatoes $3.25 per lb

6. What is the value of $\frac{3}{8}x - 4.5$ when $x = 0.4$?

7. What is the value of $8.4n - 3.2p$ when $n = 2$ and $p = 4$?

Practice & Problem Solving

Leveled Practice For 8–10, fill in the boxes to complete the problems.

8. Evaluate $10.2x + 9.4y$ when $x = 2$ and $y = 3$.

   $10.2(\boxed{}) + 9.4(\boxed{})$

   $= \boxed{} + 28.2$

   $= \boxed{}$

9. Evaluate $\frac{1}{2}t + \frac{3}{8}$ when $t = \frac{1}{4}$.

   $\frac{1}{2}(\boxed{}) + \frac{3}{8}$

   $= \boxed{} + \frac{3}{8}$

   $= \boxed{}$

10. Write an expression that represents the height of a tree that began at 6 feet and increases by 2 feet per year. Let y represent the number of years.

    $\boxed{} + \boxed{}\,y$

For 11–14, evaluate each expression for the given value of the variable(s).

11. $3d - 4$

    $d = 1.2$

12. $0.5f - 2.3g$

    $f = 12, g = 2$

13. $\frac{2}{3}p + 3$

    $p = \frac{3}{5}$

14. $34 + \frac{4}{9}w$

    $w = -\frac{1}{2}$

15. **Model with Math** What expression can be used to determine the total cost of buying g pounds of granola for $3.25 per pound and f pounds of flour for $0.74 per pound?

16. **Model with Math** Which expression can be used to determine the total weight of a box that by itself weighs 0.2 kilogram and contains p plaques that weigh 1.3 kilograms each?

    Ⓐ $1.3p + 0.2$

    Ⓑ $0.2p + 1.3$

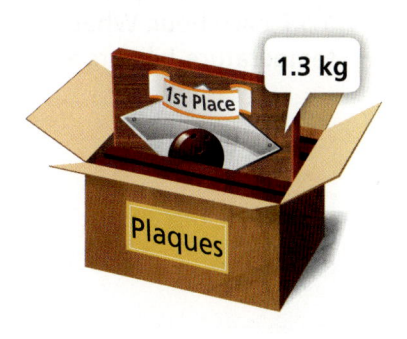

    Ⓒ $0.2 - 1.3p$

    Ⓓ $1.2p$

17. The expression $-120 + 13m$ represents a submarine that began at a depth of 120 feet below sea level and ascended at a rate of 13 feet per minute. What was the depth of the submarine after 6 minutes?

18. **Be Precise** A full grain silo empties at a constant rate. Write an expression to determine the amount of grain left after s seconds.

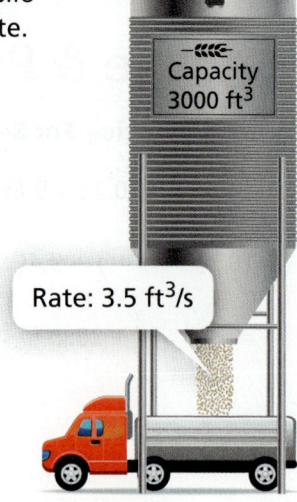

Capacity 3000 ft³

Rate: 3.5 ft³/s

19. **Higher Order Thinking** For the expression $5 - 5x$ to have a negative value, what must be true about the value of x?

Assessment Practice

20. Joe bought g gallons of gasoline for $2.85 per gallon and c cans of oil for $3.15 per can.

    PART A
    What expression can be used to determine the total amount Joe spent on gasoline and oil?

    PART B
    If he bought 8.4 gallons of gasoline and 6 cans of oil, how much will he have spent in all?

21. The outside temperature was 73°F at 1 P.M. and decreases at a rate of 1.5°F each hour. What expression can be used to determine the temperature h hours after 1 P.M.?

Explore It!

A shipment of eggs contains some cartons with a dozen eggs and some cartons with a half-dozen eggs.

Lesson 4-2
Generate Equivalent Expressions

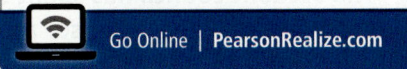

Go Online | PearsonRealize.com

I can...
write equivalent expressions for given expressions.

A. How can you represent the total number of eggs in the shipment using diagrams or images? Explain your diagram.

B. How can you represent the total number of eggs in the shipment using expressions? What variables do you use? What do they represent?

Focus on math practices

Construct Arguments How do the two representations compare? How are they different?

195

? Essential Question What are equivalent expressions?

EXAMPLE 1 — Use Properties of Operations to Write Equivalent Expressions

The student council has spent $300 on the supplies needed to sponsor a dance concert fundraiser. Three council members wrote the following expressions to represent the total amount raised for t tickets sold. Can they all be correct? Explain.

$6t - 300$ $6(t - 50)$ $-300 + 6t$

Reasoning How can you use the properties of operations to determine whether the expressions are equivalent?

STEP 1 Verify that one of the expressions represents the amount raised for t tickets sold.

$6t - 300$
- $6t$ — The amount made selling tickets
- 300 — The cost of supplies

STEP 2 Use properties of operations to write equivalent expressions.

$6(t - 50)$
$= 6 \cdot t - 6 \cdot 50$ Use the Distributive Property.
$= 6t - 300$

$-300 + 6t$
$= 6t + (-300)$ Use the Commutative Property.
$= 6t - 300$

The council members wrote equivalent expressions. They are all correct.

✓ Try It!

Nancy wrote the expression $3x - 12$ to represent the relationship in a table of values. Use properties of operations to write two equivalent expressions.

$3(x - \boxed{})$

$\boxed{} + 3x$

Convince Me! What property can you use to write an equivalent expression for $-5(x - 2)$? Explain.

196   4-2 Generate Equivalent Expressions

EXAMPLE 2: Write Equivalent Expressions by Combining Like Terms

Write equivalent expressions by combining like terms.

a. $-5x + 2y + 3x$

$-5x + 3x + 2y$ — Use the Commutative Property.

$(-5 + 3)x + 2y$ — Use the Distributive Property.

$-2x + 2y$

b. $\frac{1}{3}x + \left(\frac{1}{6}x + y\right)$

$\left(\frac{1}{3}x + \frac{1}{6}x\right) + y$ — Use the Associative Property.

$\frac{3}{6}x + y$

Look for Relationships
How can you check whether the expressions are equivalent?

Try It!

Use properties of operations to write two expressions that are equivalent to $\frac{3}{4}n + \left(8 + \frac{1}{3}z\right)$.

EXAMPLE 3: Identify Equivalent Expressions

Which of the expressions below are equivalent to $-\frac{2}{3}x - 2$?

$-\frac{2}{3}x + (-2)$

$= -\frac{2}{3}x - 2$ — Subtract the additive inverse.

The expression is equivalent to $-\frac{2}{3}x - 2$.

$2 - \frac{2}{3}x$

$= -\frac{2}{3}x + 2$ — Use the Commutative Property.

The expression is NOT equivalent to $-\frac{2}{3}x - 2$.

$-x + \left(\frac{1}{3}x + (-2)\right)$

$\left(-x + \frac{1}{3}x\right) + (-2)$ — Use the Associative Property.

$-\frac{2}{3}x + (-2)$

The expression is equivalent to $-\frac{2}{3}x - 2$.

Try It!

Write two expressions that are equivalent to $-\frac{5}{4}x - \frac{3}{4}$.

4-2 Generate Equivalent Expressions

KEY CONCEPT

You can use properties of operations to write equivalent expressions.

$$-\frac{1}{2}(x + 8)$$

$$= -\frac{1}{2}x + \left(-\frac{1}{2}\right) \cdot 8 \quad \text{← Use the Distributive Property.}$$

$$= -\frac{1}{2}x + (-4)$$

$$= -4 + \left(-\frac{1}{2}x\right) \quad \text{← Use the Commutative Property.}$$

The expressions $-\frac{1}{2}(x + 8)$, $-\frac{1}{2}x + (-4)$, and $-4 + \left(-\frac{1}{2}x\right)$ are equivalent.

Do You Understand?

1. **? Essential Question** What are equivalent expressions?

2. **Make Sense and Persevere** For which operations is the Commutative Property true?

3. How can the Associative Property be applied when writing equivalent expressions with variables?

Do You Know How?

4. Write an expression equivalent to $-3 + \frac{2}{3}y - 4 - \frac{1}{3}y$.

5. Complete the tables to determine if the expressions are equivalent. If the expressions are equivalent, name the property or properties that make them equivalent.

$3(x - 5)$

x	Value of Expression
1	
2	
3	

$3x - 15$

x	Value of Expression
1	
2	
3	

6. Use the properties of operations to write an expression equivalent to $4x + \frac{1}{2} + 2x - 3$.

Practice & Problem Solving

For 7–9, write an equivalent expression.

7. $-3(7 + 5g)$

8. $(x + 7) + 3y$

9. $\frac{2}{9} - \frac{1}{5} \cdot x$

10. Which expression is equivalent to $t + 4 + 3 - 2t$?

    Ⓐ $t + 7$

    Ⓑ $-t + 7$

    Ⓒ $6t$

    Ⓓ $10t$

11. The distance in feet that Karina swims in a race is represented by $4d - 4$, where d is the distance for each lap. What is an expression equivalent to $4d - 4$?

12. Use the Associative Property to write an expression equivalent to $(w + 9) + 3$.

13. Nigel is planning his training schedule for a marathon over a 4-day period. He is uncertain how many miles he will run on two days. One expression for the total miles he will run is $12 + y + 17 + z$.

    Use the Commutative Property to write an equivalent expression.

    Marathon Training Plan

Day	Miles to Run
1	12
2	y
3	17
4	z

4-2 Generate Equivalent Expressions

14. Maria said the expression $-4n + 3 + 9n - 4$ is equivalent to $4n$. What error did Maria likely make?

15. Write an expression equivalent to $x - 3y + 4$.

16. Andre wrote the expression $-2 + 4x \div 3$ to represent the relationship shown in the table.

Write two other expressions that also represent the relationship shown in the table.

x	Value of Expression
0	−2
6	6
12	14

17. Higher Order Thinking To rent a car for a trip, four friends are combining their money. The group chat shows the amount of money that each puts in. One expression for their total amount of money is 189 plus p plus 224 plus q.

a. Use the Commutative Property to write two equivalent expressions.

b. If they need $500 to rent a car, find at least two different pairs of numbers that p and q could be.

☑ Assessment Practice

18. Which expressions are equivalent to $\frac{3}{5}x + 3$? Select all that apply.

☐ $\frac{2}{5}x + 3\frac{1}{5}x$

☐ $\frac{4}{5}x - \frac{1}{5}x + 3$

☐ $\frac{2}{5}x + 3\frac{3}{5}x - 1$

☐ $1 + \frac{3}{5}x + 2$

☐ $1 + \frac{x}{5} + 2$

☐ $1 + \frac{2}{5}x + 3$

200 4-2 Generate Equivalent Expressions

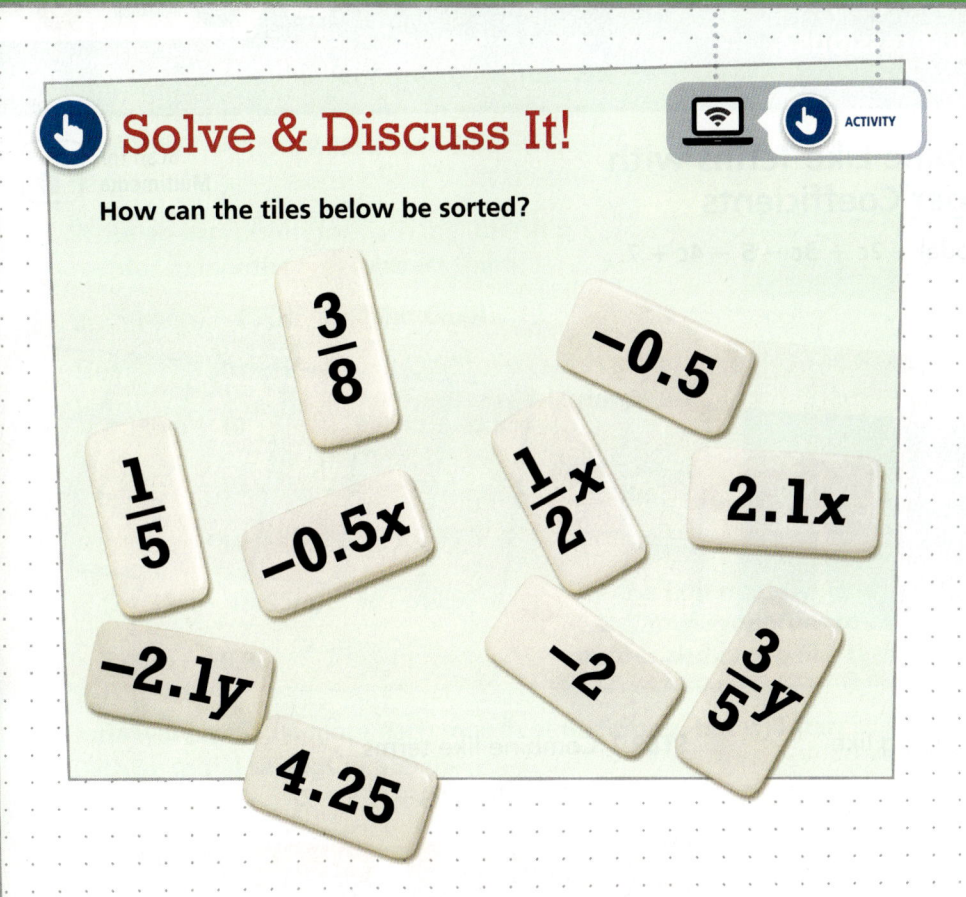

Lesson 4-3
Simplify Expressions

Go Online | PearsonRealize.com

I can... use properties of operations to simplify expressions.

Solve & Discuss It!

How can the tiles below be sorted?

$\frac{3}{8}$ -0.5 $\frac{1}{5}$ $-0.5x$ $\frac{1}{2}x$ $2.1x$ $-2.1y$ -2 $\frac{3}{5}y$ 4.25

Focus on math practices

Reasoning Would sorting the tiles with positive coefficients together and tiles with negative coefficients together help to simplify an expression that involves all the tiles? Explain.

201

Essential Question How are properties of operations used to simplify expressions?

EXAMPLE 1 — Combine Like Terms with Integer Coefficients

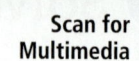

A teacher used algebra tiles to model $-2c + 3c - 5 - 4c + 7$.

Simplify the expression.

STEP 1 Write the expression by grouping like terms together.

Use the Commutative and Associative Properties to reorder and group like terms.

$-2c + 3c - 5 - 4c + 7$

$= -2c + 3c - 4c - 5 + 7$

$= -2c - 4c + 3c - 5 + 7$

$= (-2c - 4c + 3c) + (-5 + 7)$

STEP 2 Combine like terms.

$(-2c - 4c + 3c) + (-5 + 7)$

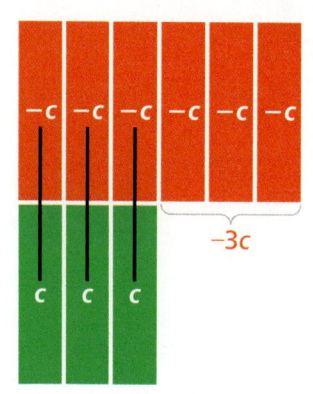

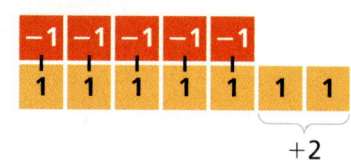

Use Structure Why can you not combine unlike terms?

The simplified expression is $-3c + 2$.

Try It!

Simplify the expression $-6 - 6f + 7 - 3f - 9$.

☐ $- 3f -$ ☐ $+ 7 -$ ☐

☐ $-$ ☐

Convince Me! How do you decide in what way to reorder the terms of an expression when simplifying it?

4-3 Simplify Expressions

EXAMPLE 2 — Combine Like Terms with Rational Coefficients

Simplify the expression $-3 + \frac{1}{3}x + (-4.5) - \frac{1}{5}x$.

$-3 + \frac{1}{3}x + (-4.5) - \frac{1}{5}x$

$= \left(\frac{1}{3}x - \frac{1}{5}x\right) + (-3 + (-4.5))$ *Use the Commutative and Associative Properties to reorder and group like terms.*

$= \left(\frac{5}{15}x - \frac{3}{15}x\right) + (-3 + (-4.5))$

$= \frac{2}{15}x + (-7.5)$ *Combine like terms.*

The simplified expression is $\frac{2}{15}x - 7.5$.

Use Structure Include the signs of terms when reordering the terms.

Try It!

Simplify each expression.

a. $59.95m - 30 + 7.95m + 45 + 9.49m$

b. $-0.5p + \frac{1}{2}p - 2.75 + \frac{2}{3}p$

EXAMPLE 3 — Combine Like Terms with Two Variables

Simplify the expression $4a - 5b - 6 + 2b - 3a$.

$4a - 5b - 6 + 2b - 3a$

$= (4a - 3a) + (-5b + 2b) - 6$ *Use the Commutative and Associative Properties to reorder and group like terms.*

$= 1a - 3b - 6$

The simplified expression is $a - 3b - 6$.

Try It!

Simplify the expression $-3.7 + 5g + 4k + 11.1 - 10g$.

($\boxed{}$ $- 10g) + 4k + ($ $\boxed{}$ $+ 11.1)$

$= \boxed{} + 4k + \boxed{}$

The simplified expression is $\boxed{}$.

Go Online | PearsonRealize.com

4-3 Simplify Expressions

KEY CONCEPT

When simplifying algebraic expressions, use properties of operations to combine like terms.

To simplify the expression below, group like terms.

$$\frac{3}{10}y - 3.5x - \frac{3}{8} + 0.53x + 5.25 - 2.75y - 12$$

$$(-3.5x + 0.53x) + \left(\frac{3}{10}y - 2.75y\right) + \left(-\frac{3}{8} + 5.25 - 12\right)$$

Then combine like terms.

$$-2.97x - 2.45y - 7.125$$

Do You Understand?

1. **Essential Question** How are properties of operations used to simplify expressions?

2. **Make Sense and Persevere** Explain why constant terms expressed as different rational number types can be combined.

3. **Reasoning** How do you know when an expression is in its simplest form?

Do You Know How?

4. Simplify $-4b + (-9k) - 6 - 3b + 12$.

5. Simplify $-2 + 6.45z - 6 + (-3.25z)$.

6. Simplify $-9 + \left(-\frac{1}{3}y\right) + 6 - \frac{4}{3}y$.

4-3 Simplify Expressions

Practice & Problem Solving

In 7–10, simplify each expression.

7. $-2.8f + 0.9f - 12 - 4$

8. $3.2 - 5.1n - 3n + 5$

9. $2n + 5.5 - 0.9n - 8 + 4.5p$

10. $12 + (-4) - \frac{2}{5}j - \frac{4}{5}j + 5$

11. Which expression is equivalent to $-5v + (-2) + 1 + (-2v)$?

Ⓐ $-9v$
Ⓑ $-4v$
Ⓒ $-7v - 1$
Ⓓ $-7v + 3$

12. Which expression is equivalent to $\frac{2}{3}x + (-3) + (-2) - \frac{1}{3}x$?

Ⓐ $x + 5$
Ⓑ $-\frac{1}{3}x - 5$
Ⓒ $\frac{1}{3}x - 1$
Ⓓ $\frac{1}{3}x - 5$

13. The dimensions of a garden are shown. Write an expression to find the perimeter.

$\frac{1}{2}x - 7$

x

14. Simplify the expression $8h + (-7.3d) - 14 + 5d - 3.2h$.

4-3 Simplify Expressions

15. Simplify $4 - 2y + (-8y) + 6.2$.

16. Simplify $\frac{4}{9}z - \frac{3}{9}z + 5 - \frac{5}{9}z - 8$.

17. Construct Arguments Explain whether $11t - 4t$ is equivalent to $4t - 11t$. Support your answer by evaluating the expression for $t = 2$.

18. The signs show the costs of different games at a math festival. How much would it cost n people to play Decimal Decisions and Ratio Rage?

MATHFEST

PROBABILITY POSSIBILITIES
Cost ($) of 1 Game: $5.5n - 3$

DECIMAL DECISIONS
Cost ($) of 1 Game: $12.70 - n + 9$

RATIO RAGE!
Cost ($) of 1 Game: $\frac{n}{4}$

19. Higher Order Thinking In the expression $ax + bx$, a is a decimal and b is a fraction. How do you decide whether to write a as a fraction or b as a decimal?

Assessment Practice

20. Which expressions are equivalent to $-6z + (-5.5) + 3.5z + 5y - 2.5$? Select all that apply.

☐ $-8 + 5y + 2.5z$

☐ $-2.5z + 5y - 8$

☐ $-8 + 5y + (-2.5z)$

☐ $2.5y + (-2.5z) - 5.5$

☐ $5y - 8 - 2.5z$

206 4-3 Simplify Expressions

Lesson 4-4
Expand Expressions

Go Online | PearsonRealize.com

I can... expand expressions using the Distributive Property.

Solve & Discuss It!

The school is planning to add a weight room to the gym. If the total area of the gym and weight room should stay under 5,500 square feet, what is one possible length for the new weight room? Show your work. Are there other lengths that would work? Why or why not?

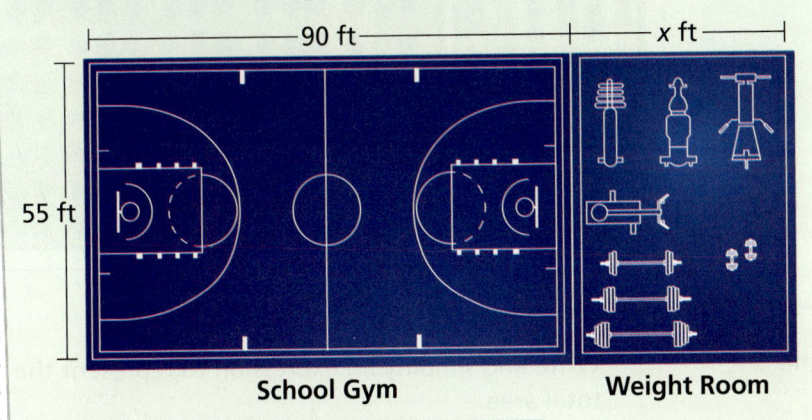

- School Gym: 90 ft by 55 ft
- Weight Room: x ft by 55 ft

Look for Relationships What is the relationship between the areas of the gym and weight room?

Focus on math practices

Model with Math What is an expression using x that represents the total area of the gym and the weight room?

Essential Question How does the value of an expression change when it is expanded?

EXAMPLE 1 — Expand Expressions Using the Distributive Property

A family farm plans to add a blueberry patch to the end of their apple orchard. What is the total area of land that will be covered by the blueberry patch and apple orchard?

Model with Math An area model can be used to represent the Distributive Property.

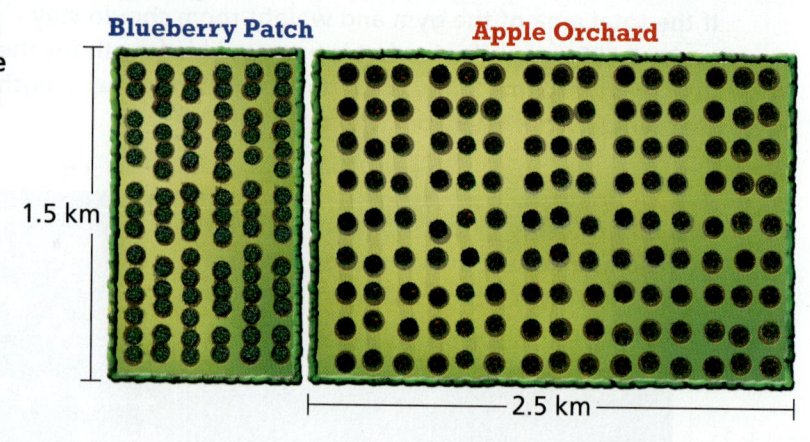

Blueberry Patch — 1.5 km
Apple Orchard — 2.5 km

Use a diagram to represent the areas of the blueberry patch and apple orchard.

You can add the two lengths and multiply by the width to find the total area.

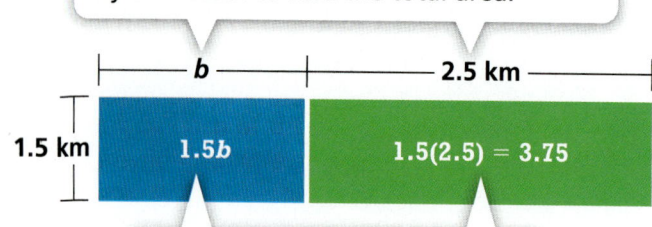

- b | 2.5 km
- 1.5 km | 1.5b | 1.5(2.5) = 3.75

You can also add the two areas to find the total area.

Write and simplify an expression to represent the total area.

$1.5(b + 2.5)$

$= 1.5b + 1.5(2.5)$

$= 1.5b + 3.75$

Use the Distributive Property to expand the expression. Multiply each term inside the parentheses by 1.5.

The expression that represents the total land area is $1.5b + 3.75$.

Try It!

What is the expanded form of the expression $3.6(t + 5)$?

$3.6(t + 5)$

$= \boxed{}\, t + \boxed{} \cdot 5$

$= \boxed{} + \boxed{}$

The expanded expression is $\boxed{}$.

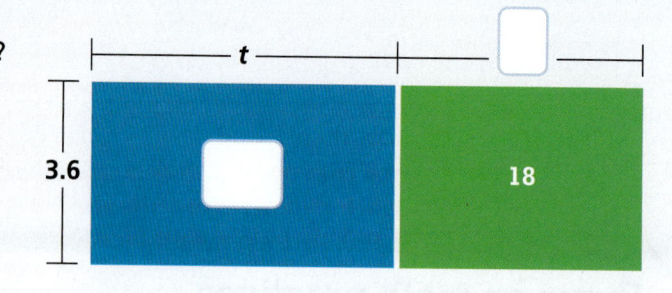

Diagram: width 3.6; lengths t and □; areas (blue) and 18 (green).

Convince Me! If you know the value of t, would the evaluated expression be different if you added the known value of t and 5 and then multiplied by 3.6? Explain.

208   4-4 Expand Expressions

EXAMPLE 2 — Expand Expressions with a Variable

Use the Distributive Property to expand the expression $x(-2 - 0.5y)$.

$x(-2 - 0.5y)$

$= (x)(-2) + (x)(-0.5y)$ — Distribute the x to both terms inside the parentheses.

$= -2x + (-0.5xy)$

$= -2x - 0.5xy$

The expanded expression is $-2x - 0.5xy$.

Try It!

Expand the expression $t(-1.2w + 3)$.

EXAMPLE 3 — Expand More Complex Expressions

Simplify the expression $-\frac{1}{3}(2 - 3x + 3)$.

ONE WAY Use the Distributive Property first to distribute the coefficient $-\frac{1}{3}$.

$-\frac{1}{3}(2 - 3x + 3)$

$= (-\frac{1}{3} \cdot 2) + (-\frac{1}{3} \cdot -3x) + (-\frac{1}{3} \cdot 3)$

$= -\frac{2}{3} + x - 1$

$= -\frac{5}{3} + x$

The simplified expression is $-\frac{5}{3} + x$.

ANOTHER WAY Simplify within parentheses first. Then distribute the coefficient $-\frac{1}{3}$.

$-\frac{1}{3}(2 - 3x + 3)$

$= -\frac{1}{3}(5 - 3x)$

$= (-\frac{1}{3} \cdot 5) + (-\frac{1}{3} \cdot -3x)$

$= -\frac{5}{3} + x$

The simplified expression is $-\frac{5}{3} + x$.

Try It!

Simplify the expression $-\frac{2}{5}(10 + 15m - 20n)$.

4-4 Expand Expressions

17. Find a difference equivalent to the product 11(x − y).

18. Use the Distributive Property to write an expression equivalent to 0.4(−5 − 7y − 13.8).

19. **Make Sense and Persevere** Use the Distributive Property to expand 7(7x − 3y) − 6.

20. Use the Distributive Property to write an expression equivalent to y(−3 − 8x).

21. An architect plans to build an extension to Meiling's rectangular deck. Let x represent the increase, in meters, of her deck's length. The expression 5(x + 8) represents the area of the deck, where 5 is the width, in meters, and (x + 8) represents the extended length, in meters. Use the Distributive Property to write an expression that represents the total area of Meiling's new deck.

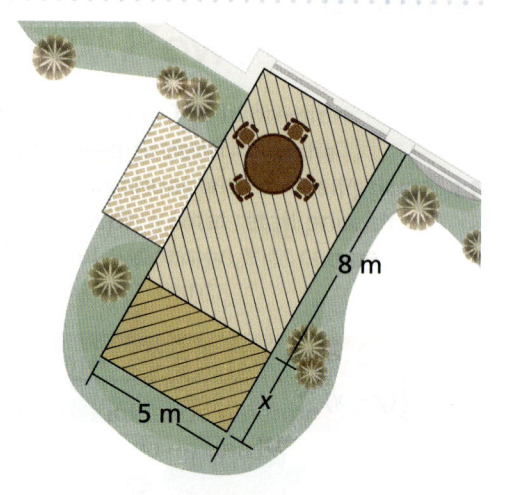

Assessment Practice

22. Which expressions are equivalent to $-\frac{1}{2}(4 - 2 + 8x)$? Select all that apply.
    ☐ −4x − 1
    ☐ 4x − 1
    ☐ 3x
    ☐ −2 + 1 − 4x
    ☐ 2 + 1 − 4x
    ☐ 4x + 1

23. Which expression is equivalent to $\frac{1}{5}(5 - 7y + 10)$?
    Ⓐ $3 - \frac{7}{5}y$
    Ⓑ $3 + \frac{7}{5}y$
    Ⓒ $\frac{22}{5}y$
    Ⓓ $-\frac{22}{5}y$

Lesson 4-5
Factor Expressions

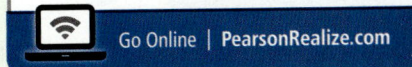

Go Online | PearsonRealize.com

Explain It!

Tasha is packing gift bags that include the same items. She has 72 glow sticks, 36 markers, and 24 bottles of bubbles. Tasha believes that she can pack no more than 6 bags using all of her supplies.

I can... use common factors and the Distributive Property to factor expressions.

Make Sense and Persevere
How can you use what you know about common factors to solve the problem?

A. **Critique Reasoning** Do you agree with Tasha? Explain.

B. If Tasha creates the greatest number of gift bags, how many of each item is in each bag? Explain how you know.

Focus on math practices

Reasoning Tasha added more markers and now has a total of 48 markers. Does this change the possible number of gift bags? Explain.

Essential Question How does the Distributive Property relate to factoring expressions?

EXAMPLE 1 Factor Expressions

Kiana painted a rectangular wall blue to start an ocean mural. She used 3 cans of paint, each of which covered x square meters, and a different-sized can that covered 12 square meters. What are possible length and height dimensions of Kiana's mural?

Model with Math The expression $3x + 12$ represents the area of the mural.

Each can covers x square meters.

covers 12 square meters.

ONE WAY Use an area model to represent the area of the mural, $3x + 12$.

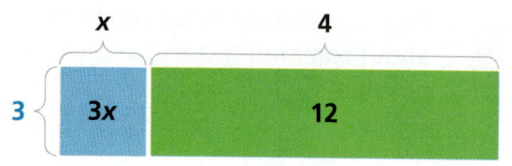

	x	4
3	3x	12

So, one possible set of dimensions of the mural could be $x + 4$ meters long and 3 meters tall.

ANOTHER WAY Use a common factor and the Distributive Property to factor the expression $3x + 12$.

$3x + 12$

$3x + (3 \cdot 4)$ — The GCF of $3x$ and 12 is 3.

$3(x + 4)$ — This represents the area of the mural as a product of two factors.

So, one possible set of dimensions of the mural could be 3 meters long and $x + 4$ meters tall.

✓ Try It!

Use factoring to write an expression for the length of the pool with the given width.

$4x + 20 = \boxed{}(x + \boxed{})$

So, the length of the pool is $\boxed{}$ meters.

? meters

4 meters { 4x | 20

Convince Me! How can you use the Distributive Property to check the factored expression? Use the factored expression for Example 1 in your explanation.

214 4-5 Factor Expressions

EXAMPLE 2 — Factor Expressions with Negative Coefficients

Rodrigo and Jordan each factor the expression $-2x - 6$. Who factored the expression correctly?

Rodrigo uses a positive common factor, 2, to factor the expression.

2 is a common factor of $-2x$ and -6.

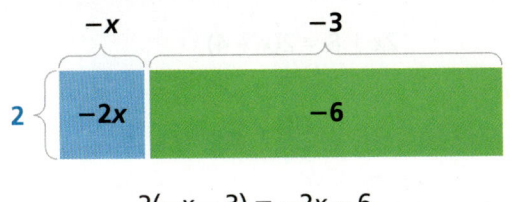

$2(-x - 3) = -2x - 6$

Jordan uses a negative common factor, -2, to factor the expression.

-2 is a common factor of $-2x$ and -6.

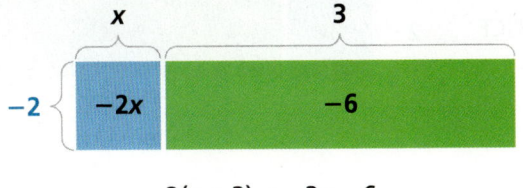

$-2(x + 3) = -2x - 6$

$2(-x - 3)$ and $-2(x + 3)$ are equivalent expressions. So, both Rodrigo and Jordan are correct.

Try It!

Show two different ways to factor $-4x - 28$.

EXAMPLE 3 — Factor Three-Term Expressions

Use the GCF to factor the expression $6x - 18 - 12y$.

STEP 1 Find the GCF of $6x$, -18, and $-12y$.

Factors of 6: 1, 2, 3, **6**

Factors of 18: 1, 2, 3, **6**, 9, 18

Factors of 12: 1, 2, 3, 4, **6**, 12

The GCF is 6.

STEP 2 Use the GCF and the Distributive Property to factor the expression.

$6x - 18 - 12y$

$= (6)(x) - (6)(3) - (6)(2y)$

$= 6(x - 3 - 2y)$

The factored expression of $6x - 18 - 12y$ is $6(x - 3 - 2y)$.

Try It!

Write an equivalent expression for the expression above using a negative factor.

4-5 Factor Expressions

KEY CONCEPT

The greatest common factor (GCF) can be used to factor expressions.

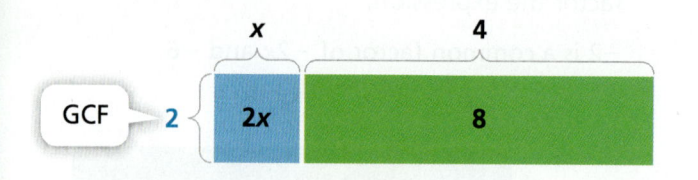

The Distributive Property can be applied to factor an expression. Factoring an expression creates an equivalent expression.

$$2x + 8 = 2(x + 4)$$

Do You Understand?

1. **Essential Question** How does the Distributive Property relate to factoring expressions?

2. Susan incorrectly factored the expression below.

   $$12a - 15b + 6$$
   $$3(4a + 5b + 3)$$

   a. Explain any errors Susan may have made when factoring.

   b. Factor the expression correctly.

Do You Know How?

3. Sahil is putting together supply kits and has 36 packs of x pencils, 12 packs of y crayons, and 24 erasers.

   a. Write an expression to show the total number of items.

   b. Use factoring to show many kits Sahil can make while putting every type of item in each kit.

   c. Use the factored expression to find the number of each item in each kit.

4. Show two different ways to factor $-12x + 24 - 18y$.

5. How can you use the Distributive Property to factor the expression $6x + 15$?

4-5 Factor Expressions

Practice & Problem Solving

Leveled Practice In 6–9, factor the expression.

6. $16a + 10$.

The GCF of $16a$ and 10 is 2.

$2 \times \boxed{} = 16a$ $2 \times \boxed{} = 10$

The factored expression is $\boxed{}$.

7. $-9y - 3$.

The positive GCF of $-9y$ and -3 is 3.

$3 \times \boxed{} = -9y$ $3 \times \boxed{} = -3$

The factored expression is $\boxed{}$.

8. $14x + 49$

9. $12y - 16$

10. This model shows the area of a garden. Write two expressions that represent the area.

| x | x | x | x | x | 1 | 1 | 1 | 1 | 1 | 1 | 1 | 1 | 1 | 1 |

11. Use the GCF to write the factored form of the expression $18x + 24y$.

12. Find the dimensions of the sports field at the right if the width is at least 60 yards.

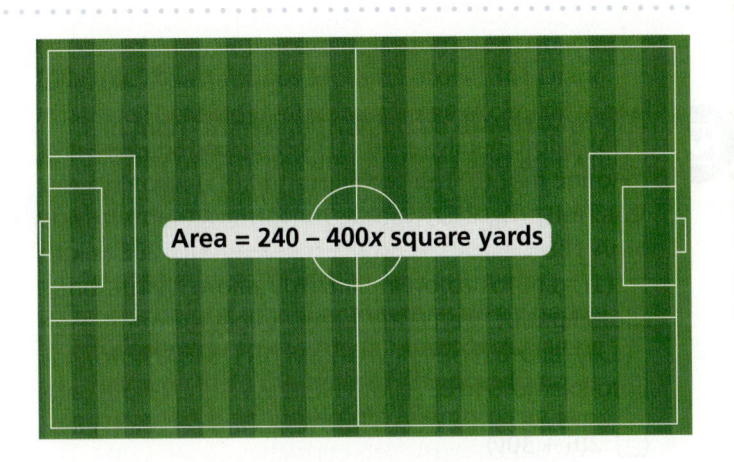

Area = $240 - 400x$ square yards

13. Your friend incorrectly factors the expression $15x - 20xy$ as $5x(3 - 4xy)$.

a. Factor the expression correctly.

b. What error did your friend likely make?

14. You are given the expression $12x + 18y + 26$.

a. **Make Sense and Persevere** What is the first step in factoring the expression?

b. Factor the expression.

4-5 Factor Expressions   217

15. **Higher Order Thinking** A hotel manager is adding a tile border around the hotel's rectangular pool. Let x represent the width of the pool, in feet. The length is 3 more than 2 times the width, as shown. Write two expressions that give the perimeter of the pool.

16. Use the expressions below.

    $14m + mn$ $2y + 2x + 4$

    $-\frac{3}{4}m + 8m + m$ $4 - 3p$

    $5.75t + 7.75t - t$ $8xy - 6xy$

    a. Circle the expressions that have like terms.

    b. Explain why the other expressions do not have like terms.

17. **Construct Arguments** Ryan says the expression $3 + 5y$ cannot be factored using a GCF. Is he correct? Explain why or why not.

Assessment Practice

18. Which of the following expressions is equivalent to $12 + 30y$? Select all that apply.
    - ☐ $3(4 + 10y)$
    - ☐ $4(3 + 10y)$
    - ☐ $6(2 + 5y)$
    - ☐ $2(6 + 30y)$
    - ☐ $6(3 + 10y)$

19. Write an expression that is the product of two factors and is equivalent to $-2x - 10$.

4-5 Factor Expressions

Name: _____

MID-TOPIC CHECKPOINT

TOPIC 4

1. **Vocabulary** If you write an expression to represent the following situation, how can you determine which is the constant and which is the coefficient of the variable? *Lesson 4-1*

   The zoo charges the Garcia family an admission fee of $5 per person and a one-time fee of $3 to rent a wagon for their young children.

2. An online photo service charges $20 to make a photo book with 16 pages. Each extra page costs $1.75. The cost to ship the completed photo book is $5. Write an expression to determine the total cost in dollars to make and ship a photo book with *x* extra pages. *Lesson 4-1*

3. Write an expression equivalent to $2a + (8a + 5b)$ by combining like terms. *Lesson 4-2*

4. Which expression is equivalent to $3y - 8 + (-7y) + 9$? *Lesson 4-3*

   Ⓐ $-10y + 1$ Ⓑ $-4y + 1$ Ⓒ $-9y$ Ⓓ $-3y$

5. Ray wants to buy a hat that costs $10 and some shirts that cost $12 each. The sales tax rate is 6.5%. The expression $0.065(10 + 12s)$ can be used to determine the amount of sales tax that Ray will pay on his entire purchase. Expand the expression. *Lesson 4-4*

6. Factor the expression $28r + 42s - 35$. *Lesson 4-5*

7. How can the Distributive Property be used to write equivalent expressions? *Lessons 4-4 and 4-5*

How well did you do on the mid-topic checkpoint? Fill in the stars.

TOPIC 4: MID-TOPIC PERFORMANCE TASK

Alison is a buyer for a chain of 6 flower shops. This means that she buys flowers in bulk from a supplier and then distributes them to the 6 flower shops in the chain.

PART A

This week Alison bought 108 bunches of carnations and 96 bunches of roses from the supplier. Let c represent the number of carnations in each bunch, and let r represent the number of roses in each bunch. Write an expression to show the total number of carnations and roses that Alison bought.

PART B

Alison wants to distribute the carnations and roses equally among the 6 flower shops. Factor the expression from Part A using 6 as the common factor. How does the factored expression help Alison determine how many carnations and how many roses each flower shop should get?

PART C

There are 24 carnations in each bunch and 12 roses in each bunch. Use your answer to Part B to determine the total number of carnations and the total number of roses Alison will distribute to each flower shop this week.

PART D

Jake manages one of the flower shops. He wants to use the carnations and roses to make bouquets. He wants each bouquet to have the same combination of carnations and roses, with no flowers left over. Determine a way that Jake can divide the flowers to make the bouquets. How many bouquets will there be?

3-ACT MATH

3-Act Mathematical Modeling: I've Got You Covered

Go Online | PearsonRealize.com

ACT 1

1. After watching the video, what is the first question that comes to mind?

2. Write the Main Question you will answer.

3. **Construct Arguments** Predict an answer to this Main Question. Explain your prediction.

4. On the number line below, write a number that is too small to be the answer. Write a number that is too large.

   Too small ←——————————————→ Too large

5. Plot your prediction on the same number line.

Topic 4 3-Act Mathematical Modeling 221

ACT 2

6. What information in this situation would be helpful to know? How would you use that information?

7. Use Appropriate Tools What tools can you use to get the information you need? Record the information as you find it.

8. Model with Math Represent the situation using the mathematical content, concepts, and skills from this topic. Use your representation to answer the Main Question.

9. What is your answer to the Main Question? Is it higher or lower than your prediction? Explain why.

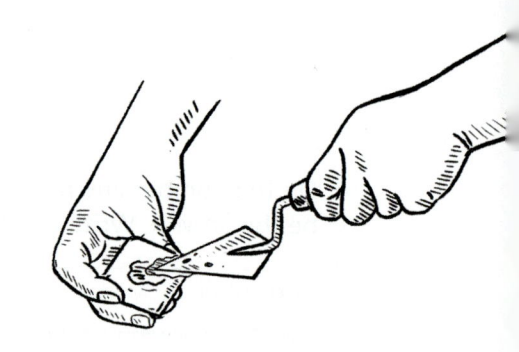

ACT 3

10. Write the answer you saw in the video.

11. Reasoning Does your answer match the answer in the video? If not, what are some reasons that would explain the difference?

12. Make Sense and Persevere Would you change your model now that you know the answer? Explain.

Topic 4 3-Act Mathematical Modeling 223

ACT 3 Extension

Reflect

13. Model with Math Explain how you used a mathematical model to represent the situation. How did the model help you answer the Main Question?

14. Generalize What pattern did you notice in your calculations? How did that pattern help you solve the problem?

SEQUEL

15. Reasoning A classmate says that another object needs 512 tiles. What do you know about the dimensions of the object?

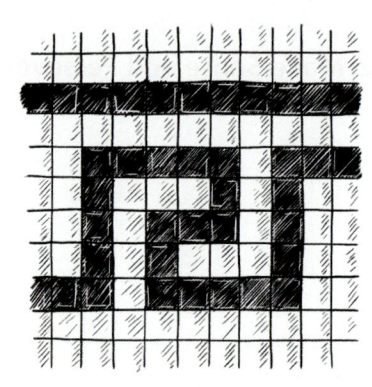

Lesson 4-6
Add Expressions

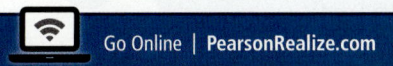

Go Online | PearsonRealize.com

I can... add expressions that represent real-world problems.

Solve & Discuss It!

The Smith family took a 2-day road trip. On the second day, they drove $\frac{3}{4}$ the distance they traveled on the first day. What is a possible distance they could have traveled over the 2 days? Is there more than one possible distance? Justify your response.

Make Sense and Persevere
How are the quantities in the problem related?

Focus on math practices

Use Structure How can two different expressions be used to represent the total distance?

? Essential Question How can properties of operations be used to add expressions?

EXAMPLE 1 Add Expressions by Using Properties

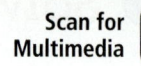

Delilah signs up for a health club and a rock-climbing gym. What expression represents her total fitness cost after m months?

RUDY'S Rock-in' Climbers
$65 Initial Fee
$40 Monthly Fee

ACE Health Club
Initial fee $80
Monthly fee $50

Model with Math Each bill can be represented with an expression.

Use bar diagrams to represent the situation and write an expression for the cost of each club.

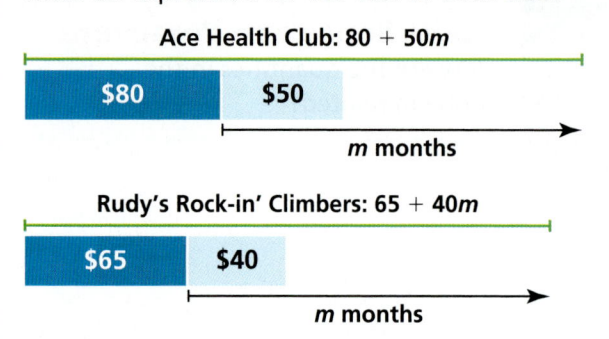

Ace Health Club: $80 + 50m$

| $80 | $50 |

m months

Rudy's Rock-in' Climbers: $65 + 40m$

| $65 | $40 |

m months

Add the expressions to find the combined cost.

$(80 + 50m) + (65 + 40m)$

$= (80 + 65) + (50m + 40m)$ — Use the Commutative and Associative Properties.

$= 145 + 90m$

The expression $145 + 90m$ can be used to determine the total cost for the health club and rock-climbing gym after m months.

✓ Try It!

Sophia and Ollie each deposit $120 to open a joint account. They each make monthly deposits as shown. What expression represents the amount in the account after m months?

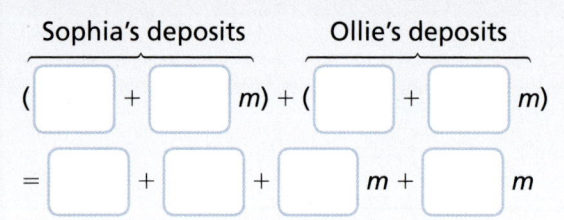

Sophia's deposits   Ollie's deposits
(☐ + ☐ m) + (☐ + ☐ m)

= ☐ + ☐ + ☐ m + ☐ m

Sophia's deposits
| $120 | $150 |
m months

Ollie's deposits
| $120 | $135 |
m months

The amount of money in the joint account after m months is ☐ + ☐ .

Convince Me! Explain why the initial deposits and monthly deposits are not combined into one term?

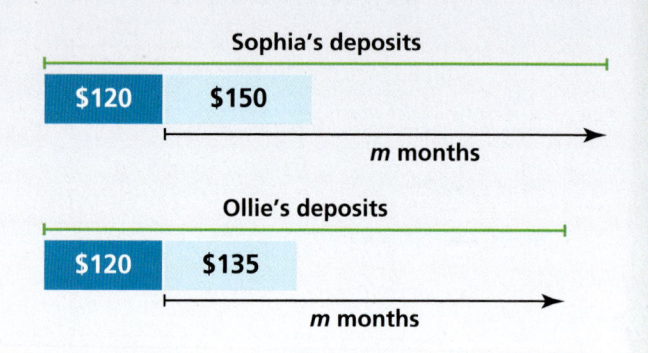

EXAMPLE 2: Add Expressions with More Than One Variable

Cindy spent $125 on ingredients for muffins and $92.40 on ingredients for bagels. Write an expression to represent Cindy's profit for m muffins and b bagels.

muffin income — cost of ingredients
$$2.40m - 125$$

bagel income — cost of ingredients
$$1.80b - 92.40$$

Muffin $2.40
Bagel $1.80

$(2.40m - 125) + (1.80b - 92.40)$
$= 2.40m + 1.80b + (-125 - 92.40)$ — Use the Commutative and Associative Properties.
$= 2.40m + 1.80b - 217.4$

The expression $2.40m + 1.80b - 217.4$ represents the profit from selling the muffins and bagels.

EXAMPLE 3: Add More Complex Expressions

Add the expressions.

$\left(\frac{1}{2}x - 3 - 2y\right) + \left(\frac{1}{4}x - 2y + 5\right)$

$= \left(\frac{1}{2}x + \frac{1}{4}x\right) + (-2y + (-2y)) + (-3 + 5)$ — Use the Commutative and Associative Properties to reorder and group like terms.

$= \frac{3}{4}x \quad + \quad (-4y) \quad + \quad 2$

$= \frac{3}{4}x - 4y + 2$

Try It!

Find each sum.

a. $(9.74c - 250.50) + (-5.48p + 185.70)$

b. $\left(\frac{2}{11}x - 3 - 5y\right) + \left(-\frac{3}{11}x + 5y + 5.5\right)$

c. $(-14.2b - 97.35) + (6.76d - 118.7 - 3.4d)$

d. $\left(\frac{3}{8} - \frac{1}{6}m + 5t\right) + \left(\frac{7}{10}m + 9t + \frac{1}{4}\right)$

KEY CONCEPT

Adding expressions may require combining like terms.

Terms with the same variables are added together and constants are added together.

When adding terms with the same variables, the rules for adding rational numbers apply to their coefficients.

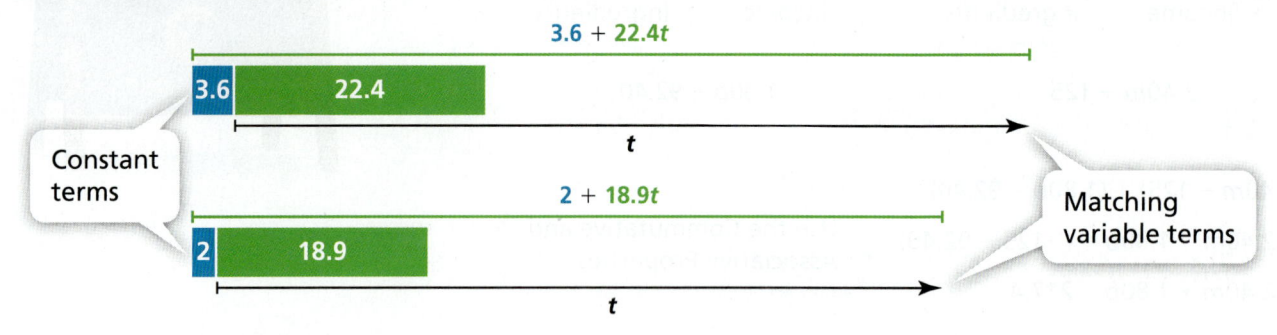

Constant terms: 3.6, 2

Matching variable terms: 22.4t, 18.9t

$(3.6 + 22.4t) + (2 + 18.9t) = 5.6 + 41.3t$

Do You Understand?

1. **Essential Question** How can properties of operations be used to add expressions?

2. **Reasoning** Explain whether the coefficients of two terms with different variables can be added to make one new term.

3. **Be Precise** Which properties of operations could be used to show that $(-5p + 9) + (-2 + p)$ is equivalent to $(-5p) + p + 9 - 2$?

Do You Know How?

4. Dillon says that $4b$ and $-2b$ are not like terms because $4b$ is positive and $-2b$ is negative. Is he correct? Explain.

5. Joel spent $28 for an Internet data service and pays $14.50 per month. He spent $24.50 to join an online movie streaming site and pays $13.25 per month. Write an expression to represent Joel's total cost for both memberships after m months.

6. Add $\frac{1}{3}n + \frac{2}{3}$ and $-\frac{1}{6}n + \frac{1}{6}m$.

7. Find the sum.

$(-3.5t - 4s + 4.5) + (-7.1 - 0.3s + 4.1t)$

228   4-6 Add Expressions

Name: _____

Practice & Problem Solving

Leveled Practice For 8–9, fill in the boxes to add the expressions.

8. $(2a + 8) + (4a + 5)$

   $= (2a + \boxed{}) + (8 + \boxed{})$

   $= \boxed{} + 13$

9. $\left(\dfrac{2}{7}x - 7\right) + \left(\dfrac{1}{7}x + 8\right)$

   $= \left(\boxed{} + \boxed{}\right) + \left(-7 + \boxed{}\right)$

   $= \boxed{}\,x + \boxed{}$

10. Find the sum.
    $(8b + 7) + (6x - 4) + (5c + 8)$

11. Combine like terms.
    $(-3y - 5) + (5m + 7y) + (6 + 9m)$

12. Felipe is going to plant b sunflower seeds in one garden and $5b + 10$ sunflower seeds in another. How many seeds is Felipe going to plant altogether?

13. An art class is making a mural for the school that has a triangle drawn in the middle. The length of the bottom of the triangle is x. Another side is 1 more than three times the length of the bottom of the triangle. The last side is 2 more than the bottom of the triangle. Write and simplify an expression for the perimeter of the triangle.

14. On a math test, Sarah has to identify all the coefficients and constants of the expression $4 + n + 7m$. Sarah identifies the only coefficient as 7 and the only constant as 4.

    a. Identify all the coefficients of the expression.

    b. Identify all the constants of the expression.

    c. What error did Sarah likely make?

Go Online | PearsonRealize.com

4-6 Add Expressions 229

15. The width of a rectangle is 5x − 2.5 feet and the length is 2.5x + 8 feet. Find the perimeter of the rectangle.

16. Nina has x coins. Clayton has 5 fewer coins than six times the number of coins Nina has. Write an expression for the total number of coins Nina and Clayton have altogether. Then simplify the expression.

17. Use the expression (8x + 2) + (−9x + 7).

    a. Find the sum.

    b. **Reasoning** Explain how you know when to combine terms with variables.

18. Gabe goes to the mall. He bought k model planes and spent $24 on books. Then he spent another $25 at another store.

    a. Write an expression that represents the amount Gabe spent at the mall.

    b. How much did Gabe spend in all if he bought 3 model planes?

    Each model plane costs $14.99.

Assessment Practice

19. A middle school with x students ran a survey to determine the students' favorite activities. The table indicates the number of students who enjoy each activity.

    PART A Write an expression in the table for each activity to represent the number of students who enjoy that activity most.

Activity	Dance	Soccer	Baseball
Word Description	25 more than one-tenth of the students	20 fewer than three-tenths of the students	21 more than one-tenth of the students
Expression			

    PART B Write a simplified expression to represent students whose favorite activity is either dance or baseball.

230 4-6 Add Expressions

Explore It!

**Lesson 4-7
Subtract Expressions**

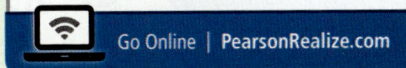

Go Online | PearsonRealize.com

The East Side Bulldogs and the West Side Bears are playing a football game. A fan is keeping score using T for a touchdown plus extra point, worth 7 points total, and F for a field goal, worth 3 points.

I can...
subtract expressions using properties of operations.

	East Side Bulldogs	West Side Bears
1st quarter	TT F	FFF
2nd quarter	TT F	T FF
3rd quarter	T FF	TTT
4th quarter	TT FF	T

A. How can you represent the score of each team using expressions?

B. How can you represent the difference of the teams' scores using an expression?

C. How can you determine how many more points the winning team had than the losing team?

Focus on math practices

Look for Relationships How can looking at the coefficients help you determine which team scored the greater number of points?

Essential Question How can properties of operations be used to subtract expressions?

EXAMPLE 1 — Subtract Expressions by Using Properties

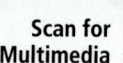

Lita's family wants to put a tiled border around their swimming pool. What expression represents the total area of the border?

Make Sense and Persevere
How can you use subtraction to find the area of the tiled border?

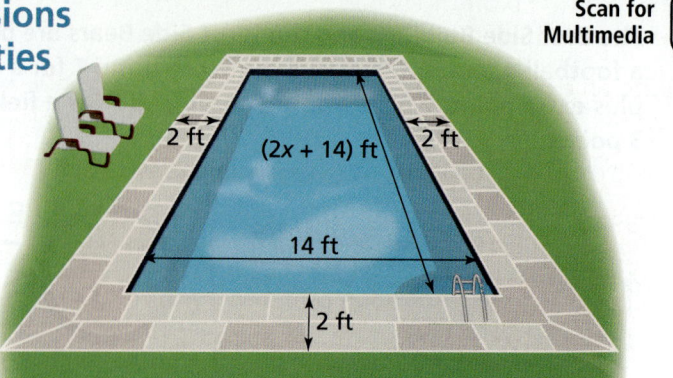

Write an expression for the area of the pool only. Then write an expression for the area of the pool plus the tiled border.

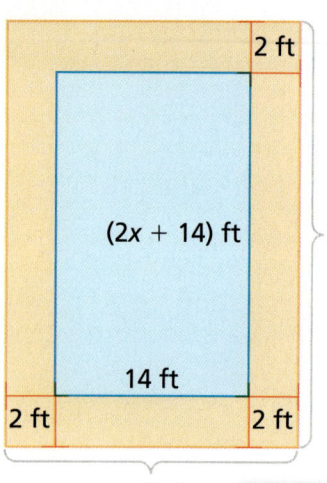

length of tiled border:
$2 + (2x + 14) + 2$
$2x + 18$

width of outer edge of walkway: $2 + 14 + 2$

Area of pool:
width • length
$14 \times (2x + 14)$ ft^2

Area of pool and tiled border:
$18 \times (2x + 18)$ ft^2

Use properties of operations to subtract the expressions.

(area of pool + tiles) − (area of pool)

$= 18(2x + 18) - 14(2x + 14)$ First, use the Distributive Property.
$= 36x + 324 - 28x - 196$
$= 36x - 28x + 324 - 196$
$= 8x + 128$

Then, use the Commutative Property.

The area of the tiled border is $8x + 128$ ft^2.

Try It!

A frame holds a picture that is 15 inches long and x inches wide. The frame border is 3 inches wide around the picture. What expression represents the area of the frame border?

Area of frame border = Area of entire frame − Area of photo = ☐ − ☐

The area of the frame is ☐ in^2.

Convince Me! Why can you choose to add or subtract when subtracting an expression?

232   4-7 Subtract Expressions   Go Online | PearsonRealize.com

EXAMPLE 2 — Subtract Expressions with Rational Coefficients

Jada is comparing membership costs for two gyms. What is the difference in membership costs after m months if she joins Be Strong instead of Zippy Health Club?

Zippy Health Club — $49.95 to join, $19.95/month

BE STRONG — $10 off the first month! $24.99/month

Write an expression for each membership cost for m months and subtract them.

(Be Strong) − (Zippy's Health Club)

$(24.99m - 10) - (19.95m + 49.95)$

$= 24.99m - 10 + (-1)(19.95m + 49.95)$

$= 24.99m - 10 + (-1)(19.95m) + (-1)(49.95)$ ← Use the Distributive Property.

$= 24.99m - 10 - 19.95m - 49.95$

$= (24.99m - 19.95m) - 10 - 49.95$ ← Use the Commutative and Associative Properties to reorder and group like terms.

$= 5.04m - 59.95$

Use Structure How did the signs of the terms in the second expression change after distributing −1?

Jada will pay $5.04 more each month at Be Strong, but will start with an initial savings of $59.95.

Try It!

Subtract $(0.95x - 0.04) - (0.99x - 0.13)$.

EXAMPLE 3 — Subtract More Complex Expressions

Subtract the expressions.

$\left(5j - 2q + \frac{2}{5}\right) - \left(4 - 3j - \frac{1}{2}q\right)$

$= \left(5j - 2q + \frac{2}{5}\right) + \left(-4 + 3j + \frac{1}{2}q\right)$ ← Distribute the minus sign, or −1, to all terms in the second expression.

$= 5j - 2q + \frac{2}{5} - 4 + 3j + \frac{1}{2}q$

$= 5j + 3j - 2q + \frac{1}{2}q + \frac{2}{5} - 4$

$= 8j - 1\frac{1}{2}q - 3\frac{3}{5}$

The simplified expression is $8j - 1\frac{1}{2}q - 3\frac{3}{5}$.

Try It!

Subtract $(17 + 4.5m + 8k) - (7.5m - 9 + 4k)$.

KEY CONCEPT

To subtract expressions, you can use properties of operations.

Write the subtraction as addition and use the Distributive Property to multiply -1 to the terms in the expression being subtracted.

$$5 - (-2x - 7)$$
$$= 5 + (-1)(-2x - 7)$$
$$= 5 + (-1)(-2)x + (-1)(-7)$$
$$= 5 + 2x + 7$$

$$5 - (-2x - 7)$$
$$= 5 + 2x + 7$$

You can use the Distributive Property to distribute the minus sign to the second expression, which changes the signs of the terms.

Do You Understand?

1. **Essential Question** How can properties of operations be used to subtract expressions?

2. **Use Structure** How is subtracting $-4x$ from $9x$ similar to subtracting -4 from 9?

3. Is adding the quantity $-12 + 8r$ to an expression the same as subtracting $-8r + 12$ from the same expression? Explain your reasoning.

Do You Know How?

4. Subtract.
   a. $(21x) - (-16 + 7x)$
   b. $(-13n) - (17 - 5n)$
   c. $(4y - 7) - (y - 7)$
   d. $(-w + 0.4) - (-w - 0.4)$

5. Jude has 5 pairs of sunglasses that cost the same in his online shopping cart, but then decides to get only 2. Each pair of sunglasses is the same price. Let p represent the cost of each pair. Write an expression for the original cost, the updated cost, and the difference in cost.

   Power Shades 3000
   In Stock Online
   Add to Cart
   Buy 3 or more, get shipping for $1.49*
   *Regular shipping: $6.49

6. Subtract and simplify.

   $$\tfrac{1}{6}m - \left(-\tfrac{5}{8}m + \tfrac{1}{3}\right)$$

Practice & Problem Solving

Leveled Practice In 7–9, fill in the missing signs or numbers.

7. Rewrite the expression $14m - (5 + 8m)$ without parentheses.

$14m \bigcirc 5 \bigcirc 8m$

8. Rewrite the expression $13d - (-9d - 4)$ without parentheses.

$13d \bigcirc 9d \bigcirc 4$

9. Write an equivalent expression to $8k - (5 + 2k)$ without parentheses. Then simplify.

$8k - (5 + 2k) = 8k \bigcirc 5 \bigcirc 2k$

$= 8k \bigcirc 2k \bigcirc 5$

$= \boxed{} k \bigcirc 5$

10. A company has two manufacturing plants with daily production levels of $5x + 11$ items and $2x - 3$ items, respectively, where x represents a minimum quantity. The first plant produces how many more items daily than the second plant?

11. Two communications companies offer calling plans. With Company X, it costs 35¢ to connect and then 5¢ for each minute. With Company Y, it costs 15¢ to connect and then 4¢ for each minute.

Write and simplify an expression that represents how much more Company X charges than Company Y, in cents, for n minutes.

12. Make Sense and Persevere
The base and height of a triangle are each extended 2 cm. What is the area of the shaded region? How do you know?

(Triangle with base 8 cm extended by 2 cm, height x cm extended by 2 cm)

13. Two friends shop for fresh fruit. Jackson buys a watermelon for $7.65 and 5 pounds of cherries. Tim buys a pineapple for $2.45 and 4 pounds of cherries. Use the variable p to represent the price, in dollars, per pound of cherries. Write and simplify an expression to represent how much more Jackson spent.

14. Yu's family wants to rent a car to go on vacation. EnvoCar charges $50.50 and 8¢ per mile. Freedomride charges $70.50 and 12¢ per mile. How much more does Freedomride charge for driving d miles than EnvoCar?

15. A rectangular garden has a walkway around it. Find the area of the walkway.

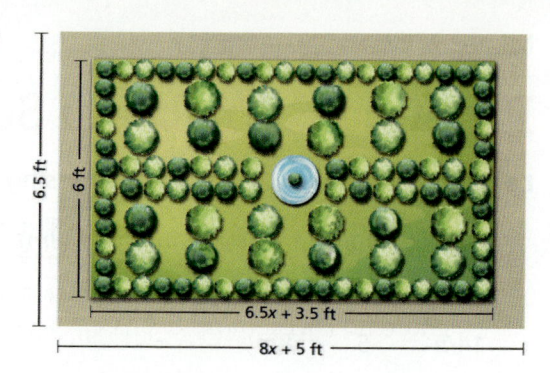

    Dimensions: 6.5 ft, 6 ft, 6.5x + 3.5 ft, 8x + 5 ft

16. **Critique Reasoning** Tim incorrectly rewrote the expression $\frac{1}{2}p - \left(\frac{1}{4}p + 4\right)$ as $\frac{1}{2}p + \frac{1}{4}p - 4$. Rewrite the expression without parentheses. What was Tim's error?

17. **Higher Order Thinking** Find the difference.
    $$\left(7x - 6\frac{2}{3}\right) - \left(-3x + 4\frac{3}{4}\right)$$

18. Each month, a shopkeeper spends $5x + 11$ dollars on rent and electricity. If he spends $2x - 3$ dollars on rent, how much does he spend on electricity?

19. Use the expression $\frac{1}{4}p - \left(1 - \frac{1}{3}p\right)$.

    a. Rewrite the expression without parentheses. Simplify. Show your work.

    b. Use a different method to write the expression without parentheses. Do not simplify.

Assessment Practice

20. Which is equivalent to $(0.25n - 0.3) - (0.8n - 0.25)$?

    Ⓐ $-0.55n + 0.55$

    Ⓑ $-0.55n - 0.05$

    Ⓒ $0.55n + 0.55$

    Ⓓ $0.55n - 0.05$

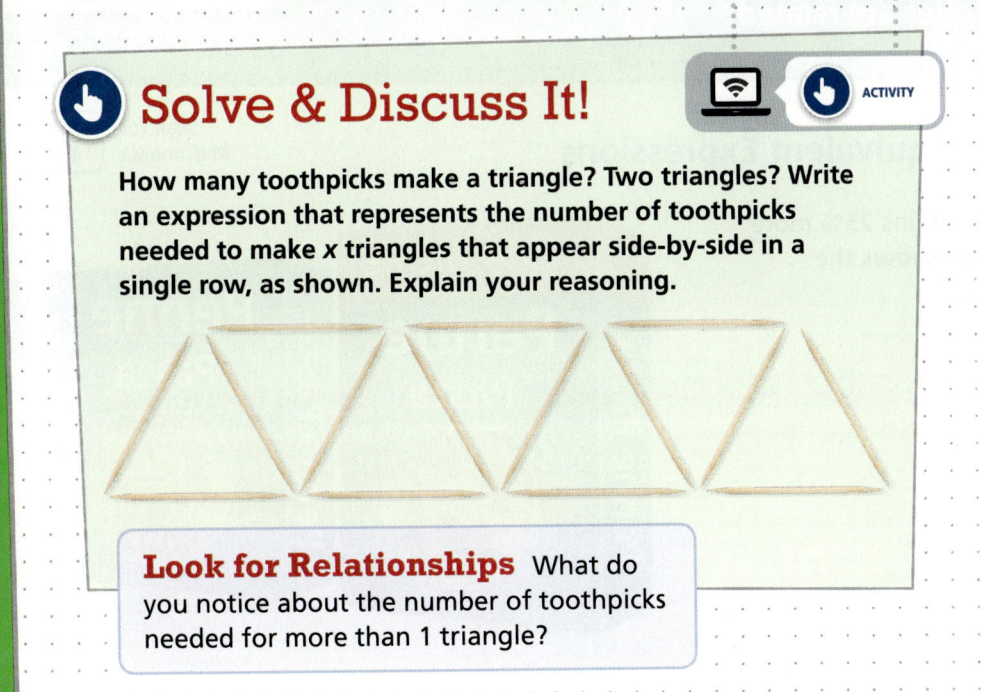

Lesson 4-8
Analyze Equivalent Expressions

Go Online | PearsonRealize.com

Solve & Discuss It!

How many toothpicks make a triangle? Two triangles? Write an expression that represents the number of toothpicks needed to make x triangles that appear side-by-side in a single row, as shown. Explain your reasoning.

Look for Relationships What do you notice about the number of toothpicks needed for more than 1 triangle?

I can...
use an equivalent expression to find new information.

Focus on math practices

Reasoning Can there be more than one expression that represents the total number of toothpicks needed to make x triangles in the arrangement shown? Explain.

? **Essential Question** How can writing equivalent expressions show how quantities are related?

EXAMPLE 1 Write Equivalent Expressions

A new box of pasta claims that it contains 25% more than the usual box. What expression shows the amount of pasta, p, in the new box?

Use Structure What expressions can you write to represent a percent greater than the original amount?

Draw a bar diagram to represent the problem situation. Then write an expression to represent the amount of pasta in the new box.

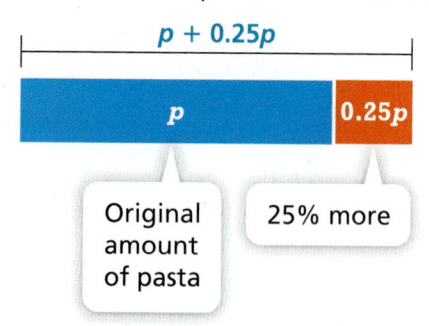

$p + 0.25p$

| p | $0.25p$ |

Original amount of pasta | 25% more

$p + 0.25p$

Combine like terms to write an equivalent expression.

The coefficient of p is 1.

$(1)p + 0.25p$
$= 1.25p$

25% more than 100% is the same as 125%.

Try It!

Joe is buying gift cards that are on sale for 15% off. He uses $c - 0.15c$ to determine the sale price of gift cards. What is an equivalent expression that Joe could also use to determine the sale price of a gift card?

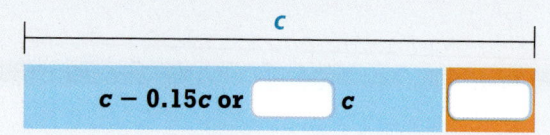

c

$c - 0.15c$ or ☐ c ☐

Convince Me! How do you know if an expression is describing a percent increase or a percent decrease?

238   4-8 Analyze Equivalent Expressions

EXAMPLE 2 Analyze Equivalent Expressions

Some middle school students will use 1-foot tiles to create a frame around a large square mural painting with side lengths s feet. Three students each wrote an expression to determine the number of tiles needed. Are these expressions equivalent? Explain.

$4(s + 1)$ $s + s + s + s + 4$ $2s + 2(s + 2)$

Look for Relationships
What does each expression tell you about the relationship among quantities and variables?

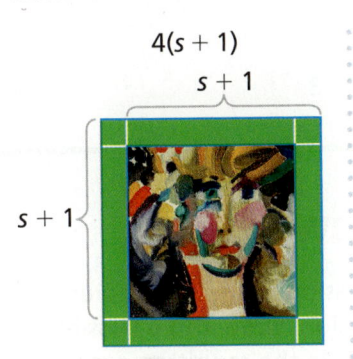

Each section requires $s + 1$ tiles and there are 4 sections.

Each side requires s tiles and there are 4 sides, so $s + s + s + s$, plus 4 corner tiles.

The top and bottom of the frame require $s + 2$ tiles and the two sides require s tiles.

The three expressions are equivalent because they each represent the number of tiles needed for the frame around the painting.

EXAMPLE 3 Interpret Equivalent Expressions

A table with a rectangular top has been extended with a table leaf as shown.

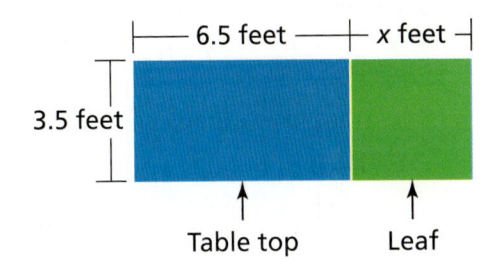

Multiply $3.5(6.5 + x)$ to write an equivalent expression for the total area of the extended table. What does each term of the equivalent expression tell you about the table?

$3.5(6.5 + x)$
$= (3.5 \cdot 6.5) + (3.5 \cdot x)$
$= 22.75 + 3.5x$

Area, in ft², of table leaf

Area, in ft², of original table

6.5 feet   x feet
3.5 feet

Table top   Leaf

✓ Try It!

The total area, in square feet, of a rectangular stage that has been widened by x feet is represented by $1{,}900 + 76x$. Use the Distributive Property to factor the expression. What does each factor in the equivalent expression tell you about the stage?

original stage
extension

4-8 Analyze Equivalent Expressions   239

KEY CONCEPT

Rewriting expressions can clarify relationships among quantities or variables.

When you *rewrite* an expression, you are writing an *equivalent* expression.

$4x + 12$ is equivalent to $4(x + 3)$ is equivalent to $x + x + x + x + 3 + 3 + 3 + 3$

Do You Understand?

1. **Essential Question** How can writing equivalent expressions show how quantities are related?

2. **Use Structure** The total area, in square feet, of a rectangular mural that has been extended by x feet is represented by $5.5(7.5 + x)$. Expand the expression using the Distributive Property. What do each of the terms in the equivalent expression tell you about the mural?

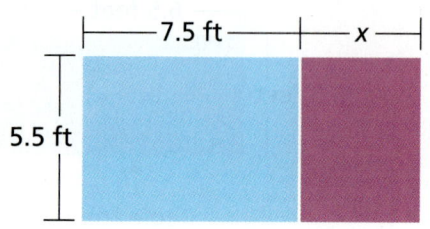

3. The expression $(2x + 6) + x$ represents the perimeter of an isosceles triangle. If x represents the length of one side of the triangle, explain how you can use the Distributive Property to find the length of each of the two equivalent sides?

Do You Know How?

4. Rewrite the expression $12x + 8$ to find an equivalent expression. Show three possible expressions. What do the rewritten expressions tell you about the relationships among the quantities?

5. A rope is used to make a fence in the shape of an equilateral triangle around a newly planted tree. The length of the rope is represented with the expression $9x + 15$.

   a. Rewrite the expression to represent the three side lengths of the rope fence.

   b. What is the length of one side?

6. The expression $(x - 0.35x)$ represents 35% off the cost of an item x. How is this equivalent to multiplying x by 0.65?

Practice & Problem Solving

7. Reasoning Eric is planning an event at a hotel. Let g stand for the number of Eric's guests. The two expressions represent the difference between the cost of the rooms. Expression 1: $(326 + 37g) - (287 + 23g)$. Expression 2: $39 + 14g$. What can you tell about Expression 2 and Expression 1?

Hotel Function Rooms

Ocean
Booking Fee $326
Price per Guest $37

Harbor
Booking Fee $287
Price per Guest $23

8. A student received a coupon for 17% off the total purchase price at a clothing store. Let b be the original price of the purchase. Use the expression $b - 0.17b$ for the new price of the purchase. Write an equivalent expression by combining like terms.

9. Kirana buys boxes of crackers that each have the same cost, c. She represents the cost of 3 boxes of cheese crackers, 2 boxes of poppy seed crackers, and 2 boxes of plain crackers using the expression $3c + 2c + 2c$. What equivalent expression can represent the cost?

10. A student received a coupon for 14% off the total purchase price at a clothing store. Let c be the original price of the purchase. The expression $c - 0.14c$ represents the new price of the purchase. Write an equivalent expression to show another way to represent the new price.

11. A farmer recently sold a large plot of land. The sale decreased his total acreage by 8%. Let v be the original acreage.

  a. Find two equivalent expressions that will give the new acreage.

  b. Use the expressions to describe two ways to find the new acreage.

12. An art teacher enlarged the area of a copy of a painting by 49%. Let d represent the area of the original painting. The expression $d + 0.49d$ is one way to represent the area of the new painting. Write two additional expressions that will give the area of the new painting.

4-8 Analyze Equivalent Expressions   241

13. Use Structure The area of a rectangular playground has been extended on one side. The total area of the playground, in square meters, can be written as $352 + 22x$.

Rewrite the expression to give a possible set of dimensions for the playground.

14. The manager of a store increases the price of a popular product by 7%. Let t be the original price of the product. The new price is $t + 0.07t$.

a. Find an expression equivalent to $t + 0.07t$.

b. If the original price was $19.99, estimate the new price by first rounding the original price to the nearest dollar.

15. Higher Order Thinking A customer at a clothing store is buying a pair of pants and a shirt. The customer can choose between a sale that offers a discount on pants, or a coupon for a discount on the entire purchase. Let n represent the original price of the pants and s represent the price of the shirt.

a. Write two expressions that represent the "15% off sale on all pants" option.

b. Write two expressions that represent the "10% off her entire purchase" option.

c. If the original cost of the pants is $25 and the shirt is $10, which option should the customer choose? Explain.

Assessment Practice

16. At a college, the cost of tuition increased by 10%. Let b represent the former cost of tuition. Use the expression $b + 0.10b$ for the new cost of tuition.

PART A
Write an equivalent expression for the new cost of tuition.

PART B
What does your equivalent expression tell you about how to find the new cost of tuition?

242   4-8 Analyze Equivalent Expressions

REVIEW TOPIC 4

❓ Topic Essential Question

How can properties of operations help to generate equivalent expressions that can be used in solving problems?

Vocabulary Review

Complete each definition and then provide an example of each vocabulary word.

Vocabulary   coefficient   constant   variable   factor   expression

Definition	Example
1. A term that contains only a number is a _____.	
2. The number part of a term that contains a variable is a _____.	
3. A _____ is a letter that represents an unknown value.	

Use Vocabulary in Writing

Membership in a digital library has a $5 startup fee and then costs $9.95 per month. Membership in a video streaming service costs $7.99 per month with no startup fee. Use vocabulary words to explain how this information could be used to write an expression for the total cost of both memberships after m months.

Topic 4 Topic Review   243

Concepts and Skills Review

LESSON 4-1 Write and Evaluate Algebraic Expressions

Quick Review
You can use an algebraic expression to represent and solve a problem with unknown values. The expression can consist of coefficients, constants, and variables. You can substitute values for variables to evaluate expressions.

Example
A farm charges $1.75 for each pound of strawberries picked and $2 for a basket to hold the strawberries. What is the total cost to pick 5 pounds of strawberries?

Write an expression to represent the total cost in dollars to pick p pounds of strawberries.

$1.75p + 2$

Substitute 5 for p.

$1.75(5) + 2 = 8.75 + 2 = 10.75$

It costs $10.75 to pick 5 pounds of strawberries.

Practice
1. Haddie makes and sells knit scarves. Next week she will pay a $25 fee for the use of a booth at a craft fair. She will charge $12 for each scarf she sells at the fair. Write an expression to determine Haddie's profit for selling s scarves after paying the fee for the use of the booth.

2. The cost to buy p pounds of potatoes at $0.32 per pound and n pounds of onions at $0.48 per pound can be determined by using the expression $0.32p + 0.48n$. How much will it cost to buy 4.5 pounds of potatoes and 2.5 pounds of onions?

LESSONS 4-2 AND 4-3 Generate Equivalent Expressions and Simplify Expressions

Quick Review
You can use properties of operations and combine like terms to simplify expressions. Like terms are terms that have the same variable part.

Example
Simplify the expression below.

$-7 + \frac{1}{3}n - \frac{4}{3} + 2n$

Use the Commutative Property to put like terms together.

$\frac{1}{3}n + 2n - 7 - \frac{4}{3}$

Combine like terms.

$2\frac{1}{3}n - 8\frac{1}{3}$

Practice
Simplify each expression below.

1. $\frac{5}{8}m + 9 - \frac{3}{8}m - 15$

2. $-8w + (-4z) + 2 + 6w + 9z - 7$

3. $-6 + (-2d) + (-4d) + 3d$

LESSON 4-4 Expand Expressions

Quick Review
The Distributive Property allows you to multiply each term inside parentheses by a factor that is outside the parentheses. This means that you can use the Distributive Property to expand expressions.

Example
Expand the expression $\frac{1}{4}(h + 7)$.

$\left(\frac{1}{4} \times h\right) + \left(\frac{1}{4} \times 7\right) = \frac{1}{4}h + 1.75$

Practice
1. Expand the expression $3.5(-3n + 4)$.

2. Simplify the expression $-\frac{3}{5}\left(-8 + \frac{5}{9}x - 3\right)$.

LESSON 4-5 Factor Expressions

Quick Review
When you factor an expression, you write it as a product of two expressions. The new expression is equivalent to the original expression. The greatest common factor (GCF) and the Distributive Property are tools that you use when you need to factor an expression.

Example
Factor the expression $12x - 9y + 15$.

The GCF of 12x, 15, and −9y is 3.

Rewrite each term using 3 as a factor.

$12x = 3 \cdot 4x$

$-9y = 3 \cdot (-3y)$

$15 = 3 \cdot 5$

Use the Distributive Property to factor the expression.

$3(4x - 3y + 5)$

Practice
Factor each expression.

1. $63a - 42b$

2. $81y + 54$

3. Which show a way to factor the expression $32t - 48$? Select all that apply.
   - ☐ $2(16t - 24)$
   - ☐ $4(12t - 48)$
   - ☐ $6(26t - 42)$
   - ☐ $8(4t - 6)$
   - ☐ $16(2t - 3)$

LESSONS 4-6 AND 4-7 | Add and Subtract Expressions

Quick Review
Adding and subtracting expressions may require combining like terms. This means that you must use the Commutative and Associative Properties to reorder and group terms as needed.

Example
Kerry has n markers. Rachel has 1 marker fewer than twice the number of markers Kerry has. Write and simplify an expression for the total number of markers they have.

Number of markers Kerry has: n

Number of markers Rachel has: $2n - 1$

Total number of markers:

$n + (2n - 1)$

$(n + 2n) - 1$

$3n - 1$

Practice
Add the expressions.

1. $(5.2c - 7.35) + (-3.9c + 2.65)$

2. $(6x - 2y - 5) - (-5 + 9y - 8x)$

3. Last week Jean ran 2 fewer than $4m$ miles. This week she ran 0.5 miles more than last week. Write and simplify an expression for the total number of miles Jean ran in the two weeks.

LESSON 4-8 | Analyze Equivalent Expressions

Quick Review
Equivalent expressions can help to show new information about a problem. Sometimes the equivalent expression will be an expanded expression. In other cases, it will be a factored expression.

Example
The perimeter of a square is represented with the expression $84 + 44s$. What is the length of one side of the square?

A square has 4 sides, so factor 4 out of each term in the expression for the perimeter.

$84 + 44s = 4 \cdot 21 + 4 \cdot 11s = 4(21 + 11s)$

The factor within the parentheses represents the length of one side of the square.

The length of one side is $21 + 11s$.

Practice
1. Hal earns n dollars per hour. Next month he will receive a 2% raise in pay per hour. The expression $n + 0.02n$ is one way to represent Hal's pay per hour after the raise. Write an equivalent simplified expression that will represent his pay per hour after the raise.

2. The area of a garden plot can be represented by the expression $84z - 54$. The garden will be divided into six sections for planting six different vegetables. The sections will be equal in area. Write an expression that represents the area of each section.

Hidden Clue

For each ordered pair, solve the percent problems to find the coordinates. Then locate and label the corresponding point on the graph. Draw line segments to connect the points in alphabetical order. Use the completed picture to help you answer the riddle below.

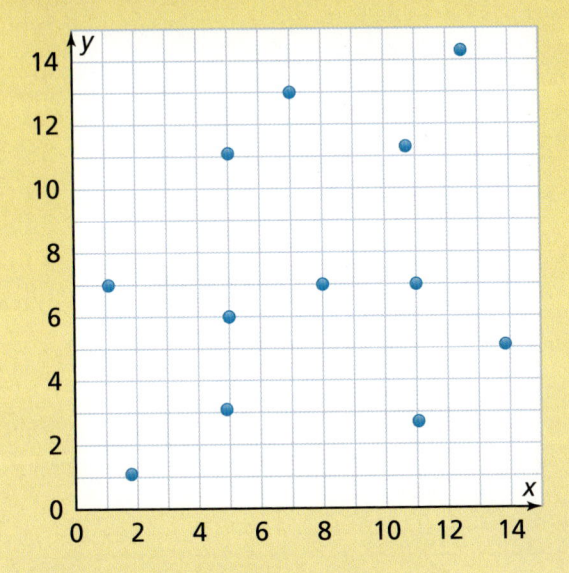

Fluency Practice
TOPIC 4

I can... represent and solve percent problems.

What occurs once in every minute, twice in every moment, yet never in a thousand years?

A (x is 85% of 13, 60% of 4.5 is y) ____ , ____

B (x is 110% of 10, y% of 50 is 3.5) ____ , ____

C (x% of 31 is 3.317, 4.407 is 39% of y) ____ , ____

D (1.36 is 17% of x, 1.05 is y% of 15) ____ , ____

E (x% of 60 is 3.006, 10% of 111 is y) ____ , ____

F (x is 16% of 31.25, y is 24% of 25) ____ , ____

G (78% of x is 3.822, y% of 8 is 0.248) ____ , ____

Go Online | PearsonRealize.com

GLOSSARY

ENGLISH   **SPANISH**

A

action In a probability situation, an action is a process with an uncertain result.

acción En una situación de probabilidad, una acción es el proceso con un resultado incierto.

additive inverses Two numbers that have a sum of 0.

inversos de suma Dos números cuya suma es 0.

Example 7 and −7 are additive inverses.

adjacent angles Two angles are adjacent angles if they share a vertex and a side, but have no interior points in common.

ángulos adyacentes Dos ángulos son adyacentes si tienen un vértice y un lado en común, pero no comparten puntos internos.

Example ∠ABD and ∠DBC are adjacent angles.

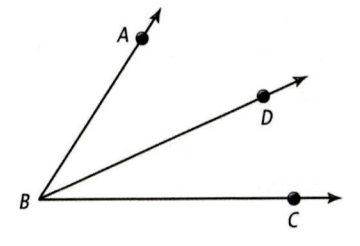

B

balance The balance in an account is the principal amount plus the interest earned.

saldo El saldo de una cuenta es el capital más el interés ganado.

Example You deposit $100 in an account and earn $5 in interest. The balance is $105.

biased sample In a biased sample, the number of subjects in the sample with the trait that you are studying is not proportional to the number of members in the population with that trait. A biased sample does not accurately represent the population.

muestra sesgada En una muestra sesgada, el número de sujetos de la muestra que tiene la característica que se está estudiando no es proporcional al número de miembros de la población que tienen esa característica. Una muestra sesgada no representa con exactitud la población.

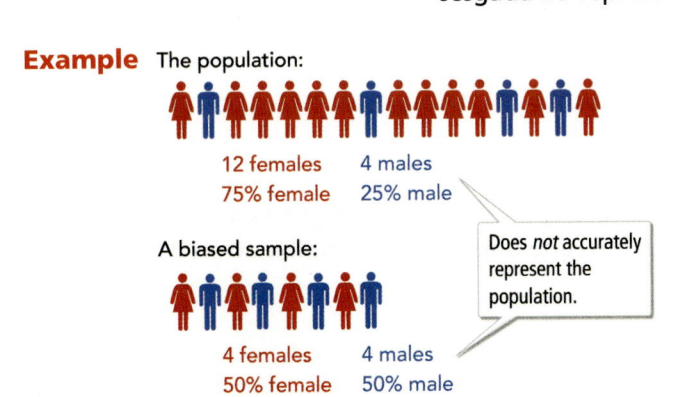

Example The population:

12 females   4 males
75% female   25% male

A biased sample:

4 females   4 males
50% female   50% male

Does not accurately represent the population.

ENGLISH | SPANISH

C

circumference of a circle The circumference of a circle is the distance around the circle. The formula for the circumference of a circle is $C = \pi d$, where C represents the circumference and d represents the diameter of the circle.

circunferencia de un círculo La circunferencia de un círculo es la distancia alrededor del círculo. La fórmula de la circunferencia de un círculo es $C = \pi d$, donde C representa la circunferencia y d representa el diámetro del círculo.

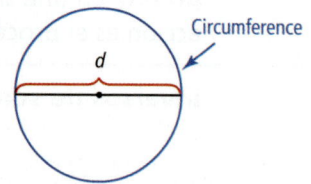

Example

---

comparative inference A comparative inference is an inference made by interpreting and comparing two sets of data.

inferencia comparativa Una inferencia comparativa es una inferencia que se hace al interpretar y comparar dos conjuntos de datos.

Example Inference: Based on Sample A, 65% of Population A loves to sing.

Inference: Based on Sample B, 30% of Population B loves to sing.

Comparative Inference: Based on Sample A and Sample B, a greater percent of Population A loves to sing than Population B.

---

complementary angles Two angles are complementary angles if the sum of their measures is 90°. Complementary angles that are adjacent form a right angle.

ángulos complementarios Dos ángulos son complementarios si la suma de sus medidas es 90°. Los ángulos complementarios que son adyacentes forman un ángulo recto.

Example

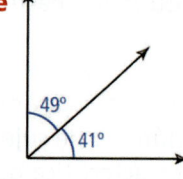

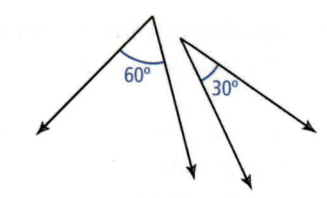

complex fraction A complex fraction is a fraction $\frac{A}{B}$ where A and/or B are fractions and B is not zero.

fracción compleja Una fracción compleja es una fracción $\frac{A}{B}$ donde A y/o B son fracciones y B es distinto de cero.

Example $\frac{\frac{1}{2}}{\frac{3}{4}}$

---

composite figure A composite figure is the combination of two or more figures into one object.

figura compuesta Una figura compuesta es la combinación de dos o más figuras en un objeto.

G2 Glossary

ENGLISH

compound event A compound event is an event associated with a multi-step action. A compound event is composed of events that are the outcomes of the steps of the action.

Example Action: Toss a coin. Roll a number cube.

Compound event: tails, 3

constant of proportionality In a proportional relationship, one quantity y is a constant multiple of the other quantity x. The constant multiple is called the constant of proportionality. The constant of proportionality is equal to the ratio $\frac{y}{x}$.

Example In the equation $y = 4x$, the constant of proportionality is 4.

cross section A cross section is the intersection of a three-dimensional figure and a plane.

Example

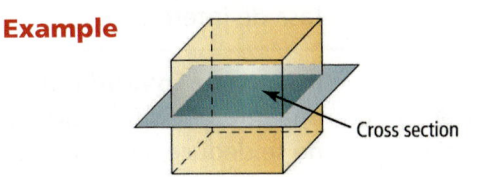

event An event is a single outcome or group of outcomes from a sample space.

Example Sample space for rolling a number cube:

Rolling a 3 is an event with one outcome.

Rolling an even number is an event with three outcomes.

experimental probability You find the experimental probability of an event by repeating an experiment many times and using this ratio:

$P(\text{event}) = \frac{\text{number of times event occurs}}{\text{total number of trials}}$

Example Suppose a basketball player makes 19 baskets in 28 attempts. The experimental probability that the basketball player makes a basket is $\frac{19}{28} \approx 68\%$.

SPANISH

evento compuesto Un evento compuesto es un evento que se relaciona con una acción de varios pasos. Un evento compuesto se compone de eventos que son los resultados de los pasos de una acción.

constante de proporcionalidad En una relación proporcional, una cantidad y es un múltiplo constante de la otra cantidad x. El múltiplo constante se llama constante de proporcionalidad. La constante de proporcionalidad es igual a la razón $\frac{y}{x}$.

corte transversal Un corte transversal es la intersección de una figura tridimensional y un plano.

evento Un evento es un resultado simple o un grupo de resultados de un espacio muestral.

probabilidad experimental Para hallar la probabilidad experimental de un evento, debes repetir un experimento muchas veces y usar esta razón: $P(\text{evento}) = \frac{\text{número de veces que sucede el evento}}{\text{número total de pruebas}}$

ENGLISH

I

independent events Two events are independent events if the occurrence of one event does not affect the probability of the other event.

Example Action: Pick a marble out of a bag, and then replace it. Then pick a second marble from the same bag. The events are independent because the probability of picking the second marble is not affected by the choice of the first marble.

inference An inference is a judgment made by interpreting data.

Example If 25% of a representative sample has Characteristic X, then a valid inference is that 25% of the population has Characteristic X.

interest rate Interest is calculated based on a percent of the principal. That percent is called the interest rate (r).

invalid inference An invalid inference is false about the population, or does not follow from the available data. A biased sample can lead to invalid inferences.

isolate a variable When solving equations, to isolate a variable means to get a variable with a coefficient of 1 alone on one side of an equation. Use the properties of equality and inverse operations to isolate a variable.

Example To isolate x in $2x = 8$, divide both sides of the equation by 2.

M

markdown Markdown is the amount of decrease from the selling price to the sale price. The markdown as a percent decrease of the original selling price is called the percent markdown.

Example A shirt that was originally $28 is on sale for $21. The markdown is $28 - 21 = 7$. The percent markdown is $\frac{7}{28} = \frac{1}{4} = 0.25$, or 25%.

SPANISH

eventos independientes Dos eventos son eventos independientes cuando el resultado de un evento no altera la probabilidad del otro.

inferencia Una inferencia es una opinión que se forma al interpretar datos.

tasa de interés El interés se calcula con base en un porcentaje del capital. Ese porcentaje se llama tasa de interés, (r).

inferencia inválida Una inferencia inválida es una inferencia falsa acerca de una población, o no se deduce a partir de los datos disponibles. Una muestra sesgada puede llevar a inferencias inválidas.

aislar una variable Cuando resuelves ecuaciones, aislar una variable significa poner una variable con un coeficiente de 1 sola a un lado de la ecuación. Usa las propiedades de igualdad y las operaciones inversas para aislar una variable.

rebaja La rebaja es la cantidad de disminución de un precio de venta a un precio rebajado. La rebaja como una disminución porcentual del precio de venta original se llama porcentaje de rebaja.

ENGLISH

markup Markup is the amount of increase from the cost to the selling price. The markup as a percent increase of the original cost is called the percent markup.

SPANISH

margen de ganancia El margen de ganancia es la cantidad de aumento del costo al precio de venta. El margen de ganancia como un aumento porcentual del costo original se llama porcentaje del margen de ganancia.

Example The original cost of a shirt is $16, and a store is selling it for $28. The markup is 28 − 16 = 12. The percent markup is $\frac{12}{16} = \frac{3}{4} = 0.75$, or 75%.

O

outcome An outcome is a possible result of an action.

resultado Un resultado es un desenlace posible de una acción.

Example One outcome of rolling a number cube is getting a 3.

P

percent equation The percent equation describes the relationship between a part and a whole. You can use the percent equation to solve percent problems. part = percent · whole

ecuación de porcentaje La ecuación de porcentaje describe la relación entre una parte y un todo. Puedes usar la ecuación de porcentaje para resolver problemas de porcentaje. parte = por ciento · todo

percent error Percent error describes the accuracy of a measured or estimated value compared to an actual or accepted value.

error porcentual El error porcentual describe la exactitud de un valor medido o estimado en comparación con un valor real o aceptado.

Example A person guesses that there are 36 passengers on a bus. The actual number of passengers is 45.

$$\text{percent error} = \frac{|\text{measured or estimated value} - \text{actual value}|}{\text{actual value}}$$

$$= \frac{|36 - 45|}{45}$$

$$= \frac{|-9|}{45}$$

$$= 0.20, \text{ or } 20\%$$

So the guess "36 passengers" is off by 20%.

ENGLISH	SPANISH
percent of change Percent of change is the percent something increases or decreases from its original measure or amount. You can find the percent of change by using the equation: percent of change = $\frac{\text{amount of change}}{\text{original quantity}}$	**porcentaje de cambio** El porcentaje de cambio es el porcentaje en que algo aumenta o disminuye en relación a la medida o cantidad original. Puedes hallar el porcentaje de cambio con la siguiente ecuación: porcentaje de cambio = $\frac{\text{cantidad de cambio}}{\text{cantidad original}}$

Example The number of employees changed from 14 to 21.
amount of change = 21 − 14 = 7
percent change = $\frac{7}{14} = \frac{1}{2} = 0.5$, or 50%

population A population is the complete set of items being studied.	**población** Una población es todo el conjunto de elementos que se estudian.

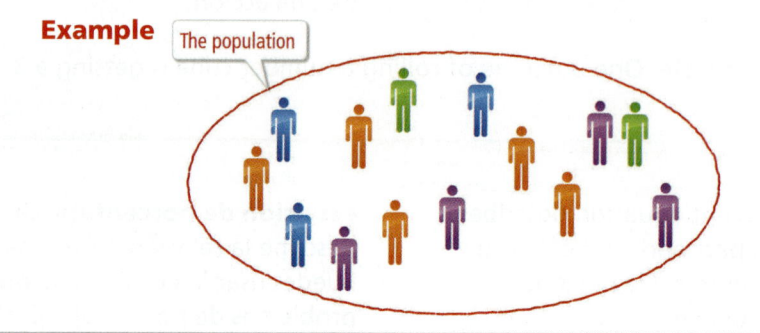

Example The population

principal The original amount of money deposited or borrowed in an account.	**capital** La cantidad original de dinero que se deposita o se pide prestada en una cuenta.

Example You open a savings account with $500. The principal is $500.

probability model A probability model consists of an action, its sample space, and a list of events with their probabilities. The events and probabilities in the list have these characteristics: each outcome in the sample space is in exactly one event, and the sum of all of the probabilities must be 1.	**modelo de probabilidad** Un modelo de probabilidad consiste en una acción, su espacio muestral y una lista de eventos con sus probabilidades. Los eventos y las probabilidades de la lista tienen estas características: cada resultado del espacio muestral está exactamente en un evento, y la suma de todas las probabilidades debe ser 1.

Example Action: Spin the spinner once
Sample space: red, blue, green
Probabilities: $P(\text{red}) = \frac{1}{3}$, $P(\text{blue}) = \frac{1}{3}$, $P(\text{green}) = \frac{1}{3}$

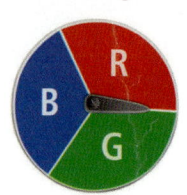

ENGLISH

probability of an event The probability of an event is a number from 0 to 1 that measures the likelihood that the event will occur. The closer the probability is to 0, the less likely it is that the event will happen. The closer the probability is to 1, the more likely it is that the event will happen. You can express probability as a fraction, decimal, or percent.

SPANISH

probabilidad de un evento La probabilidad de un evento es un número de 0 a 1 que mide la probabilidad de que suceda el evento. Cuanto más se acerca la probabilidad a 0, menos probable es que suceda el evento. Cuanto más se acerca la probabilidad a 1, más probable es que suceda el evento. Puedes expresar la probabilidad como una fracción, un decimal o un porcentaje.

Example

	Impossible	Unlikely	As Likely as Not	Likely	Certain
Probability (fraction):	0	$\frac{1}{4}$	$\frac{1}{2}$	$\frac{3}{4}$	1
Probability (decimal):	0	0.25	0.50	0.75	1
Probability (percent):	0%	25%	50%	75%	100%

proportion A proportion is an equation stating that two ratios are equal.

proporción Una proporción es una ecuación que establece que dos razones son iguales.

Example $\frac{2}{3} = \frac{6}{9}$ and $\frac{9}{12} = \frac{x}{4}$

proportional relationship Two quantities x and y have a proportional relationship if y is always a constant multiple of x. A relationship is proportional if it can be described by equivalent ratios.

relación de proporción Dos cantidades x y y tienen una relación de proporción si y es siempre un múltiplo constante de x. Una relación es de proporción si se puede describir con razones equivalentes.

Example The equation $y = 4x$ shows a proportional relationship between x and y.

R

random sample In a random sample, each member in the population has an equal chance of being selected.

muestra aleatoria En una muestra aleatoria, cada miembro en la población tiene una oportunidad igual de ser seleccionado.

relative frequency relative frequency of an event $= \frac{\text{number of times event occurs}}{\text{total number of trials}}$

frecuencia relativa frecuencia relativa de un evento $= \frac{\text{número de veces que sucede el evento}}{\text{número total de pruebas}}$

Example For 40 trials, the relative frequency of 2 is $\frac{12}{40}$, or 30%.

Outcome	1	2	3	4
Frequency	10	12	4	14

ENGLISH	SPANISH
representative sample A representative sample is a sample of a population in which the number of subjects in the sample with the trait that you are studying is proportional to the number of members in the population with that trait. A representative sample accurately represents the population and does not have bias.	**muestra representativa** Una muestra representativa es una muestra de una población en la que el número de sujetos de la muestra que tiene la característica que se estudia es proporcional al número de miembros de la población que tienen esa característica. Una muestra representativa representa la población con exactitud y no está sesgada.

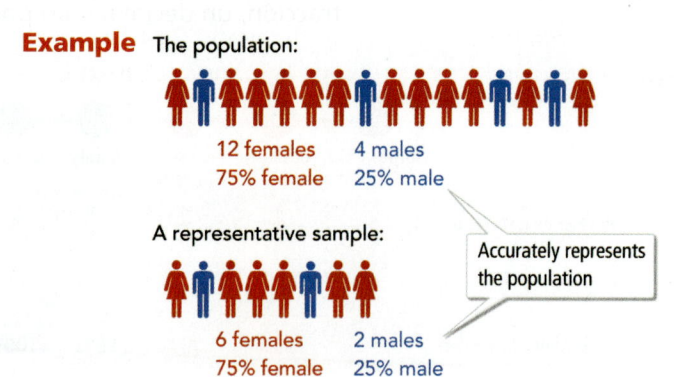

Example The population:

12 females 4 males
75% female 25% male

A representative sample:

6 females 2 males
75% female 25% male

Accurately represents the population

S

sample of a population A sample of a population is part of the population. A sample is useful when you want to find out about a population but you do not have the resources to study every member of the population.	**muestra de una población** Una muestra de una población es una parte de la población. Una muestra es útil cuando quieres saber algo acerca de una población, pero no tienes los recursos para estudiar a cada miembro de esa población.

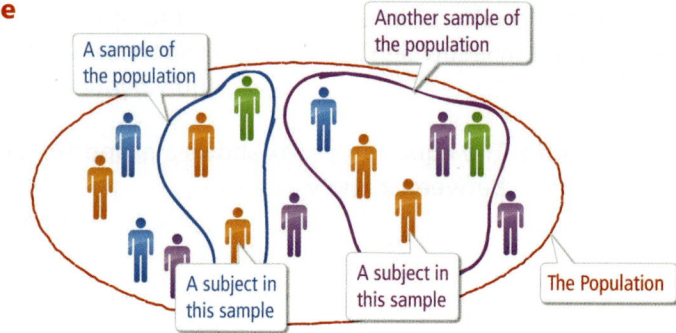

Example

A sample of the population
Another sample of the population
A subject in this sample
A subject in this sample
The Population

sample space The sample space for an action is the set of all possible outcomes of that action.	**espacio muestral** El espacio muestral de una acción es el conjunto de todos los resultados posibles de esa acción.

Example The sample space for rolling a standard number cube is 1, 2, 3, 4, 5, 6.

scale drawing A scale drawing is an enlarged or reduced drawing of an object that is proportional to the actual object.	**dibujo a escala** Un dibujo a escala es un dibujo ampliado o reducido de un objeto que es proporcional al objeto real.

Example Maps and blueprints are examples of scale drawings.

ENGLISH | SPANISH

simple interest Simple interest is interest paid only on an original deposit.

interés simple El interés simple es el interés que se paga sobre un depósito original solamente.

---

simulation A simulation is a model of a real-world situation that is used to find probabilities.

simulación Una simulación es un modelo de una situación de la vida diaria que se usa para hallar probabilidades.

---

supplementary angles Two angles are supplementary angles if the sum of their measures is 180°. Supplementary angles that are adjacent form a straight angle.

ángulos suplementarios Dos ángulos son suplementarios si la suma de sus medidas es 180°. Los ángulos suplementarios que son adyacentes forman un ángulo llano.

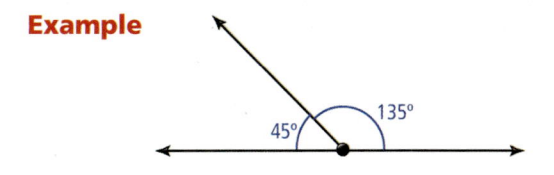

Example

(45°, 135°)

T

terminating decimal A terminating decimal has a decimal expansion that terminates in 0.

decimal finito Un decimal finito tiene una expansión decimal que termina en 0.

Example Both 0.6 and 0.7265 are terminating decimals.

---

theoretical probability When all outcomes of an action are equally likely, $P(\text{event}) = \frac{\text{number of favorable outcomes}}{\text{number of possible outcomes}}$.

probabilidad teórica Cuando todos los resultados de una acción son igualmente probables, $P(\text{evento}) = \frac{\text{número de resultados favorables}}{\text{número de resultados posibles}}$.

Example The theoretical probability of rolling a 6 on a standard number cube is $\frac{1}{6}$.

---

trial In a probability experiment, you carry out or observe an action repeatedly. Each observation of the action is a trial.

prueba En un experimento de probabilidad, realizas u observas una acción varias veces. Cada observación de la acción es una prueba.

U

unbiased sample A sample in which every item or individual in the population has an equal chance of being selected.

muestra no sesgada Muestra en la que cada elemento o individuo de la población tiene la misma probabilidad de ser escogido.

---

uniform probability model A uniform probability model is a probability model based on using the theoretical probability of equally likely outcomes.

modelo de probabilidad uniforme Un modelo de probabilidad uniforme es un modelo de probabilidad que se basa en el uso de la probabilidad teórica de resultados igualmente probables.

Example You can use a uniform probability model to determine the probability of rolling yellow on a color cube on which one side is yellow and the remaining five sides are blue. Each face of the color cube is equally likely to land up.

ENGLISH

V

valid inference A valid inference is an inference that is true about the population. Valid inferences can be made when they are based on data from a representative sample.

Example If 25% of a representative sample has Characteristic X, then a valid inference is that 25% of the population has Characteristic X.

vertical angles Vertical angles are formed by two intersecting lines and are opposite each other. Vertical angles have equal measures.

Example

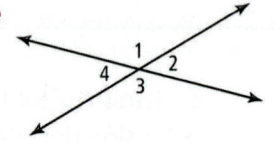

∠1 and ∠3 are vertical angles.
∠2 and ∠4 are vertical angles.

SPANISH

inferencia válida Una inferencia válida es una inferencia verdadera acerca de una población. Se pueden hacer inferencias válidas si están basadas en los datos de una muestra representativa.

ángulos opuestos por el vértice Los ángulos opuestos por el vértice están formados por dos rectas secantes y están uno frente a otro. Los ángulos opuestos por el vértice tienen la misma medida.

ACKNOWLEDGEMENTS

Photographs

Photo locators denoted as follows: Top (T), Center (C), Bottom (B), Left (L), Right (R), Background (Bkgd)

Cover senina/Shutterstock.

F18 (TL) Gelpi/Fotolia, (TR) Hogan Imaging/Fotolia; **F19** (T) Cherries/Fotolia, (C) Donatas1205/Fotolia; **F20-F21** Macrovector/Fotolia; **003** mycteria/Shutterstock; **004** (penguin) Kotomiti/Fotolia, (skull) Željko Radojko/Fotolia, (glasses) Th3fisa/Fotolia, (snowballs) Ilya Akinshin/Fotolia, (top hat) Elisanth/Fotolia, (sticks) Dule964/Fotolia, (map) Cunico/Fotolia, (bike) Mbruxelle/Fotolia, (iPad) yossarian6/Fotolia, (icicles) Mr Twister/Fotolia, (hat) leona_44/Fotolia, (iceberg) siempreverde22/Fotolia, (snowman) destina/Fotolia; **007** (C) 3dsculptor/Fotolia, (BR) Destina/Fotolia; **013** (C) Djahan/Fotolia, (TC) Bacalao/Fotolia, (CL) Djahan/Fotolia, (T) Rawpixel/Fotolia; **014** (TCR) 103tnn/Fotolia, (TR) Pete Saloutos/Shutterstock; **018** NRT/Shutterstock; **019** Ras-slava/Fotolia; **020** (C) Brostock/Fotolia, (T) Violetkaipa/Fotolia; **021** (CR) Nik_Merkulov/Fotolia, (TCR) david_franklin/Fotolia, (TR) tashka2000/Fotolia; **022** (CR) Eric Isselée/Fotolia, (R) Modella/Fotolia, (BCR) Ravenna/Fotolia; **023** (BCR) dampoint/Fotolia, (BR) Vitaly Krivosheev/Fotolia; **025** castelberry/Fotolia; **039** (TC) Thomas Barrat/Shutterstock, (C) Natis/Fotolia; **041** (TR) Igor Mojzes/Fotolia, (TCR) totophotos/Fotolia; **045** (C) Nataliia Pyzhova/Fotolia, (TC) Thanakorn Thaneewach/Fotolia; **055** (BR) Maximmmmum/Shutterstock, (BCR) Aleksei Lazukov/Shutterstock; **057** Elvirkin/Fotolia; **063** (C) Georgejmclittle/Fotolia, (TC) Rasulov/Fotolia; **065** Georgejmclittle/Fotolia; **069** mycteria/Shutterstock; **079** Stockphoto/Getty Images; **081** (TC) Foonia/Shutterstock, (T) Mylisa/Shutterstock; **082** (TR) Somchai Som/Shutterstock, (BR) yossarian6/Fotolia, (BCR) nito/Fotolia; **087** (C) Scattoselvaggio/Shutterstock, (R) Bernhard Richter/Shutterstock, (TCR, TR) Javier Brosch/Shutterstock; **089** (BR) Rawpixel/Shutterstock, (BCR) Alphalight Pro Stock/Shutterstock; **091** (Bkgd) Sorapop Udomsri/Shutterstock, (CL) Pete Pahham/Shutterstock, (BC) Takayuki/Shutterstock, (C) kak2s/Shutterstock, (TC, BCR) ChiccoDodiFC/Shutterstock, (CR) leungchopan/Shutterstock, (BR) kak2s/Shutterstock; **092** Technotr/E+/Getty Images; **097** (BL) Jiang Hongyan/Shutterstock, (TR) Quaoar/Shutterstock, (TL) Somchai Som/Shutterstock, (BR) Eric Isselee/Shutterstock, (B) khunaspix/123RF; **099** Kelly Nelson/123RF; **105** (TC) Erik Isakson/Getty Images, (T) Sergey Nivens/Fotolia; **111** (TC) Foonia/Shutterstock, (T) Mylisa/Shutterstock; **115** luanateutzi/Shutterstock; **116** Mango Productions/Corbis/Glow Images; **121** (BCR) Arina P Habich/Shutterstock, (BR) Arina P Habich/Shutterstock, (B) Viktor/Fotolia; **123** Purestock/Getty Images; **125** Peter Anderson/Dorling Kindersley; **126** Andrii Pokaz/Fotolia; **133** photastic/Shutterstock; **134** (TC) Tupungato/Fotolia, (TR) Andrey Popov/Fotolia, (TCL) lucadp/Fotolia, (CL) manaemedia/Fotolia, (R) Nikolai Tsvetkov/Fotolia, (TCR) Stephen VanHorn/Fotolia, (CR) Lasse Kristensen/Fotolia, (BCR) Andrey Popov/Fotolia, (BR) yossarian6/Fotolia; **137** (Bkgd) Sergey Yarochkin/Fotolia, (BR) Denys Prykhodov/Fotolia, (BL) Africa Studio/Fotolia, (TL) Leo Lintang/Fotolia, (TR) BillionPhotos/Fotolia, (C) Maxal Tamor/Fotolia; **149** (CR, CL) Semen Lixodeev/Shutterstock, (C) Sorapop Udomsri/Shutterstock; **150** iko/Shutterstock; **151** Luisa Leal Photography/Shutterstock; **152** (CR) Anterovium/Fotolia, (R) LoopAll/Shutterstock; **158** (TCR) adogslifephoto/Fotolia, (TR) adogslifephoto/Fotolia; **159** juserdiuk/Fotolia; **163** photastic/Shutterstock; **167** (CL) David Pereiras/Fotolia, (C) Verve/Fotolia; **169** (CR) GraphicCompressor/Fotolia, (C) Andrey Kuzmin/Fotolia; **170** Goir/Fotolia; **173** (CL) Guzel Studio/Fotolia, (CR) lzf/Fotolia, (C) Zorabc/Fotolia; **175** (TCR) Gennady Poddubny/Fotolia, (TR) georgerudy/Fotolia; **185** Derek Hatfield/Shutterstock; **186** (BR) yossarian6/Fotolia, (CR) Stephen VanHorn/Fotolia, (CL) macrovector/Fotolia; **195** (L, CL) Kungverylucky/Fotolia, (TCL) Sripfoto/Fotolia, (C) Picsfive/Fotolia, (CR) David_franklin/Fotolia, (R) Yevgeniy11/Fotolia, (TCR) Gomolach/Fotolia; **201** Portokalis/Fotolia; **205** (R) Orlando Bellini/Fotolia, (CR) Dmitriy Syechin/Fotolia, (BCR) Nipaporn/Fotolia; **207** Halfbottle/Fotolia; **213** (T) Michaeljung/Fotolia, (TC) Elnur/Fotolia, (C) FreedomMan/Fotolia, (CL) Guzel Studio/Fotolia, (CR) Casejustin/Fotolia; **221** Derek Hatfield/Shutterstock; **225** (Bkgd) Beemar/Fotolia, (C) Determined/Fotolia, (CL) Altanaka/Fotolia, (CR) Davit85/Fotolia, (R) Mat Hayward/Fotolia; **226** (C) milphoto/Fotolia, (CR) .shock/Fotolia, (TC) tarapong/Fotolia; **230** Sofya Apkalikova/Shutterstock; **231** (CL) Somjring34/Fotolia, (CR) Pixelrobot/Fotolia; **237** Dmitriy Syechin/Fotolia; **239** slava_samoilenko/Fotolia.